MARGARET THATCHER

Margaret Thatcher

FROM CHILDHOOD TO LEADERSHIP

GEORGE GARDINER, MP

WILLIAM KIMBER · LONDON

First published in 1975 by
WILLIAM KIMBER & CO. LIMITED
Godolphin House, 22a Queen Anne's Gate,
London SW1H 9AE

© George Gardiner, 1975
ISBN 0 7183 0204 4

Made and printed in Great Britain by
The Garden City Press Limited
Letchworth, Hertfordshire
SG6 1JS

Contents

List of Illustrations

Foreword

I am sure no biography of a contemporary political figure can be impartial, and I make no such claim for this book. I admire Margaret Thatcher, I share most of her political values, and with a number of other backbench colleagues I helped her in the contest which made her Party Leader. However, I had never worked closely with her before the 1975 leadership election, and it struck me forcibly then how her personality differed in many respects from the image that many of the public and Press had of her. In this book I therefore try to present her to the reader as she appeared to me then, and as she has since.

To understand Margaret Thatcher we have to go back to her roots in Grantham and to the strong values of her father and family, and see how she made the most of what opportunities came her way. Regrettably she is not a hoarder; all letters, speeches and personal records have been thrown away as soon as they ceased to have immediate relevance. So the first part of this book has been built substantially on recollection. I began by arranging with her a series of lengthy conversations, covering the different stages of her life, recording them on tape for my information and guidance. I also had shorter conversations with her sister Muriel, her husband Denis, and a number of other friends and colleagues. To all of them, but to Margaret particularly, I am deeply indebted for their help and advice.

In Part I, starting with her childhood in Grantham, I have tried to avoid drawing too many conclusions, rather leaving the reader to draw his own from the narrative. Part II covers her period shadowing and then in charge of the Department of Education and Science, and in fitting her various policies and actions into a framework I have necessarily exercised my own judgement. Part III is very much my personal view and assessment of the events leading to the Conservative Party's 1974 election defeats and to the subsequent choice of Margaret as

Leader. Though I am grateful to her and to other colleagues for their views on these events, the conclusions presented in these pages are of course my own.

A few of my Parliamentary colleagues may feel I have been rather critical of some actions and policies in which they were involved. But when a party has been through a period of defeat and internal dissent there is merit in recording those past differences, if only to help us and others to learn from them. By the time this book was written there was a general agreement that the party's revival must be based on those historic principles of individual freedom with responsibility which have always linked it most closely with the aspirations of the majority of citizens.

Finally, I should like to thank all those who have helped me in researching and preparing the material for this book, including Helen Hackett, Karen and Geoffrey Irvine, Susan and Paul Beardsall, Carole Irving and in particular my former colleague in journalism, Gordon Leak. I also record my thanks to the Department of Education and Science for supplying me with published material from the period when Margaret was Education Secretary, and to the staff of Conservative Central Office, notably Gerry Mulligan, Alan Leonard and Jill Jackson, for other documentary material. And specially I thank my wife Juliet for all her help—and patience.

House of Commons
June, 1975

PART I

The Roots of Understanding

CHAPTER ONE

Home and Family in Grantham
1925-1943

The first woman to become leader of one of Britain's major political parties, and so alternative Prime Minister, was born on October 13, 1925, in a room over a grocer's shop on a busy street corner in Grantham. Beneath the bedroom window the traffic of the Great North Road flowed past. From a little farther away came the clanking of the railway shunting yards, interrupted regularly by the noise of an express train thundering through. This was the home of Alfred and Beatrice Roberts. The child just born was their second daughter, and they decided to call her Margaret Hilda.

It was in this home that Margaret Roberts spent the first eighteen years of her life. It was hard-working, strictly Nonconformist in belief and practice, rich in culture and through Alfred Roberts took a close interest in local, national and world affairs. One cannot begin to understand the personality of Mrs. Margaret Thatcher, as she now is, without first comprehending the very strong character of her father, as well as the values of his family and household.

Looking back, Margaret Thatcher reflects that she was brought up 'in a rather puritan way'. Her sister Muriel, four years older, says they both received 'a very strict upbringing, with very strict principles'. But neither regrets it.

As Margaret puts it now : 'I owe everything in my life to two things : a good home, and a good education. My home was ordinary, but good in the sense that my parents were passionately interested in the future of my sister and myself. At the same time they gave us a good education—not only in school, but at home as well.'

The strongest single influence was undoubtedly her father. Indeed, Alfred Roberts seems to have exerted a strong influence on all around him. He was a striking man, standing 6 feet 3 inches

tall and with a shock of platinum blond hair. In later years it
turned pure white, but stayed as thick as ever. He was a pillar
of the local Methodist Church, and a lay preacher. He was elected
to the Town Council as an Independent when Margaret was
four or five, served as a distinguished chairman of its Finance
Committee, and in 1945 became Mayor of Grantham. He was
a leading figure in the town's Rotary Club, and involved himself
in a whole range of charitable activities. He had a most inquiring
mind, read voraciously, and always wished that he had been able
to be a schoolteacher. But such an opportunity had never come
his way.

He was not a native of Grantham, but of Ringstead, in North-
amptonshire, where he was the eldest of a family of seven. His
father was a shoemaker, as had been at least two previous
generations. His father Benjamin was dead by the time Margaret
was born, but she can still remember occasional visits to her
paternal grandmother, who lived in a fairly humble cottage.
Margaret had the impression that at some stage her grandfather
had hit on hard times. But one limb of the family in Northampton-
shire had managed to do rather better.

'My great-uncle was John Roberts, who made all the organs
for the churches around that area, and some pianos too. At the
bottom of his garden was a great barn in which he had two
organs, and I can remember trying to play them.'

When visiting these separate limbs of the family as a small
child Margaret was struck by the contrast in life styles. 'There
was the big house, and there was the small cottage.'

However, Alfred Roberts decided against following the family
craft of shoemaking, perhaps because of his poor eyesight, so
when he left school at thirteen he went into the grocery business.
Then in the early years of the century he moved to Grantham to
become manager of a grocery store in the town. He worked hard,
saved hard, and before the First World War married Beatrice
Ethel Stephenson. Her father worked on the railway, but she had
trained as a dressmaker and ran a flourishing business from her
home. During the war the couple managed with their combined
savings to buy a family grocery business of their own on the
corner of North Parade, a little way from the centre of Grantham.
This was a busy spot; the Great North Road ran beneath Margaret's bedroom window, and as she grew up the lorry and long
distance bus traffic built up considerably, by night as well as day.
Some two hundred yards farther on was the main railway line.

'We were brought up to traffic noise,' Margaret recalls. 'There were traffic lights on the corner, so we had all the lorries stopping and starting, and we always knew when the express trains were going through.'

The shop took up the ground floor of what was a substantial brick building of three storeys, and the family lived in the rooms above. The arrangement of rooms was a little peculiar; the family had to go through a bedroom to reach their sitting room. At the top of the house each of the sisters had a small bedroom. On the ground floor was a small lean-to kitchen, there was no garden, and the lavatory was outside in the yard. The house was filled with good, solid furniture, some of which Alfred Roberts bought in the auction sales which were then held twice a week in Grantham. 'Nearly all of it was typical Victorian dark-red mahogany furniture—the beds, dressing tables, and we each had our own bedroom wash-stand.'

Hard work was taken for granted in the Roberts household. The lives of the whole family had to be organised round the shop, which included a sub-Post Office and also sold cigarettes and tobacco, sweets and chocolate and a little greengrocery. It was a substantial business employing three assistants as well as the energies of Mr. and Mrs. Roberts and their daughters—Margaret more than Muriel, since she was in her teens in the war years when assistants were harder to get. Husband and wife made it a rule that one or other of them would always be on duty in the shop during its opening hours—which in those days included Saturday evenings. As a result it was rare for the whole family to sit down together for a meal during the week. Early closing was on Thursdays.

'The shop always seemed to be very busy,' Margaret recalls. 'On Saturday nights we did very brisk business, but even on other nights customers would often call after we had closed if they suddenly ran out of something.'

The main grocery business in an area was clearly much more a focus of social life, too, than a supermarket is today. Customers, including some of the most influential citizens of the town, would often stay half-an-hour or more chatting to Alfred Roberts over matters ranging from Hitler's designs in Europe to Grantham's rates bill. In those days, too, a substantial part of a good grocer's business was obtained by calling on a round of households and taking orders for delivery later that week. This Alfred Roberts did, making up the orders and cashing up the day's takings in the evening after the shop had closed. The orders were delivered by a boy on a bike; not until the war did the business acquire a delivery van.

Margaret can still recall vividly the scene inside the shop, which was quite large with polished mahogany fittings.

'The whole place was spotless, and we had a cat to keep the mice away. At the back was a great big bake-house; we didn't use it for baking, but all the great sides of bacon were hung there, and the sugar and flour stored in big sacks. So much was delivered in bulk in those days, you had to have quite a bit of warehousing space. There was a separate room in which we stored all the soap and soap flakes. A small passageway led from the shop to a sort of dining room, to which people like travellers were shown if they wanted to see my father.'

As she grew up Margaret was expected to do her bit helping in the shop, particularly since it was war-time. One of the main tasks was to weigh the different goods into the bags in which they would be sold. One of the earliest tasks she can remember was weighing the sugar into bags, which was done when business was slacker. The same had to be done with dried fruit and other dried commodities, such as lentils, pearl barley and peas, which were then a staple part of any weekly shopping basket. Tea, too, arrived in chests, and the quality teas were kept in polished canisters. There were also many different drums of coffee beans. 'We stocked a very wide choice. We kept spices too—every single spice you could think of.'

Treacle came in big barrels, and had to be decanted into tins or jars. Butter, margarine and lard were delivered in large packs too, and though quantities required by customers were often shaped by assistants with pats in the shop, it helped to make up pound and half-pound packets when the shop was closed. 'We used to count out bulk orders for eggs, too. When eggs were cheap in the summer people used to buy them in bulk to preserve in waterglass.' All these jobs were undertaken by Margaret at different times, occasionally after school, but always in the school holidays. Then when she was in her teens she would frequently help out by serving behind the counter too. When she was younger her maternal grandmother was also part of the family, and helped with the running of the house. She died, however, when Margaret was ten.

Alfred Roberts' business clearly prospered, but only in consequence of the hard work and long hours put into it by the members of his family. At some point between the wars he also acquired another grocery shop on the other side of the town, which had better living accommodation attached to it. But this business was never built up in the same way, probably because the original shop, the Town Council, the Methodist Church and the Rotary Club together took up all of his time. Not until Margaret was nineteen, and starting her career at Oxford, did the family finally move out from above the shop into a rather handsome semi-detached Edwardian house not far up the road. Then, for the first time, they had a garden—but there was never one for Margaret to play in as a child.

Just as the whole family could rarely sit down together to a meal during the week, so Mr. and Mrs. Roberts had to split their annual holiday so that one could remain behind to take care of the shop. Mrs. Roberts would take her two daughters each year on the train for a week at Skegness.

'In those days it was almost unheard of in Grantham for any-one to take more than a week away on holiday,' Margaret explains. 'Indeed, we felt we were very lucky to get that. Skegness was the nearest holiday resort, so that was where we went.'

In fact, she looks back with great pleasure on those childhood holidays.

'We went to the same boarding house for years—the kind where you hired rooms but took your own food and cooked it yourselves.'

On holiday there were a number of treats to which the girls looked forward every year. One was going to the fun fair, and going on the big dipper and the dodgem cars. Another was going on the boating lake. But going to what she describes as a 'typical old music hall' was the highlight of every holiday. 'We didn't have a lot of money, so these were real treats, and in those days we looked forward to them for a long time.' But most of their holiday pleasures were free—days spent on the miles of sand at Skegness, or standing outside the open front of the rock-maker's shop watching the large lumps of different colours being rolled out by hand on the marble into yards and yards of stripey rock. Then there were 'physical recreation' sessions organised for children in the gardens, and obstacle races. On one occasion, when she was older, Margaret went with a school-friend's family to Skegness for just a week-end—but that was an unusual luxury. As for Alfred Roberts, he took his holiday in Skegness during

Bowls Week, which gave him the company of other Grantham friends while enjoying the tournaments.

At New Year the girls would be taken to a pantomime, perhaps in Nottingham, where Margaret also went to some music festivals, but there were few other excursions away from Grantham. It was not till after the war that Alfred Roberts acquired a car—a second-hand Ford. So for Margaret there were no drives out into the country to neighbouring places of interest.

Though the family business clearly prospered, Alfred Roberts was always very careful with money. Great emphasis was placed on thrift. Margaret clearly remembers him telling her how when he got his first job he earned 14 shillings a week (one shilling equals 5p), of which 12 shillings went to his landlady, one shilling was spent and one shilling was saved. Even as he grew more prosperous the family continued to live very carefully; Margaret recalls how even a grapefruit was considered a luxury in the household right up until the war, when such imports were cut off anyway. For the same prudence guided Beatrice Roberts' running of her household.

She did not have Alfred's forceful character, and is described as being very kind and gentle. But she did have considerable musical talent, and it was she who encouraged Margaret in her piano lessons. She employed domestic cleaning help, since this was essential if she was to meet the heavy demands on her time from the shop. She was a trained dressmaker, and so continued to make all the girls' clothes—a skill which she passed on to her daughters as they grew up. She also did her own cooking, including the family's main daily meal. According to Margaret her mother was a great cook, and according to Denis Thatcher it is certainly a talent which she passed on to her daughters.

There were two baking days each week—on Thursday afternoon, when the shop was closed, and very early on Sunday mornings. By the time Margaret sat down to her Sunday breakfast the house was full of the smells of home-baked bread and cakes. Margaret also recalls how it was a regular part of her mother's routine to bake a few extra loaves and cakes for those they knew who might be sick or have fallen on hard times, and how she would then deliver them.

'It was all done very quietly,' she recalls. 'We were always encouraged to think in terms of *practical* help, and to think very little of people who thought that their duty to the less well-off started and finished by getting up and protesting in the market

place. That was ducking it, passing off your responsibilities to
someone else. The crucial thing was what you were prepared to
do yourself out of your own slender income. So twice a week
Mama baked, and twice a week loaves or cakes went out to anyone
she knew who really needed them.'

The same high regard for thrift shown by the parents was
passed on to the children 'We took our pocket money to school
each week to buy savings stamps, which we put towards buying
savings certificates,' Margaret recalls. 'I think we took it every
Monday morning with the milk money.' Of course, this domestic
pressure would have been reinforced soon after war broke out,
when Margaret was fourteen, by Government propaganda too.
But it was an established part of her childhood long before that.
Neither was this saving undertaken with a view to subsequent
withdrawal in order to buy some coveted object. 'We simply saved
in order to have a little behind us, perhaps when we went on to
college or started work. After all, those were pretty uncertain days.
In our home it was also a rule that all birthday money had to
go into savings too. Of course, in those days money had a stable
value.'

So we can see how the values of the successful private shop-
keeper were an essential part of the family environment in which
the young Margaret grew up. Hard work was the lot of all, and
accepted without question. The business came first, for Alfred
Roberts the Town Council second, and all other pleasure and
pastimes had to fit into the routine dictated by these. The entire
business was governed by careful budgeting and accounting, and
great care with money was exercised throughout the household.
Here, indeed, were the virtues of small private enterprise at their
best, and they go a long way to explain Margaret Thatcher's
deep regard now for all who work to sustain their own businesses.

But there was one dominant influence on the whole Roberts
family which fortified and guided all the others, and that was
the Methodist Church. Both father and mother were active
members, and indeed probably first met through its activities.
The girls were brought up in it, and took part in the whole range
of Methodist Church activities. We have already noted Margaret's
view that she was brought up 'in a rather puritan way', and her
husband Denis describes the household even when he knew it as
being 'very Nonconformist'. Grace was said before and after
every meal. Both parents were teetotal, though they were tolerant
to the extent of keeping some sherry and cherry brandy in order to

be able to offer hospitality to visitors. No newspapers were allowed into the house on Sundays, and the grandmother, who was very strict in this respect, would not even allow the girls to sew or knit on Sundays either.

For them, of course, Sunday was a very special day. As we have seen, it began very early for Mrs. Roberts, who got up long before breakfast to do half the week's baking. After breakfast both Muriel and Margaret would go to Sunday School, and from there to Morning Service, at which they would join their parents. The girls would return to Sunday School again in the afternoon and, when older, go with their parents to church again in the evening. Alfred Roberts was a lay preacher in some demand, and as they got older the girls sometimes went to hear him preach. On Sunday evenings the church would have a visiting preacher, and after the service he would generally return with other church people to the Roberts household for supper and further religious discussion.

Thus Sundays were set aside entirely for church activity, and there was no question of the girls using the day to play with friends. One of Margaret's closest school friends was a girl called Jean Farmer, and it often struck her that her friend led a freer and in some ways gayer life than she did herself. Indeed, she once asked her father why she could not sometimes be as free on Sundays as her friend.

'Margaret,' replied her father, 'never do things just because other people do them. Make up your own mind what you are going to do and persuade people to go *your* way.'

But one should not be left with the impression that religion for the Roberts family was of a negative, kill-joy kind. A wealth of social and cultural activity went on around the Methodist Church, to which the family contributed fully and therefore drew from too in good measure. There were regular church socials, either to raise funds for a Methodist charity or to help maintain the church itself. Every Wednesday afternoon Mrs. Roberts slipped away from the shop to attend the church sewing meeting, and frequently Margaret would join her there after school in order to improve her stitching. Then on Tuesday evenings there was the Methodist Guild for young people, to which both girls belonged. Each Christmas they would join in a Nativity play. And then there was the splendid music of the church.

'People living in London often don't realise that the musical talent existing in every provincial town is very considerable,' Margaret remarks. 'This was certainly so in Grantham. In the

Methodist Church we had an excellent organist and a good choir. They were a joy to hear.'

Margaret herself took piano lessons from the age of five, and apparently performed very well, often entering local music festivals and Eisteddfods. The very first time she entered she won a prize for her piano piece. In later years more medallions followed, for her readings and recitations as well as for her piano performances. She kept up her piano lessons till she was fifteen, latterly from quite an advanced teacher who travelled once a week from Lincoln to teach about a dozen pupils in Grantham, but then gave them up as the pressure of her academic studies became greater.

She also had a good singing voice, and joined the church choir for a while. Then when she was older she joined a local Dramatic Society from which sprang a concert party. But much of her musical activity was within the church.

'The high point in the church's musical life were the oratorios performed once or twice a year. Three or four lead singers would be brought in, and the music was magnificent.'

An important part of church life was also the recognition of responsibility to those less fortunate. We have already seen how Mrs. Roberts baked a number of extra loaves and cakes each week for those she felt could do with them. Those of their weekly pennies that the girls did not save were often directed towards Methodist charities and missions. Denis Thatcher, on his first meeting with Alfred Roberts, clearly remembers him opening out a Methodist newspaper in which were pages of advertisements for a wide variety of charities. Then he remarked sadly, 'I dream of the day when I have a lot of money, so that I can subscribe to all those I'd like to.'

Thus, in addition to the example of hard work and commercial prudence set by her parents, the Methodist Church with all its activities and works was a very strong influence on Margaret as she grew up. Though in later years she moved away from strict Nonconformity, and indeed came to take in the Anglican position, the values she acquired from that bustling Methodist Church in Grantham are with her still. It is perhaps revealing to reflect that Margaret Thatcher, in her way, is as much the child of the Nonconformist conscience as Harold Wilson is in his.

CHAPTER TWO

Broadening Horizons
1930–1943

The Grantham into which Margaret Roberts was born was a fairly prosperous railway town. The express trains from London to Scotland used to stop here to change engines and crews, and in one way or another the railway provided many jobs. Large and powerful steam engines were made at Ruston and Hornsby's works, whose manager was among the customers at Alfred Roberts' shop. Grantham was also a busy market town, and every Wednesday farmers came in from a wide area around. Saturday saw a different kind of market—'rows and rows of stalls in the Market Place and the length of Castlegate,' Margaret recalls, 'at which you could buy everything from greengrocery to china and haberdashery.' She went to it regularly, and also with her father 'prowled around' the auction sales that were held twice weekly. She can remember bidding herself for some Queen Anne-type mahogany dining chairs—and getting them for £1 each.

In the thirties Grantham was inevitably affected by the depression. 'I remember we had some friends whose father just could not get work, and who had to draw the dole,' she says. 'Everyone did what they could to help, but the parents had great pride and went without many things to support their children. I still remember the great thrill we all had when he eventually got a job.' The war brought a kind of artificial prosperity. There was a large munitions works, and the town was full of Air Force people from Grantham Aerodrome.

Margaret began her school career at Huntingtower Road Elementary School just before her fifth birthday. This was not the nearest school to her home, but it had the best reputation among the council schools of Grantham. Alfred Roberts would have been a schoolmaster if he had had the chance, and he was determined that both his daughters should receive the very best education available to them. He accordingly took great pains to secure their

admission to Huntingtower Road. This was about a mile away
from their home—a mile which five-year-old Margaret walked
four times a day, as lunches were not served at the school so she
and her sister would return home for them. Margaret never had
a bicycle until, as an adult, she got her first job.

She still remembers this first school very clearly, her first
teacher, Miss Dabbs, and the name of each teacher as she pro-
gressed through it. The teaching was traditional, and thorough.
The classes numbered around forty, but she can recall no discipline problems, and the teachers seem to have succeeded in
opening out the minds of their infants.

Though the rich would not send their children to a council
school, this one nevertheless drew its pupils from a fairly broad
social background.

'It drew from the ordinary life of Grantham,' she recalls, 'from
families who were fortunate, and from those who weren't. They
were tough days for some people—very tough. One or two
children used to go to the soup kitchen for lunch; I can remember
one young boy who did, in fact a very gay and cheerful child.' The
school also drew pupils from an orphanage across the playground.
'It always seemed a great pity that they were the only ones in
uniform, blue with white pinnies.'

Margaret herself did well at school from the very start. She had
not been there long before she was moved up to a class for
children a year older than herself. She was good all round, and
describes herself at this stage of her academic career as always
being 'near the top of the class'.

And so at the age of ten she came to take the scholarship
examination for the Kesteven and Grantham Girls' School. This
school had a good reputation, sustained by the examination suc-
cesses of its senior girls. About half the pupils were boarders, and
about a quarter were there on scholarships. Muriel was already
there as a fee-paying pupil, but it was quite important to their
father that Margaret should win a scholarship. In practical terms
this did not make a great deal of difference, since it was means-
tested and he would end up paying the fees for her too. But it was
an insurance that, in the event of his death, she could continue
at the school as a maintained pupil. Certainly when she sat the
examination Margaret was deeply aware how important it was,
but given her record at Huntingtower Road School she was
justifiably confident of passing—'though that didn't stop me
feeling pretty elated when I did'.

Once she was at Kesteven there was no holding her back. She shone in nearly all subjects, and at the end of nearly every term came out top of her class. 'I was never much good at art,' she recalls, 'and my marks in that tended to pull me down. But it was always very competitive. In those days I think we were all very conscious of striving to make the most of our opportunities.'

Margaret did not greatly enjoy ball games, but persevered with hockey, and in time became vice-captain of her school team. Out of school hours she enjoyed swimming. She joined the Debating Society and took an active part. But her studies took pride of place. Several in Grantham still remember her as the girl who could never fasten her satchel because it was packed with so many books.

She did not have a large circle of friends, but was very close to one or two like Jean Farmer and Margaret Goodrich—both, like her, pretty serious girls. It was during her career through this school that she began to reveal that streak of utter determination that has characterised everything that she has done since.

Her headmistress, Miss Dorothy Gillies, must at times have found this rather irritating, but reacted with tolerance. There was the occasion when she asked Margaret whether she had given any thought to her future career. Margaret, who may have been influenced by her avid reading of Kipling, replied that she would like to join the Indian Civil Service.

Miss Gillies remarked that this was a career which very few women succeeded in entering, to which Margaret replied, 'That sounds a very good reason for trying to get into it.'

Her response to more immediate challenges at school was much the same. As her sister Muriel recalls, 'At school Margaret always knew what she wanted to do, and did it.' As we shall see, it was only by applying this same determination that she got to Somerville College, Oxford.

In those days children generally sat for their School Certificate at the age of sixteen, and passes in a set number of subjects secured what was called Matriculation. This was in 1940–41, and Margaret can remember swotting up her subjects under the dining room table at home during air raids.

'Though Grantham was not often their main target, the enemy planes came over frequently and sometimes unloaded their bombs. We got up when the sirens went, and climbed under the dining room table. It was large and solid, and made the best air raid shelter we had.' Such distractions, of course, did not prevent her securing Matriculation, and she went on into the sixth form to study chemistry, biology and French for Higher School Certificate, the examination which was then generally taken at the age of eighteen.

By this time she was starting to concentrate on the sciences— 'One then knew that science was the coming thing. That was a period when we were dazzled by what it could achieve. We thought there were no problems that could not ultimately be answered by science.'

During this period it also became clear that Margaret had the gift of great concentration which in later life enabled her to master so many Shadow and Departmental briefs. 'When I took one of the papers for my School Certificate I can remember going in, looking at the questions, and realising that I should be able to work through them fairly easily. So I put my head down and got on with it. When the exam was over someone remarked on the heavy thunderstorm there had been part way through. But I'd been concentrating so hard on answering the questions that I'd never even noticed it.'

We shall never know at what point in her school career Alfred Roberts realised that his second daughter was something rather exceptional. He had, as we have seen, given her every encouragement from a very early age. But during her teens it is clear that he made a great effort to involve her in any activity which would have the effect of broadening her intellectual horizons.

He was first elected to Grantham's Borough Council as an Independent soon after Margaret was born, and he went on to serve the Council for thirty-four years. In the Council Chamber he grew in stature, and soon came to be regarded as a leading figure in the community—which, with his additional involvement in the Methodist Church and the Rotary Club, he indeed was. Mr. Percy Willard, the town's librarian, has described him as 'the most skilled debater the Council ever had'.

The town was then run largely by Independent or Ratepayer councillors, challenged by Socialists. Most of the former were local shopkeepers or professional people, and as party politics were brought more and more into council affairs they came to be identified more as what they really were—Conservatives.

Alfred Roberts and his wife were originally Liberals, which historically one might have expected from their strong Nonconformist background. But during the inter-war years they became firmly Conservative, though on the Council he did not invariably vote with the other Conservatives.

In due course he became an alderman, and for several years was the respected chairman of the Council's key Finance Committee. Finally, not long before Margaret left home, he was made Grantham's Mayor.

Thus over many years he was a highly respected local figure, and anyone wishing to consult him always knew where to find him—at the shop. Indeed, a day rarely passed without some other councillors or leading figures in the town calling in to discuss something, and Margaret recalls the conversations could easily last for half-an-hour or more. To other members of the family it often seemed that the shop was an annexe to the Council Chamber.

However, the conversations were by no means restricted to local affairs, often ranging over national events and the ominous developments in Europe—the expansion of Nazi Germany, Mussolini's ambitions in Africa and the Spanish Civil War. But the important point concerning us is that, as she grew older, whenever Margaret was in the shop her father would deliberately involve her in these discussions. Thus not only did she become exceptionally well-informed on such matters for a girl of her age, but also gained experience in discussing them and putting forward views of her own.

'I also used to go about with him a lot,' she recalls. 'If he was doing anything interesting he would take me along. This was part of one's education.' Looking back, it is as if Alfred Roberts was deliberately schooling his younger daughter for a role in public life.

He was also a man of inquiring intellect, and a voracious reader. Every week Margaret was sent to the public library to get two books—one of current fiction for her mother, the other a biography or historical or political work for her father.

As he read these books he would mark passages which he thought particularly interesting to draw to her attention, and in school holidays, when she was unburdened with homework, she would read some of the books in their entirety. She can still remember some of the titles: *Berlin Diary*, a book about communism called *Out of the Night*, *Guns or Butter*, and *The Seven Pillars of Wisdom*.

He would then seek her opinions, and convey his own, this conversation between father and daughter often being conducted as the more routine tasks of running the shop were undertaken. Another of Alfred Roberts' favourite pastimes, on a rare empty evening, was to move round the dial of their radio picking up English-language programmes from across Europe. It is to all this that Margaret is referring when she speaks of the good education she received, 'not only in school, but at home as well'.

Whenever a prominent national politician came to Grantham Margaret was taken along to meet or hear him. 'I can remember Herbert Morrison coming at the beginning of the war to visit the local ARP [Air Raid Precautions] service, and I was taken along to that. Then we had our National Savings Week; Grantham was saving towards a frigate, and Pa was chairman of the National Savings Committee. During this another Labour man, A. V. Alexander, who was First Lord of the Admiralty, came to speak from the Town Hall steps, and I went to hear him.'

When she was only ten she acquired her first taste of national politics being fought out on the ground in the 1935 general election, when she helped the Conservative effort to return Sir Victor Warrender.

'I helped fold election addresses, and on election day I helped run the numbers of those who'd voted from the tellers at the Polling Station to our committee room.'

At the age of sixteen she was even more involved when, following Sir Victor's elevation to the House of Lords, there was a by-election in March 1942. The Conservative candidate was Sir Arthur Longmore, but he was challenged by an Independent, William Kendall, who ran a very prosperous local munitions works. It was a straight fight, and the Roberts family were backing the Conservative. Margaret helped in pushing leaflets through the doors.

On polling day the Conservatives were toppled by 367 votes, and William Kendall became MP. But of course Alfred Roberts knew him well too, and occasionally borrowed books from him. But to this day Margaret has strong views about him, for though like her father he was a self-made man, to her the munitions works clearly represented the superficial prosperity which the war had brought to Grantham.

'He was a flamboyant character, had a very glamorous wife— and a flamboyant home, built with the sort of things in it many people didn't have. Undoubtedly extrovert, and talented, he certainly had something, and was going places.'

The Kendalls' life style obviously offended the Roberts family's idea of the example which those in public life should set. But William Kendall must have been popular in Grantham generally, for in the 1945 general election he boosted his majority from 367 to 15,513, in a three-cornered fight. The Conservatives did not get their revenge till 1950, after which the Kendalls left Grantham.

Thus by the time she reached the sixth form at Kesteven Margaret had a fairly broad knowledge of national and world affairs, had read quite widely beyond the strict range of her school subjects, and had some practical experience of politics at work—just flavoured with the taste of defeat. Meanwhile, she was beginning to distinguish herself particularly at chemistry, having been brought on by a particularly good teacher at Kesteven. And so, as she worked for her Higher School Certificate, the question arose of which university she should proceed to later. Pupils at Kesteven had established quite a good record at winning university places, and Margaret duly lodged her application with two or three, including Bedford and Holloway Colleges at London University. However, it was at this point that Margaret made one of those distinctive and typically strong decisions of her life; she was going to aim high, and try for a scholarship at Somerville College, Oxford.

The whole idea was riddled with difficulties, as Miss Gillies soon told her. First of all, the usual approach was to join in the stiff competition for a scholarship at Oxford or Cambridge during a third year in the sixth form, after acquiring Higher School Certificate. But if Margaret did this she would have to go for a curtailed two-year degree, instead of the obviously more highly-rated full degree course. This was because, at that point in the war, all women were called up for military service at the age of twenty—so fitting in a three-year degree course meant in her case winning a place at seventeen. On top of this, one needed School Certificate in Latin or Greek to enter Oxford. Margaret had never even studied Latin, leave alone obtained a School Certificate in the subject.

From all this Miss Gillies concluded, not unreasonably, that the idea of going for a scholarship at Somerville was a non-starter. So Margaret went home to ponder the situation, which looked pretty bleak, and to talk it over with her father. But, as sister Muriel said: 'At school Margaret always knew what she wanted to do, and did it.' So she unfolded her plan to her father, who typically decided to back it, despite all the obstacles.

The first was her lack of any qualification in Latin, which seems not to have been taught at Kesteven. So her father arranged to pay for a concentrated course of lessons out of school hours from the classics master at the boys' school, which if successful would enable Margaret to obtain the necessary School Certificate in a matter of months. As soon as this was fixed up Margaret went to Miss Gillies and told her, but still the headmistress said it was an impossible course on which she was seeking to embark.

Back Margaret went to her father, and the next day returned to Miss Gillies' study with a cheque covering the examination entrance fee in her hand. 'I have decided to go in for this exam, so will you please send off my forms?' she asked. So Miss Gillies, recognising that this kind of determination could often overcome apparently insuperable obstacles, fell in with the plan too.

From then on for Margaret it was one fast slog to reach the required standard, and to acquire the basic qualification in Latin, which she did.

The scholarship examination had to be taken at Somerville College in late winter, and involved staying in college overnight. This was Margaret's first visit to Oxford, and the atmosphere of the 'city of dreaming spires' obviously made a great impression on the girl from Grantham, making her all the more determined that this was the university for her. The examination involved written papers in her chosen subjects, a general paper, and an interview. All the discussion and reading inspired by her father equipped her well to tackle the general paper, and after all the hours of discussion with him and other citizens of the town she should have been able to give a reasonably good account of herself in an interview.

The result of the whole exercise was that Margaret just missed the scholarship she was after; it was awarded to a girl who already had experience of competing for it the previous year. But she was awarded a place, and shone enough to be told by the college authorities that if she needed financial help to take it up they would see that she obtained it. That was all Margaret needed! With various bursaries arranged by the college, and the savings of her childhood behind her, she was all set to go to Somerville College, Oxford. Her determination, and her father's faith in her, had paid off.

However, it is worth noting that even after this success she still had a very open mind on what career she should pursue. Some of her schoolfellows have since claimed that she had her sights set on getting into Parliament from an early age, but Margaret claims that all she did was to seize the different chances as they came.

Indeed, after winning her place and financial backing at Somerville to read chemistry, she did have some regrets that it was not an opening to read law instead. This arose from another of Alfred Roberts' exercises in broadening the horizons of his daughter. For during his Mayoral year, shortly before she went up to Oxford, he used to sit on the Bench at Grantham's Quarter Sessions with the Recorder, Norman Winning, QC. After this the Recorder and the local magistrates would lunch together at the Angel Hotel.

When Margaret was sixteen—the minimum age for admission to the public gallery of the court—her father had encouraged her to watch the proceedings, and she was fascinated by them. Subsequently he took her with him to the Angel Hotel. There she got to know Norman Winning, and after gaining her place at Somerville confided in him that she would as soon be reading law. But his advice was to take up the chance she had to read chemistry, and if she wished to combine this qualification with law later to aim for the Patent Bar. Then he clinched the argument by revealing that he himself had read physics at Cambridge. In fact, Margaret began reading for the Bar some seven years later. But, whether she had cast herself in her mind during her schooldays for politics or not, the conversation in the Angel Hotel is proof that she already saw herself as becoming a woman of many parts.

CHAPTER THREE

Oxford: The Path of Politics
1943-1947

Margaret Roberts arrived at Oxford with her trunk filled with books and her wartime ration of clothes in the autumn of 1943, a few days away from her eighteenth birthday. The contrast between life in a provincial town such as Grantham, where her father had become the leading citizen, and the sophisticated and even in the war academically rarified atmosphere of Oxford must have struck her sharply. She was at Somerville, which had a good reputation; in any event, academic standards in the women's colleges were on average higher than in the men's, for the simple reason that there were far fewer of them and therefore competition to enter them was rather more intense.

The university generally would also have contained a number of fairly wealthy people—though Margaret puts them in a minority—whereas she had to plan very carefully to make ends meet. In fact, her income was assembled from a variety of sources. As promised by the college authorities at the time of her scholarship examination, she received a bursary from some charitable trust, and, as she recalls, 'we had to rustle around for a number of small grants from other bodies—but we just about got enough together'. There were also the savings she had accumulated through childhood, and if she had really found herself in difficulties she could have fallen back on a scholarship from Kesteven Girls' School in return for undertaking to teach there for a period subsequently. However, this never became necessary.

For her first two years she had a small but comfortable room in college. But wartime Oxford was a rather peculiar place, populated by students cramming in short courses before call-up, some young ones like Margaret planning to get in a three-year course, others exempted from military service on medical grounds, and a few who had been invalided out. Margaret recalls 'a sort of general feeling of unease whether we ought to be there at all, but joined up instead and leaving our studies till later. I think this feeling was particularly strong among the arts people.'

And so while a war was being fought across Europe it was accepted that everyone should undertake some kind of voluntary work. Margaret's was to help twice a week in a forces' canteen at Carfax, in the centre of the city. There 'you just did anything that had to be done—washed up, made sandwiches, served at the counter. You did anything.'

Meanwhile she worked hard at her studies, which entailed laboratory work in the mornings. Her own tutor was Dorothy Hodgkin, though of course she had others. Her work was to a consistent standard, and she was expected to do well in her finals. 'I enjoyed every moment of Oxford life,' she recalls, 'both the work and everything else. But I didn't go in for any sports—I wasn't really good enough.'

However, she developed plenty of interests outside her college, most of them continuations of those she had had in Grantham. She continued her interest in music by joining the Bach Choir, and she went occasionally to sing with the Balliol Choir as well. She attended the Methodist Church, and later in her Oxford career broadened her religious interest to take in Anglican Churches too.

But her main activity, in the footsteps of her father, was politics. She joined the Oxford University Conservative Association (OUCA), which after the war developed into a powerhouse of political energy. She attended the weekly meetings to hear visiting speakers of note. She was elected to OUCA's committee, and in subsequent terms served as its general agent, treasurer and eventually president—the top of the Tory tree at Oxford. This political activity, culminating at the end of each term in elections to the main OUCA offices, can easily become almost full-time unless one is very careful; but, though this was her main activity, Margaret kept her interests broad.

For a male undergraduate such political activity generally spilt over into the Oxford Union, whose famous debates took place every Thursday evening. But in those days, and for a long time afterwards, women were not admitted as members, and to hear the debates had to be invited into a gallery as a guest, as Margaret was frequently. In fact, this was the only discrimination against women of which she was aware at Oxford, and it does not seem to have irritated her unduly; her attitude was rather that she would not have been very keen to join in the Union debates

Three years old and looking alert, Margaret sits with her elder sister Muriel.

Margaret as a schoolgirl, feeding pigeons.

The earliest picture: Margaret as a toddler, held firmly for the camera by her father, Alfred Roberts.

anyway. 'They were conducted in a way that would not particularly appeal to women. The approach at that time was very witty, certainly, and "clever", but it lacked gravitas. It was excellent entertainment, and some of the debates were superb, but many of them were rather frothy.' Politics were Margaret's dominant interest—and they were serious.

Meanwhile, she appears to have led a fairly full social life, many of her friends being drawn from outside Somerville. She had a number of men friends, but denies having any in particular. 'I was a pretty serious person. One was asked out and about, but by quite a number of people.' The more glamorous side of Oxford's life, such as the big college commemoration balls, was not revived after the war until about the time she was leaving.

We have seen how at Oxford she had to budget rather carefully, and one thing that every undergraduate needs in this university is a bicycle to get to laboratories, lectures, social engagements and, eventually, one's lodgings. Now throughout her Grantham childhood Margaret had never enjoyed such a luxury, having always walked to and from school, and during her first year at Oxford she determined that in the next summer vacation she would take a job and buy herself a new bicycle.

And so it came about that, in the August of 1944, Margaret Roberts took a job teaching chemistry, mathematics and general science at Grantham's Central School for Boys. In those war years a school term was arranged in August so that the pupils could be released to pick rose hips later in the year. Right across the country school terms were made much more flexible to meet local harvesting needs, and the special late summer term in Grantham meant that the future Secretary of State for Education got in six weeks' experience as a teacher!

She is rather modest over how she made out. 'I just don't know, but I enjoyed it. I used to go on until I knew they'd got it, and I wasn't prepared to let them go on until they'd got it. And you might have to come at it several different ways, particularly in mathematics.'

It is characteristic of Margaret Thatcher that she never exploited this experience as a teacher for propaganda purposes while at the Department of Education, or indeed while shadowing it earlier, since she recognised how minimal her formal qualification to teach then had been. The important thing was that it met a war need back home in Grantham—and provided the money with which to buy a bicycle the following term.

It was during her second year at Oxford that the war was won, thus clearing the way for her not only to complete her three-year course before taking her finals but also the fourth year of research necessary before getting an honours degree in chemistry.

1945 was also the year of the general election, and Margaret threw herself fully into the campaign, both in Oxford and then after term ended in Grantham. The MP for Oxford City since the famous by-election of 1938 was Quintin Hogg, and he now returned from military service to defend it against a Labour challenge from Frank Pakenham. Margaret well remembers a meeting in Oxford Town Hall with Quintin using 'real old-fashioned electioneering tactics'. She herself canvassed for him in a rough area of small streets, since demolished, round the gasworks.

Then a letter arrived from George Worth, the Conservative candidate at Grantham, asking if she would help him in his campaign as soon as term was over. He was the son-in-law of Sir Arthur Longmore, the defeated Tory candidate in the 1942 by-election. She readily agreed, and back in Grantham her role was to go to the surrounding villages speaking on his behalf. 'I was the "pot-boiler" who kept the meeting going until the candidate arrived.' They were, of course, challenging the Independent William Kendall, for whom Margaret had no more regard than she had during the by-election.

The national result was a Labour landslide—though Margaret correctly recalls how this took many Tories by surprise. Led by Winston Churchill, they had assumed that his great reputation as war leader would be reflected in Conservative votes.

'I remember very vividly the long, long gap in that election between polling day and the count, while we all waited for forces' votes to come back. We were all quite confident, and it never occurred to us that we could ever lose on that scale.' So many whom one might a couple of years before have assumed would be Conservative voted for something different as a symbol of change from what they had known in the pre-war years. On the day the results were coming out Margaret recalls meeting a teacher friend in Grantham and saying to him : 'Isn't the news dreadful?' 'I was absolutely shaken to the core when he replied, "Oh, I don't know, I'm really rather pleased about it." But that sort of thing was happening all across the country.'

Quintin Hogg held Oxford City, but in Grantham William

Kendall scooped up much of the anti-Tory as well as the Tory vote to romp home. Clement Attlee's majority in the Commons was 146.

When Margaret returned to Oxford that autumn to start her third Michaelmas term she found the university a very different place. All those who had postponed their courses, or interrupted them for war service, came flooding back on good ex-servicemen's gratuities. The Oxford of this immediate post-war period has since become something of a legend. Men who had fought their way across the Western Desert and Europe were hardly likely to settle down and accept the conventions of undergraduates straight from school. There were among this generation a tough element who were determined to be a law unto themselves. But Margaret, as one of the younger students, is convinced that she and others of her generation benefited enormously from the great influx of ex-servicemen and women.

'The whole student body became so much more mature. So many of my friends were now older than I was, some much older —five, ten, even fifteen years older.' Throughout her teens Margaret had always preferred older more serious company, and one can see how the new post-war Oxford suited her perfectly.

It was this same term that she had to move into lodgings, having completed her two years of residence in Somerville. With two other girls she took lodgings quite centrally at 18 Walton Street, where the landlady was a Mrs. Cole.

'It was a comfortable house, and each of us had our own room. There was Mary Mallison, a farmer's daughter, and Mary Foss, whose father was a butcher. That was very convenient, because we used to put all our meat coupons together and send them to her father, and get a really good joint for the week-end, which Mrs. Cole would cook for us.'

Here the three girls also offered the standard student hospitality of tea parties, at which Margaret's political and musical friends would mix with those from other walks of student life brought in by the other girls. 'We had lots of discussions—discussions all the time.' Thus the great broadening of the horizons of student life due to the arrival of the ex-service generation coincided with her own increased freedom as a result of moving out of college.

One effect of this was to give a big impetus to political activity, both on the Left and the Right. Sir Edward Boyle shone from the Tory side, and William Rees-Mogg; Anthony Wedgwood Benn was a leading Labour figure, and Anthony Crosland, though he was a don. Peter Emery and Ludovic Kennedy were also among Margaret's contemporaries. The Tories' massive defeat in the 1945 election does not seem to have produced any feeling among Conservative students of having their backs to the wall; rather the spirit within OUCA seems to have been one of reconstruction and regeneration, with fertile discussion of how the Tories should reappraise their policies in the light of the new situation. Tory politicians of note came to OUCA's weekly meetings, and there was good contact with Quintin Hogg, the city's MP.

Margaret particularly remembers a visit by Peter Thorneycroft, and his advocacy of a 'dash for freedom' with a rapid scrapping of controls when the Tories next took office. 'Both he and Quintin represented a young school of Tory thought, stressing the restoration of freedom in contrast to the growth of bureaucracy.'

Another notable visitor was Sir David Maxwell-Fyfe (later Lord Chancellor Lord Kilmuir), who in the post-war years was given the task by Winston Churchill of investigating the whole organisation of the party and recommending drastic changes. These covered the procedures for selecting Parliamentary candidates, which when adopted opened the door to those with ability but no privilege—candidates such as Margaret herself.

Meanwhile, at the Conservative Research Department, R. A. Butler was starting to shape the new Tory policies which were to form the basis of the 1950 and 1951 election programmes, and indeed of Government action through the early 1950s. These did not start to blossom publicly until the time that Margaret was leaving Oxford, but she and the other deeply committed members of OUCA were certainly contributing to the background thought that was leading to them.

Her own political thinking at this time seems to have been within the mainstream of newly emerging Butlerite policies. She was clearly very impressed by the thought and arguments of Quintin Hogg, whose emphasis on the religious element in the Conservative view of society and the obligations it entailed struck an obvious chord with someone of her family background. She would appear to have supported the 'dash for freedom' school of thought after the necessary restrictions of war-time and Labour's subsequent version of the Planned Economy.

This was also a period in which her own interests were broadening again, from chemistry and law to take in economics. Many of her OUCA friends were students in the thriving philosophy, politics and economics school, and a good deal of their academic knowledge would have rubbed off on Margaret during the discussion groups, formal and informal. So some of her spare-time reading was directed to increasing her knowledge of economics too. It was to this lively, but perhaps distracting background that Margaret completed her three-year course.

It was that October, in 1946, that she attended her first annual party conference, in Blackpool, representing OUCA, and the event made a great impression on her.

'It was, as usual, an enormous party gathering. For the first time in my life I realised just how big the party was, and what it meant to be a member of such an organisation of people with the same ideals and objectives.'

Despite the scale of the 1945 defeat, she recalls that the party's 'spirit was good and morale was high'.

And so back to Oxford, to embark on the further year's research for thesis that was needed to obtain an Honours Degree in Science. The field of research was dictated very much by one's tutor's own field of activity, which in Margaret's case meant research into X-ray crystallography. This she pursued diligently, but she never saw it as leading to anything further in her case, since she had already come to the firm conclusion that on going down from Oxford she would take a scientific job which would allow her to study law in her spare time.

'I felt very much how *impersonal* work in a laboratory was,' she recalls. 'One reason why I was so active in politics was that all the time it's concerned with people,' she explains. 'I think a lot of scientists of my generation were looking for ways in which they could apply their knowledge, not in a laboratory, but out in the field.'

During this final year she also won a university prize for an essay she had submitted—and became president of OUCA. And at the end of it all she emerged with a good Second—which disappointed some of her tutors, who had thought her quite capable of getting a First.

'I was taken to task because I could have done better,' Margaret admits. 'The point was that I had been active doing so many other things.'

In fact, this tells us a good deal about the priorities she was establishing for her future life. From her record at Kesteven one might have expected her to fix on the one objective of academic distinction in her chosen subject and to pursue it with total dedication. But, though she worked hard, she certainly did not do this.

Politics played an increasingly important part in her life and this led her to spend some time studying economics. Finally, her year of laboratory research reinforced her inclination even before going up to Oxford to switch to law at the earliest opportunity. In view of this a First Class Degree, though personally gratifying, would have been of little direct benefit. Oxford's gift to Margaret, as to so many of its pupils, was to broaden her intellectual horizons to the point of enabling her to comprehend the nature of other academic disciplines.

But there was no question of her being able to move on to a second degree course in law; there was no grant or other cash available for her to do so. Her only chance was to get a scientific job in London, join one of the Inns of Court at which she would eat the necessary number of dinners, and pursue her studies in her spare time. But getting a job in London proved difficult, so instead she took a research job with a plastics firm at Colchester, and moved into fresh lodgings there. This was too far from London to enable her to join one of the Inns of Court, so she postponed this ambition for the moment—and threw herself fully into the activities of the Colchester Conservative Association.

'We had a "39–45 Group"—a discussion group for those who had returned from the Services.' Margaret had not seen military service, but this was the generation which had provided so many of her friends at Oxford. And so with her political priorities clearly established, she again felt at home.

CHAPTER FOUR

The Youngest Woman Candidate
1948-1951

'People often ask me whether at some point in the past I saw myself as a future MP, or Minister, or even Party Leader. The answer is always "No". In politics you just seize your chances as they come, and make the most of them—and that's what I've always tried to do.'

So Margaret Thatcher seeks to refute those who suggest that her career proceeded according to some kind of Grand Design. There is little doubt that, as a student and as a graduate research chemist, she did seriously consider the possibility of looking for a Parliamentary seat to fight at some time in the future.

This would be quite normal for someone devoting as much time to student politics as she did, and who immediately integrated with the local Conservative Association on getting her first job at Colchester. But what she could never have anticipated was that her first chance to put herself forward would come so soon—at the age of twenty-four.

It came when she went to the 1948 annual party conference, which was held that year in Llandudno, representing the Oxford University Graduates' Association. While there she happened to meet an old Oxford friend called John Grant, who was a director of Blackwell's Bookshop, and they sat down together in the conference hall.

As Margaret tells the story : 'Sitting the other side of him was the chairman of the Dartford Association, a chap called John Miller. He said to Miller : "Who is your candidate?" to which Miller replied, "We haven't got one, but we're considering getting one." John Grant then said, "Would you consider a woman?", then immediately turned to me and said, "Why don't you put your name in for it?" '

In fact, the Dartford chairman's initial response was sceptical. He pointed out that it was a highly industrial constituency, and that perhaps a woman candidate would not go down well. However, later that day while Margaret was taking a stroll on Llandudno pier she encountered him again, this time with the rest of his delegation, to whom he introduced her. Margaret cannot remember whether candidatures were mentioned, but she liked the Dartford delegates, and after returning to Colchester formally applied to be considered as prospective candidate for the seat.

It was, of course, a hopeless seat for a Conservative to fight, with Norman Dodds then holding it for Labour with a majority of nearly 20,000. However, even hopeless 'first try' seats within easy reach of London are generally popular with would-be candidates, and there were some twenty-four applicants for this one. Early in 1949 Margaret was invited to Dartford for an interview, and short-listed. She was the only woman on the short list, and the youngest. This being the first candidature for which she had applied she hardly expected to be selected—but selected she was to fight this rather tough North Kent seat.

One gathers from other sources that the selection committee were particularly impressed by her ability—which has continued to take people by surprise throughout her political career—to expound a complicated argument in brief and relatively simple terms, without in any way seeming to talk down to her audience. Looking back, Margaret's own feeling is that, given the social attitudes prevalent in 1949, the Dartford selection committee were rather brave in taking on a woman of twenty-four. In both the 1950 and 1951 general elections she was the youngest woman candidate in the country.

After the selection of a candidate by a committee generally representing all sections of a Conservative association, the next step in the process is an adoption meeting, at which the committee's choice is presented to all members of the association. At this meeting he or she makes a speech, answers questions, and is usually then adopted by formal resolution as that association's prospective Parliamentary candidate. The 'prospective' tag remains until the actual start of the election campaign, when the candidate becomes legally responsible for his or her election expenses. But the initial adoption meeting is a candidate's first big political occasion in the constituency, and a mistake made at this can dog him or her right through to the general election.

Margaret's adoption meeting turned out to be packed and

quite exciting because, as she puts it, 'all sorts of people turned out to see this unusual creature'. But it all went very well, she was formally adopted with great enthusiasm, and presented with an enormous bouquet. Dinner had been arranged for her that evening by some leading members of the Association. A few days before the hostess realised she would be one man short, so invited a business colleague of her husband's who was active in the association but who lived in London. After the meeting the question arose of how Margaret was to get back to Colchester, and she said by train. 'In that case you'd better come as far as London with me in the car,' the young man said—an offer which the new candidate gratefully accepted. And that was how Margaret Roberts met Denis Thatcher.

Margaret immediately set about her new task with typical dedication, and indeed rebuilt her life around it. She gave up her job at Colchester, which made the journey to Dartford difficult, and got another as research chemist with J. Lyons and Company in London. Her next move was to take lodgings in Dartford, commuting to London daily, but being on hand in the constituency most evenings and week-ends. Her first lodgings were with a widow, but later she moved to live with a couple who were active workers in the Conservative Association. 'Since I was a young single woman everyone was very kind,' she explains. 'I was asked to the houses of helpers a lot'.

The local Conservative workers rallied to their new young candidate with great enthusiasm. Indeed, given the size of the Labour majority they were up against, their organisation seems to have been in good shape, with good headquarters. The seat was a large one, with 79,000 electors, and as then defined had three centres—Erith, Crayford, and Dartford itself. Like any good candidate, Margaret's first task was to get to know her own active workers in every ward, and then spread her contact outwards to other organisations. John Miller, the chairman she had first met in the Llandudno conference hall, was a great strength to her. The various local branches organised their usual money-raising functions, most of which out of working hours she managed to attend. And of course she pitched into the local council election campaigns, canvassing alongside the Conservative candidates. Just as through her father she had been so involved in local affairs in Grantham, so she wanted to become involved in all aspects of community life in Dartford, Erith and Crayford. Looking back

she is amazed at the confidence with which she approached her
task, though admits she often found the work very tiring.

One early engagement at which she made her mark was a
mass rally organised by the North Kent group of Conservative
associations for Anthony Eden on the Dartford Football Ground.
Margaret, as the local candidate, proposed the vote of thanks,
and made a great impression. 'It was just one of those speeches
that happened to go off rather well,' she recalls.

There were some pretty rough parts to the constituency, but her
recollection is of being received with courtesy even in politically
hostile areas—perhaps an advantage of being a woman candidate.
She also fared very well in terms of Press publicity, since her
youth and sex gave added interest to whatever she said or did.
This was true not only of the local weekly papers but also to the
London evenings—then three in number.

She also seems, rather peculiarly, to have been given additional
publicity by the sitting Labour MP, Norman Dodds, who took
rather a sporting interest in his young Tory challenger. Margaret
was first introduced to him at a mayoral reception, and from the
start they got on well, treating each other with respect. But
instead of Margaret challenging the sitting MP to a public debate
—which would have been the more standard and usually un-
successful tactic—it was he who challenged her! Perhaps he felt
that with his majority he could afford such sport.

Naturally she accepted the challenge, and together they fought
it out in a school hall, with the Press taking considerable interest.
Norman Dodds was a good debator—'a hard hitter', as Margaret
puts it. But she managed to hold her own, and the challenge was
never repeated. The MP was also fond of writing letters to the
local Press taking her up on statements she had made. She would
of course reply—'and sometimes the correspondence would go on
for weeks on end.' Looking back, she is still amazed by the amount
of notice this locally popular MP took of her.

The general election campaign of February 1950 was cold
and wet and snowy. The Conservatives went into it with high
hopes of ousting the Labour Government which had swept in with
such a massive majority in 1945. The public utilities and the
railways had been nationalised as promised, and the National
Health Service created. But there had been a period of prolonged
austerity, and people were getting rather fed up with continuing
tight Government controls and the fact that Ministers seemed
unable or unwilling to foresee any end to food rationing. There

had also been the devaluation of the pound by Sir Stafford Cripps.

By this time Margaret Roberts had built up quite a reputation for herself as someone involved in the community in Dartford, and she plunged into the fight with customary enthusiasm. Election meetings played a more important role then than they do in such urban seats now. 'We had one every night, sometimes two a night,' she recalls. 'They were very well attended, sometimes packed. And there was plenty of lively heckling, sometimes very clever. But we never had the sort of attempts you sometimes get now, of groups of people creating a barrage of noise in an effort to prevent you being heard at all. The kind of heckling we had was fair game.'

Her days would begin with a morning conference with key officers at headquarters, 'then I would usually have an open-air meeting somewhere over lunch-time. The afternoon I would spend canvassing, then go home for a short rest before the evening meetings.' This is a classic electioneering pattern, though nowadays there is less enthusiasm for open-air meetings. She also went into local factories to speak in their canteens, and to the hospitals to meet the nurses in their recreation rooms. There were generally some Pressmen following her around, since as the country's youngest woman candidate she was something of a phenomenon. And there were a few shared platforms with Norman Dodds arranged by independent bodies, such as the United Nations Association. There was also a Liberal in the field, but he made little impact.

She and Denis particularly remember her eve-of-poll meeting in Crayford Town Hall. Two had been arranged for that night, the first at Erith, so a 'warm-up' speaker had to be laid on to hold the fort at Crayford until Margaret could be rushed across. On this occasion the supporting speaker had been pushing a pretty vigorous line. But somehow the meeting, which was packed and had an overflow in an adjoining room, had gone sour, challenges to fights had been tossed about, and the whole place was in uproar.

It was at this moment that a breathless Margaret arrived up the back steps from the Erith meeting to be greeted with the happy news, 'We've had to send for the police!' Swallowing hard, she walked on to the platform—and just stood there waiting to be heard. To her it seemed an age before the noise subsided, but according to others present you could have heard a pin drop after two minutes. Then she launched into her eve-of-poll speech, and took a lively but civil question session at the end.

When the votes were counted the following night the result for Dartford was:

Norman Dodds (Lab and Co-op)	38,128
Margaret Roberts (Con)	24,490
H. Giles (Lib)	5,011
Labour majority:	13,638

Labour's lead had been cut from nearly 20,000, but Margaret was a little disappointed. 'I'd hoped to get the majority down to 9,000, but it was more solid than we thought.' At the count she was desperately tired; indeed, she had found the whole campaign utterly exhausting. 'Being young and fit, I hadn't expected it to be such a physical strain. I've noticed since that you develop much more stamina as you get older. You get tired, but you don't get quite so exhausted as when you are younger. Perhaps it's the added experience in ordering your activities.'

Nationally the Conservatives just missed achieving their objective; the Attlee Government survived with a majority of six. The balance was tipped in the end by a campaign which sought to portray Winston Churchill as a 'warmonger', backed up very effectively by a *Daily Mirror* front page asking: 'Whose finger on the trigger?' In Dartford, as elsewhere, this front page appeared in the front windows of many Labour households. But there were more local compensations. In those days four North Kent constituency associations—those of Bexley, Chislehurst, Dartford and Gravesend—all shared the same president, Maurice Wheeler. He brought the candidates together frequently, and indeed they helped out by speaking in each other's constituencies.

In the run-up to the election Margaret had spoken in support of Ted Heath at Bexley and Pat Hornsby-Smith at Chislehurst, and they in turn had provided support in Dartford, so she was particularly pleased to see both of them elected. 'Because of this link-up we all knew each other very well,' she recalls. 'This was very valuable, for it stopped you feeling all isolated and alone in attacking a seat like Dartford. We had other links across Kent too. I remember going to speak in Sevenoaks, Ashford, Canterbury and Orpington. So the candidates and MPs in Kent were a friendly and closely-knit group.'

It looked as if the next general election would not be far

away, the occasion for what Winston Churchill called 'the final heave'. Conservative associations everywhere therefore made their dispositions quickly, and Margaret was naturally asked to stay on to fight Dartford again. She agreed without hesitation. In fact, the next election was twenty months in coming, the result not of by-election losses but of the deep rift within the Labour Party itself.

Unlike the far shorter gap between the two 1974 general elections, it was not a period of continuous electioneering. The Korean War was causing anxiety and a colossal inflation in commodity prices. But behind the scenes the Conservative Party's election machinery was kept in good trim. Margaret recalls almost monthly conferences for adopted candidates, attended by members of the Shadow Cabinet.

For the October 1951 election the Dartford Conservatives worked to much the same plan of campaign as in 1950, though this time it was a straight fight. 'We adopted the same approach,' says Margaret. 'We'd been through it all before, and we were much more confident. We did similar things—had similar posters, similar leaflets, and meetings in much the same places. But they weren't quite so well attended. They never are when you get one election coming fairly soon after another.'

The previous twelve months had seen the fastest rise in the cost of living that anyone could remember. This, the divisions in the Labour Party, and the Tory promise to 'Set the People Free' from an overburdening bureaucracy were the main campaign issues. And, with Britain engaged in fighting the Communists in Korea, the Labour Party could hardly play the 'warmonger' card against Winston Churchill again.

For her part, Margaret found the campaign rather less fatiguing than her first. But through most of it she was keeping a secret within a very tight circle of friends. For just as the election was announced she had become unofficially engaged to Denis Thatcher.

They first met, as we have seen, on the night that Margaret was adopted as prospective candidate early in 1949, and Denis gave her a lift in his car back to London. After that they met periodically, though it seems that their romance really began to develop in the period between the two general elections—all, however, unknown to the party workers at Dartford.

Denis Thatcher was tall, athletic, and ten-and-a-half years

older than Margaret. He was then joint general manager of the
Atlas Preservative Company, in Erith, which made paint, marine
and agricultural chemicals and some insulation products, and
sold them round the world. The firm was partly owned by
members of his own family, and Denis had a small stake in it
himself. He was on the committee of the Erith Ratepayers'
Association, joined in Conservative Association activities but
declined to hold any office. The nearest he ever came to playing
a political role himself was when he stood as a Ratepayers' candidate for Kent County Council, though clearly he would have had
the shock of his life if he had won the seat.

He liked fast cars, and owned a Jaguar and a Triumph—which
did not particularly impress Margaret, who does not much enjoy
fast driving. But they soon found they had a strong common
interest in music, and began going to concerts in London together.

'We dined out from time to time,' Margaret recalls, 'and went
to the occasional cinema or theatre. But they were still rather dark
days in 1949 and 1950; there wasn't a lot of gay life about.'

She was also very interested in economics, and Denis had
practical knowledge of running a business on a scale of which
she had no experience. During this period he took her to his
annual trade association dance, at which, towards the end of the
evening, his company chairman leaned over to mutter in his ear :
'That's it, Denis—that's the one.' By this time Denis Thatcher was
coming to the same conclusion.

At first sight, it would seem odd that their romance never came
to the attention of anyone in Dartford. But this is very largely
explained by the fact that between the 1950 and 1951 elections
Margaret gave up her lodgings in Dartford and moved back to
London to rent a flat in St. George's Mews. This was partly to
make it easier for her to study law, which she had now begun to
do. Denis Thatcher's flat was in London too, so there was nothing
remarkable in him driving her down to Dartford for the occasional party meeting or social engagement. Meanwhile, she would
still attend many functions on her own.

In September 1951, Denis returned from a motoring holiday
with a friend round France and Spain, proposed marriage to
Margaret and was accepted. This was just as the election campaign was breaking, so the couple consulted the Dartford Association chairman, John Miller, over whether to announce the fact
or not. His advice was against doing so, and Margaret agreed.
First, there was the danger that the timing of the announcement

might appear somewhat contrived, but what worried her rather
more was that the voters and some of her party workers might
fear that her mind was not fully on the task of fighting the election,
whereas of course it was. So they decided to keep their engagement a secret until the election was over.

Looking back, it seems a rather naïve hope. Margaret was again
the youngest woman candidate standing, and so attracted considerable Press interest. Inevitably the news leaked out, though
not till eve-of-poll, in the London evening papers. The consequent
publicity was terrific, though Margaret thinks it came too late to
have any significant effect on the voting figures.

When the result was declared, Margaret had reduced the
Labour majority by a further 1,300, but still not to the 9,000-odd
that had been her original target. However, by now she had a
more realistic view of the situation. The figures were :

Norman Dodds (Lab and Co-op)	40,094
Margaret Roberts (Con)	27,760
Labour majority	12,334

The national result was to return the Conservatives with a
majority of 17, and there was no apparent reason why they should
not continue to hold office for a full five-year term. Clearly the
time had come for Margaret to say goodbye to Dartford.

The marriage took place in December that year, in the Wesley
Chapel in City Road, London. This was regarded by Alfred
Roberts as very High Church, since the form of service was really
Anglican. But by this time Margaret had rather moved away
from her original strict Methodism. The couple had the usual
debate whether to have a large wedding or small, and decided to
invite about fifty close friends and relatives. Margaret decided
she did not want to marry in white lace, but in velvet—'it was
deep mid-winter, and I wasn't going to be cold.' She did not like
the idea of white velvet, and so chose sapphire blue—a long dress
with train and hat.

Then off for the honeymoon, and according to Margaret 'we've
never had another holiday like it. Denis had some business to do
in Portugal, so we went there for a few days. Then over to
Madeira, which was the real holiday part of it, and after that
Denis had to do some business in Paris, so we went there for
five days. We've never been away together for so long since. In

Portugal it was like spring, in Madeira early summer, and Paris still winter.'

They then returned to London and started married life in Denis's flat in Swan Court, Flood Street—just opposite the home they lived in later when she was MP and Minister, and indeed where they still live at the time of writing.

CHAPTER FIVE

Motherhood and the Bar
1952–1959

Most women who have already embarked on a careeer face the
difficult decision on getting married of what priority to give to
their work and how much to the possibility of raising a family.
Margaret Thatcher was no exception, though political ambition
added a further dimension to her difficulty. She was quite happy
to give up her work as an industrial research chemist. But she
had already begun to read for the Bar, and had made the first
stabs at a political career. Would all this have to go if she and
Denis were fortunate enough to have children? On this Margaret
had very decided views, and they were expressed most forcefully
in a newspaper article within three months of her marriage.

Queen Elizabeth had just ascended to the throne, and one of
the popular-style papers then published, the *Sunday Graphic*
thought it a good idea to ask what kind of challenge this presented
to women generally 'at the dawn of the new Elizabethan era'. So
it commissioned an article from Margaret, since she was only a
few months older than the Queen herself, and had been the
youngest woman candidate in the previous two general elections.
She was only too pleased to rise to the challenge, and her article
appeared on February 17, 1952 under the headline 'Wake Up,
Women'. The views expressed in it may seem unremarkable today,
but in 1952 they would have come as a shock to many, not least
within the Conservative Party.

'If, as many earnestly pray, the accession of Elizabeth II can
help to remove the last shreds of prejudice against women aspiring
to the highest places, then a new era for women will indeed be at
hand,' she began. 'I hope we shall see more and more women
combining marriage *and* a career. Prejudice against this dual
role is not confined to men. Far too often, I regret to say, it comes
from our own sex. But the happy management of home and career
is being achieved'—and she went on to cite current examples of

women known professionally by their maiden names who were in fact mothers of children. But, she added, 'the term "career woman" has unfortunately come to imply in many minds a "hard" woman, devoid of all feminine characteristics.'

Then, warming to her theme, she went on to ask : 'Why have so few women in recent years risen to the top of their professions? One reason may be that so many have cut short their careers when they marry. *In my view this is a great pity*. For it *is* possible to carry on working, taking a short leave of absence when families arrive, and returning later. In this way gifts and talents that would otherwise be wasted are developed to the benefit of the community. *The idea that the family suffers is, I believe, quite mistaken*. To carry on with a career stimulates the mind, provides a refreshing contact with the world outside—and so means that a wife can be a much better companion at home. Moreover, when her children themselves marry she is not left with a gap in her life which so often seems impossible to fill.'

But for women to play an important role in business and the professions was not good enough; at that time there were only 17 women out of 625 MPs in the House of Commons. With a greater degree of prophecy than she realised, she went on : 'Should a woman arise equal to the task, I say let her have an equal chance with the men for the leading Cabinet posts. Why not a woman Chancellor—or Foreign Secretary?' She clearly shrank from adding 'or Prime Minister.' If they made mistakes, she said, they would not be the first to do so in those jobs.

The article concluded : 'I should like to see the woman with a career holding down her responsibility with easy assurance during the Elizabethan age. I should like to see married women carrying on with their jobs, if so inclined, after their children are born. I should like to see *every* woman trying to overcome ignorance of day-to-day affairs; and *every* woman taking an active part in local life. And, above all, I should like to see more and more women at Westminster, *and in the highest places too*. It would certainly be a good thing for the women of Britain. And I'm sure it would be a good thing for the men too!'

Thus 'Seize Your Opportunities' was Margaret Thatcher's manifesto for women, and helps to explain why, twenty years later, she took a rather jaundiced view of the antics of some sections of the Women's Lib movement.

For her own part, she decided to press on with her studies for the Bar while keeping house for Denis, and to play down politics for the time being. 'If you organise yourself properly you can do two things properly, but not three,' she explains. Denis's income, which he describes then as being 'reasonable but not fantastic', obviously made this possible. His work at Erith was fairly demanding, and so were her legal studies. But from very early on they had a private understanding which goes far to explain the subsequent success of their marriage, as she has taken on successive and more demanding roles. As she puts it : 'This is a deal that we have always done : work is the most important thing, and it comes first, and therefore you do it.'

Denis confirms this, adding that the work demands of the two of them have never really come into conflict. As he puts it : 'If there were political demands on me that I didn't have time to meet, then they had to take second place. I've always taken the view that my job came first. People have often said : "You do so much for Margaret in politics". It's a beautiful theory, but it's not really true. I've had a wife and two kids to keep, and my job came first.'

In fact, life was fairly easy to manage in those early days in Swan Court. Denis left around 8.15 every morning to drive down to Erith, while Margaret would get down to her legal studies and make preparations for their evening meal. Denis would stay in Erith till his work was finished, which meant Margaret never knew exactly when he would return, though it was generally somewhere between 7.30 and 9 pm. The flat was quite spacious, with three bedrooms—and, as Margaret points out, they had no incentive to leave it because it was rent restricted, costing them about £7 a week plus excess rates.

It was a little over a year after they were married that Margaret learned she was pregnant—news which was warmly welcomed. The child was due in October, so Margaret stepped up her work for her Bar Intermediate examination, which she took in May and duly passed. The shock came when she gave birth in August seven weeks prematurely—and not until the day they were born did she know that it was going to be twins! They were a boy and a girl, and were named Mark and Carol.

The unexpected arrival of twins obviously meant a major reorganisation of the routine of the Thatcher household. The first step was to employ some help. As Margaret puts it : 'You tend to need some sort of help with twins, who wake for feeding at different hours of the day and night.' A children's nurse was recruited, who lived in. She and Margaret shared the work of

the babies, though the nurse had every Saturday off and sometimes the whole week-end.

However, Margaret was determined not to let her studies for
Bar Finals lapse, so she soon arranged things so that she could
work while the children were asleep, and after a couple of months
to slip away for lectures lasting an hour at a time. What is more,
she decided to enter her Bar Finals that December—only four
months after giving birth to the twins. Friends told her it could
not be done, but clearly Margaret had already covered some of
the ground for Finals before taking her Intermediate. She took the
Finals in December, passed, and was called to the Bar soon after
Christmas.

As Denis Thatcher puts it : 'Bar Intermediate in May, produced
twins in August, and Bar Finals in December. I'd like to meet
another woman who can equal that record !'

True to her *Sunday Graphic* manifesto, Margaret decided to
look for Chambers straight away, with a view to serving a number
of pupillages. A good nanny was employed—and Margaret is
the first to admit that it was only the ability to do this, and the
fact that they lived so conveniently in London, that made this
possible. She had started off, following the advice of Recorder
Norman Winning in Grantham, by wanting to be a patent lawyer,
but she now decided to seek a far more broadly-based legal
experience first.

'So after I got my finals,' she recalls, 'I started various pupillages. The first was at the Common Law Bar, because you need
experience of the rules of evidence. Then at Chancery, for the
wills and trust settlements, and finally at the Revenue Bar. So I
did a long pupillage. It took two years before starting on my own,
by which time the children were coming up to start at nursery
school. We were still living in London, and this is what made it
all possible.'

It was during this period that she found herself sharing
chambers with Airey Neave, who with his wife came occasionally
to dine with the Thatchers—and who more than twenty years
later was to be Margaret's campaign manager in the Conservative
leadership election.

It was also during this time that Margaret decided that
she wanted to specialise not in patent law but in tax law. This
was partly because she found this fascinating, but it was also a
very practical decision, since most of the big tax cases came to
London, and so there would be little call for her to travel away

from the twins. However, the first advice she received was that
in order to do this she should also become qualified as a chartered
accountant. Denis Thatcher arrived home one day to find all the
necessary papers on the coffee table. But his advice was that the
long period of further training was 'just not on'—advice which
Margaret in fact accepted. She went into tax chambers in
Queen's Bench Walk—in which, at the same time, were lawyer-
politicians Anthony Barber and Patrick Jenkin.

Meanwhile politics were pushed into the background—except
for one notable occasion. She and Denis kept in touch with old
friends in Dartford, then being divided to make Erith and
Crayford a separate seat. Many legal friends were aspiring politicians too, and she also joined the Inns of Court Conservative
Association, which during the 1950s produced some significant
policy reports. But most of the time Margaret worked on the
assumption that with proper organisation she could perform two
functions at once—like practising law and keeping in very close
contact with the twins—but not three.

However, in November 1954 she succumbed to the temptation
to offer herself as candidate for a by-election seat. The temptation
was undertandable, since the seat that had become vacant was
safe Orpington, with which she had had such close connections
while she was fighting Dartford. Having fought the next-door
seat in 1950 and 1951, she was in a good position to make a bid
for Orpington. 'So I decided to enter for it, and see which way
the fates went,' she recalls.

Not surprisingly, she was short-listed, but she was up against
Donald Sumner, chairman of the Orpington Conservative Asso-
ciation, who naturally presented himself strongly as the local man.
Margaret can remember hearing him tell the selection committee,
'You want someone in Parliament who knows the state of the
road in Locks Bottom.'

He got the nomination, and won the by-election easily the
following January. Ironically, nearly four years later the
Thatchers moved to live in Locks Bottom. In 1961 Donald
Sumner took legal promotion, and in the by-election the following
year the Liberals made their first spectacular break-through by
getting Eric Lubbock elected.

From then on 'Orpington Man' became a generic name for
dissident suburban Tory voters—and Margaret was able to tease
local friends that if only they had chosen 'Orpington Woman' in

1954 they would never have suffered 'Orpington Man' eight years later.

Though one can understand her leaping at the chance of a safe seat near her old battleground so quickly, it was in fact a blessing to her that she did not get it. Given her own wish to be close to the twins in their formative years before going away to boarding school, her work as an MP as early as this would have suffered, and consequently her political reputation would never have developed in the same way. Margaret seems to have taken this point herself, for she did not put herself forward for any seat in the 1955 general election.

By this time, in fact, her domestic life was becoming very important to her. The twins were emerging from the baby stage and Margaret had very definite ideas on how they should be brought up. She did not provide for them the strict Nonconformist background of her own childhood, but she keenly remembered how her father had sought to interest her in everything around her, and she was determined to do the same for her own children. She so arranged her time that she was able to play with them for a part of each day, and as they grew older she would always read to them before they went to sleep. Looking back on this period when she was practising law, Denis Thatcher insists that she always gave family needs first priority. There was one occasion, on their fourth or fifth birthdays, when she spent a couple of days making and specially icing two cakes—one in the shape of a fort for Mark, the other a car for Carol. The way she put into practice her own beliefs about education *within* the home is corroborated by her sister Muriel, a mother herself, who has always admired the way Margaret brought up the twins.

'She never shouted at them,' Muriel recalls, 'it was all sweet reason. I could have screamed at her sometimes for being so reasonable. And her attitude all the time was to *teach* the twins interesting things. Everything she did with them was teaching, but always in such a kind way. They arrived at our farm once when we were in the middle of lifting potatoes, and straight away she said, "Oh good, we can *teach* the twins how the machine works". Again, one holiday I can remember us all going out in a boat. To me it was just a trip in a boat, but Margaret immediately said to the twins, "Now you'll be able to *learn* how to crew." She was always so imaginative with them, so stimulating.'

Denis Thatcher is also proud of his wife's other domestic talents. We have already seen how she learned and practised needlework as a child in Grantham, and as a mother she made many of the twins' clothes, particularly dresses for Carol. But his highest praise is for her cooking—'supreme, always striving after absolute perfection.' In fact, Margaret has been fond of cooking and giving small dinner parties whenever possible throughout their married life, even when she was a Cabinet Minister.

'She decides what she has got to do, and how she wants to do it,' Denis explains. 'Then she either gets up very early or works on very late to get everything prepared. It's this singleness of purpose again, that comes through in everything she wants to do.'

By the 1955 general election Anthony Eden was leading the Conservative Party, and was well placed to go to the country on the Government's record of achievement since 1951. After some initial tough measures to curb public spending the economy was expanding, the most irritating machinery of Labour's controls dismantled, and all food rationing abolished.

It must have been particularly frustrating for Margaret to be sitting this one out, but following the failure of her dash for Orpington she accepted the situation philosophically. During the campaign she was enlisted to speak in support of Tory candidates in a number of Essex seats, and on eve-of-poll moved down to Erith, where of course Denis still worked, to support Edward Gardner, the new candidate there. The result of the election was that the Conservatives increased their majority to 60.

The next political convulsion, of course, was the Suez Crisis, the British invasion and then withdrawal. The nation was split over the succession of bewildering events, as indeed was the Tory Party. Margaret was caught up in it as was every party worker; she recalls hearing Sir Edward Boyle speak at an Inns of Court function a couple of days before he resigned in protest from the Eden Government. But in this crisis Margaret was not on the Boyle wing of the party, taking the view that, having once embarked on such a course, we should have seen it through to the end. The rapid resignation of Anthony Eden as Prime Minister did not surprise her, and she certainly endorsed the party's choice of Harold Macmillan as his successor, having been an admirer of his for some considerable time.

One of the acts of the first Macmillan Government was to bring some flexibility into the system of rent restriction, which was coming to have a very bad effect on the state of the nation's private housing stock. This, of course, directly affected the Thatcher family, who were still living happily in their rent controlled flat in Swan Court, Chelsea. They faced the choice of whether to pay a very substantially increased rent, or move some-where else, and so they decided it was time they bought a place of their own.

They felt they could not really afford Chelsea prices, so in 1957 they went house hunting outside London, in that band of Kent within reasonable reach of Denis's work at Erith but also with good rail links with London, so that Margaret could continue her work at the Bar.

They settled on a house in Locks Bottom, Farnborough, within the Orpington constituency. It was a sizeable detached house standing in about an acre of land, but it was in a bad state since very little renovation work had been done to it for several years, and the garden was something of a jungle.

'But we could see it had possibilities so, we bought it and started to do it up gradually and to cope with the garden,' she recalls.

The move certainly made life easier for Denis, but it meant a complete change in Margaret's life style. New schools had to be found for the twins, and Margaret drove them and neighbouring children to school each morning before catching her train into London. By mutual arrangement other parents collected them at the end of the day. The Thatchers still employed a nanny as Margaret built up her reputation in tax chambers and became a very active member of the Inns of Court Conservative Associa-tion. But she was still very careful to keep her domestic role in balance with this, arranging to spend considerable time with the twins when they were home and in the school holidays. She also developed a great love of gardening—something she had never been able to do before. The home over the shop in Grantham in which she had been brought up had had no garden at all. She and Denis laid out their new garden with roses, shrubs and herbaceous plants, had the help of a gardener to keep things tidy during the week but did a considerable amount of gardening themselves at week-ends.

Despite the fact that living in London would obviously have been much easier for her, Margaret looks back on this period of her life with considerable happiness. As the twins grew older she was able to organise all kinds of outings for them in Kent, and they began a regular pattern of annual family holidays. When they were very young they went one year to Westgate, and another to Bognor Regis, but when Mark and Carol were about five the family went to Seaview on the Isle of Wight, and continued to go there every year thereafter. The first year they stayed in a hotel, but after that would always hire the same house for about a month each summer. Denis would join them for a couple of weeks and at week-ends, coming up to his office in between while Margaret amused the children on the beach or drove them to various places of interest on the island. Naturally they made friends with whom they tended to meet up again each year.

Soon after the Suez Crisis Margaret decided that she had better start looking seriously for a seat to fight in the next election. By then the children would be at school, and it was Denis's intention that at least Mark should go away to boarding school when he was nine. By the time she next election came Margaret would be thirty-four or thirty-five, and she knew that if she missed fighting two general elections in a row her chances of ever being selected for subsequent ones would start to diminish. So she began again to submit her name to constituency selection committees. She had fought a hopeless seat twice, and this time was obviously after something that she could win. But still she restricted her sights very much to seats in Kent, or at least within easy reach of London from the other side, since she knew full well the amount of time a prospective candidate must devote to even the safest seat, and did not want to be drawn away from home and family for long periods.

Her first bid was for Beckenham, in Kent, where a by-election was due early in 1957. But this was won by Philip Goodhart, a journalist, with Margaret coming second. It was then that she became really aware of the in-built barriers to a woman, especially a mother, being selected for a safe Tory seat. At Beckenham she was honestly told the view of the majority of the selection committee : 'You're a woman with young children, and we don't think you ought to contest an election.'

This argument would obviously be somewhat weaker in a general election two or three years hence, by which time the children would be established at school, than it was in an immediate by-election situation. But still, as she went after general election vacancies, Margaret still found herself doing well but always coming second, never first. Denis went with her to these selection meetings, but stayed well in the background. Tory selectors were often intensely interested in prospective candidates' wives—but never in their husbands.

Another Kentish seat she tried hard to get was Maidstone, but

again she came second, to John Wells. 'By this time I was seriously
looking for a seat,' she recalls. 'I realised I wanted very, very
much to come back into politics. The children were at school, and
I could. But I couldn't go far away from London because I knew
I couldn't up sticks and leave home. So I just applied for any
London area seat that came up.' These included Finchley where
the Tory majority in 1955 had been 12,825.

There is no set pattern in the Conservative Party for selecting
a candidate. Some selection committees invite you to make a
speech, some do not. Some arrange an initial interview asking
only personal details, others plunge straight into sticky political
questions. In some the questioning seems slow, even desultory,
while in others each member of the selection committee has set
questions, carefully planned and co-ordinated beforehand, to
put to each applicant. In some the final choice is made from a
short list by an executive committee, in others at a meeting open
to all paid-up members of the Conservative Association.

Finchley fell into the category of those in which the selection
committee asked each would-be candidate the same battery of
questions, and awarded marks for the answers on each selector's
scorecard. Some 200 had applied to fill the vacancy, but eventually Margaret found herself on a short-list of four to appear
before the divisional council, made up of 50-60 representatives,
in mid-July. On the night this list was down to three, as one
on it, Monty Woodhouse, had just been selected to fight Oxford.

Denis was not with her on this occasion, since he was on a business visit to Africa. There, two days later, on his way from
Johannesburg to Lagos he boarded a plane that had just come
out from London, and on the seat beside him was a copy of the
previous day's *Evening Standard*. As he idly flipped through the
pages he read the news—Margaret had been selected to fight
Finchley.

CHAPTER SIX

Into Parliament—and Promotion
1959–1964

Late arrivals at Margaret Thatcher's adoption meeting in the Conservative Hall, Finchley, on August 8, 1958, were lucky to find standing room at the back. But by the end of the meeting it seems that everyone was on their feet cheering their new prospective candidate. The Finchley Press reported the following week :

> Speaking without notes, stabbing home points with expressive hands, Mrs Thatcher launched fluently into a clear-cut appraisal of the Middle East situation [two weeks before had seen the coup in Iraq], weighed up Russia's propagandist moves with the skill of a housewife measuring the ingredients in a familiar recipe, pinpointed Nasser as the fly in the mixing bowl, switched swiftly to Britain's domestic problems (showing a keen grasp of wage and trade union issues), then swept her breathless audience into a confident preview of Conservatism's dazzling future.

With this triumph behind her she set about making herself known first to her local party workers and then throughout the constituency with the same vigour she had shown nine years before at Dartford. As before, she had about a year's run-in to the election campaign.

By this time Harold Macmillan had successfully restored the Tory Party's self-confidence after the Suez debacle, the economy was expanding and the spread of consumer durable goods such as washing machines was effectively emancipating many women from household chores to which they had hitherto been bound. By this time a television set was standard in almost every home. This period has since been pilloried with the tag 'You've never had it so good'—a distortion of a remark made by Macmillan concerning the level of retirement pensions. It is easy to adopt a lofty attitude and brand such progress as materialistic, but it was undoubtedly raising the quality of life for ordinary families across the land. Many were moving from city centres to live in new housing estates in the suburbs, and, as Margaret recalls, 'all sorts of new expectations were coming up'. In all this process former class attitudes were becoming far less rigid, and much more open to change.

In 1959 the election campaign began in September. At Finchley Margaret still worked to the routine of canvassing during the day and addressing meetings at night, though television was starting to play a much more important role in election campaigning. She denies that campaigning was more sedate in Finchley than in Dartford; in her new constituency she had no factory meetings to handle, but instead far more of the voters would write in to her asking questions, all of which demanded a serious answer. Each evening she had one meeting only, but this is no less strenuous than two, since inevitably the question session goes on far longer.

There was no doubt that Margaret would win Finchley, but looking back she can recall being totally uncertain what the overall national result would be.

'We had just no idea how it was going to go. We seemed in a reasonable position to win, but it was possible our majority in Parliament would be reduced. We were attacked as the party of Suez, and Labour were trying to exploit the easing of rent restriction against us.'

But counting in the Tories' favour were Macmillan's preparations for a summit meeting of world leaders. So the Tory manifesto posed the twin questions: 'Do you want to go ahead on the lines that have brought prosperity at home?' and 'Do you want your present leaders to represent you abroad?'

Part way through the campaign, Hugh Gaitskell, the Labour Leader, suddenly promised to take sixpence (equivalent to $2\frac{1}{2}$p) in the pound off income tax. The timing of this was bad, it did not appear to relate to an overall strategy, and it backfired. 'Hugh Gaitskell, I think, made a number of errors—and it was almost as if Macmillan was waiting for him to make them. But none of us felt at all certain as we gathered back at our chairman's house on election night to watch all the results come in.'

The election turned out to be a Tory landslide, with Macmillan returning with a Commons majority of 100. The result at Finchley was :

Margaret Thatcher (Con)	29,697
Eric Deakins (Lab)	13,437
Henry Spence (Lib)	12,701
Conservative majority :	16,260

Margaret's majority was 3,435 higher than her predecessor's in 1955. Her Parliamentary career had begun.

Unlike many new Members, she did not find the House of Commons immediately bewildering. From her active membership of the Inns of Court Conservative Association and her years of political activity in Kent she found she had many friends in the House, all of whom were only too pleased to show her around. But in her first days as an MP she had an extraordinary stroke of luck. At the start of each session backbench MPs put their names in for a ballot to decide who should have priority in introducing Private Member's Bills. The list to emerge from the ballot is a long one, but due to the limited time available only the first half-dozen on it have any chance of getting a substantial or controversial Bill through the House.

Like everyone else, Margaret put her name in, and when the Speaker had conducted the draw she found she had come out second. This was an unusually lucky break for a new Member; oddly enough, it was a new Labour MP who came first in the ballot—Richard Marsh.

In those days an MP successful in the ballot had to decide the subject of his or her Bill very quickly, and in the knowledge that no help was necessarily available for the complicated task of drafting it. Her first inclination was to remedy what many lawyers saw as a defect in the law concerning the Attorney-General's fiat arising out of the Podola case, but was then told that the Government was itself contemplating legislation on this matter. So, with her deadline fast approaching, Margaret had to do some quick thinking, and settled on a Bill to provide for admission of the Press to the meetings of local councils. Its title was the Public Bodies (Admission of the Press to Meetings) Bill. 'Nobody persuaded me,' she explains. 'The decision was my own.'

There had at this time been considerable public misgivings over cases in which local councils or their committees had made executive decisions behind closed doors—decisions which consequently were never reported to the public through the Press. There had been the example of the Watch Committee of Nottingham Council, who had suspended the city's Chief Constable, Captain Popkess, for his failure to inform it of Scotland Yard inquiries involving council members. The committee's decision was taken following an oral report from the Town Clerk, and at no stage had the local Press or anyone else been allowed to witness the council's or committee's deliberations on the case.

Though most councils admitted the Press to their meetings, further evidence of how precarious its position was came during a national printing dispute involving provincial newspapers, during which journalists in Bristol succeeded in producing a 'black' newspaper. However, the Labour-controlled Bristol Council responded by barring reporters from its meetings for the duration of the dispute, in order to demonstrate solidarity with the printers. In this case many people took the view that the first duty of local councillors was to the public, who had a right to be informed of their activities, regardless of any industrial dispute that might be on at the time.

This, then, was the background to Margaret's Bill. The ballot for Private Members' time was held in November, and she had to have the Bill drafted, published and ready for debate on February 5.

'I was really thrown in at the deep end,' she recalls, 'having to dash around and consult everyone, and then turn round and start drafting the Bill.'

But she had immediate and weighty help from Sir Lionel Heald, a former Attorney-General, as well as from a number of other Tory backbenchers. The Association of Municipal Corporations began by opposing the Bill, and of course the Press were very much in its favour. But one of Margaret's first tasks was to seek the support of the Minister for Housing and Local Government, Henry Brooke. At first she found the going very tough; he and his Department thought it better to seek a voluntary Code of Practice with the local authority associations, instead of approaching the problem through legislation. But in the end the support the Bill was attracting from the Tory Benches and the Press had its effect, and Brooke agreed that his Ministry would help with the drafting. But this concession came pretty late in the day.

A newly-elected MP generally chooses a fairly early occasion on which to make his or her maiden speech, which ideally should not last more than ten or twelve minutes. Once the intention has been expressed the Speaker makes a particular effort to ensure that the new MP is called in the debate, and by kind convention he or she is not interrupted. However, due to all her rushing around on her Bill Margaret had no chance to go through these formalities, with the result that her maiden speech was her speech on February 5 in the Second Reading—that is to say, the first—Debate on her Bill.

Private Members' Bills are debated on Fridays, when most MPs have usually seized the chance to return to their constituencies. However, on this occasion her Bill had aroused such interest that more than a hundred MPs were present to hear her maiden speech introducing it. They included all three women Members of the Government—Pat Hornsby-Smith, an old friend from Dartford days, Edith Pitt and Mervyn Pike.

A maiden speaker generally starts with what can be either an amusing or boring description of his or her constituency, but Margaret tossed aside this convention.

'I know that the constituency of Finchley which I have the honour to represent would not wish me to do other than come straight to the point and address myself to the matter before the House,' she explained.

She went on to define the objective of her Bill in the words used by Arthur Henderson in introducing the then existing Act governing the Press and local council meetings in 1908.

'He specified the object and purpose as that of guarding the rights of members of the public by enabling the fullest information to be obtained for them in regard to the actions of their representatives upon local authorities.'

Then, developing the case in her own words, she continued : 'The public does not have a right of admission, either at common law or by statute, to the meetings of local authorities. Members of the public are compelled, therefore, to rely upon the local Press for information on what their elected representatives are doing.'

Local councils in England and Wales then spent some £1,400 million a year, and in Scotland £200 million.

'Less than half is raised by ratepayers' money and the rest by taxpayers' money, and the first purpose in admitting the Press is that we may know how those moneys are being spent.'

Publicity was the greatest and most effective check against any arbitrary action.

'That is one of the fundamental rights of the subject. Further, publicity stimulates the interest of local persons in local government. That is also very important. But if there is a case for publicity, there is also a case for a certain amount of private conference when personal matters are being discussed and when questions are in a preliminary stage. It is in trying to find a point of balance between these two aspects—the public right of knowledge and the necessity on occasion for private conference—that the difficulty arises.'

The loophole in the previous legislation had been created by the Local Government Act of 1933, which empowered local councils to appoint any committees they chose. A number of councils had used this to exclude the Press by resolving themselves into committee, without ever applying their minds to whether such action was justified.

'Where, previously, local authorities had to deliberate in open council, they were able to resolve themselves into committee merely as a matter of administrative convenience,' she declared. Under her Bill 'the Press will be admitted to the main council meetings of local authorities and to those meetings which effectively discharge the functions of the council—that is, the committees with substantial delegated powers.'

She then went point by point through the main provisions of her Bill. It was inevitable, she said, that on some occasions the Press should be excluded—for example, when personal circumstances or matters leading to legal proceedings were under discussion. 'There must, however, be very good reason for exclusion,' and the only reason could be that publicity for the matter to be discussed would be against the public interest. The Bill also provided for the supply of necessary background documents to the Press, and of clear and proper agenda.

Then she concluded 'I hope it is evident from what I have said that we are trying very hard to put into the form of legislation a code of practice that will safeguard the rights of the public . . . I hope that MPs will consider that a paramount function of this House is to safeguard civil liberties, rather than to think that administrative convenience should take first place in law.'

In all her speech took twenty-seven minutes—rather below the average for an MP introducing a substantial Bill. But more to the point, *it was delivered without a note.* Her performance won immediate acclaim from opponents as well as supporters, and later the Minister, Henry Brooke, said that 'she spoke with a fluency which most of us would envy. She achieved the rare feat of making a Parliamentary reputation on a Friday, a reputation

Margaret, aged nineteen, with her parents. Alfred Roberts wears his robes and chain as Mayor of Grantham. Sister Muriel is on the left.

The grocer's shop and Margaret's birthplace in Grantham, pictured about the time her father bought it. But it had changed little by 1925, when she was born.

Three generations of
Conservative Party Leaders
together at a rally at
Dartford in 1949: Sir
Anthony Eden, Edward
Heath and Margaret
Roberts.

Margaret and Denis
Thatcher on their wedding
day in 1951.

which I am sure she will now proceed to enhance on the earlier days of the week.'

Next day the Peterborough column in the *Daily Telegraph* commented :

> As a maiden speech it has not been, and is unlikely to be, excelled by any of her contemporaries new to the 1959 Parliament. As a thirty-minute exposition, without a note, of a controversial and complex Bill, it was of Front Bench quality.

She showed, the comment concluded, 'an uncanny instinct for the mood of the House which some Members take years to acquire —and many never acquire at all'. Thus did Margaret Thatcher, by thorough and single-minded application to her objective over a period of weeks, lay the foundation for her future Parliamentary reputation.

But her Bill was not without its enemies. It was, perhaps, unfortunate that all ten of its sponsors were Conservatives. Since there was Labour support for the Bill, it would have been better to enlist one or two from the other side. There were several Labour MPs who saw this as a Tory-inspired measure to give the Press, of whom they were suspicious, greater power to expose Labour councillors to attack.

In the debate that followed Margaret's speech the Labour opposition was led by Gerry Reynolds, backed up by Arthur Skeffington and Charles Pannell. There were Tory critics too, like Roy Wise. But valuable Labour backing came from Barbara Castle, whose husband was a professional journalist, and from Maurice Edelman, a journalist himself.

However, it was Labour MP Michael Stewart who, while supporting the Bill's general objective, put his finger on its essential weakness : 'Whatever the intentions of the Bill it is not, as it is framed at the moment, a Bill for the protection of the public; it is a Bill for the enlargement of the privileges of the Press.'

And when Henry Brooke joined in the debate he did so with caution. His first intention, he said, had been to seek to get a voluntary Code of Conduct supported by all the local authority associations, with the prospect of legislation kept as a fall-back power. But Margaret Thatcher's Bill had created a new situation. He would support her Bill, 'and I am ready to help her to improve

it in Committee so as to rub away the sharp corners and to remove
any causes for legitimate criticism.'

A vote was then taken, and the Bill given a Second Reading
by 152 votes to 39. It was on its way.

The Bill then went off to a Standing Committee, whose job is
to consider Bills clause by clause, amend where thought necessary
and, in Henry Brooke's phrase, rub away the sharp corners before
sending them back to the full House for Report and Third Reading. Piloting a Private Member's Bill through Committee demands
considerable political and tactical skill, and Margaret readily
admits that she had to rely heavily on the advice of her more
experienced friends.

The Government was represented on the Standing Committee
by Henry Brooke's Junior Minister, a man who some years later
was to play a very important role in Margaret's political life—Sir
Keith Joseph. He brought Government help that she very much
needed, for her main stumbling block lay in meeting the very
point raised by Michael Stewart—that is, in ensuring that journalists were not given a more privileged position in the local
government process than ordinary citizens.

The answer clearly lay in broadening the scope of the Bill to
embrace admission of *the public*, rather than just the Press, to
council meetings. But to do this she needed to change the 'long
title' of the Bill, which referred only to the Press, and this as a
backbencher she could not do. So Henry Brooke put a motion to
the Commons in Government time to change the long title, which
despite some blocking attempts MPs agreed should be done.

So her Bill became the Public Bodies (Admission to Meetings)
Bill. Other changes were also made in Committee which involved
Margaret making some concessions. But a stop was put to two
practices to which some councils had resorted; no longer could
a council resolve itself into a committee for the purpose of exclud-
ing the Press, neither could it meet as a general purposes committee in private before a short open council meeting. And all
members of the public had a right in law which they had not
possessed before. The Bill was given an unopposed Third Reading
by the Commons, during which debate Sir Keith congratulated
its sponsor on steering through 'a delicate and contentious measure, perhaps not ideally suited for a first venture into legislation.'
However, she had dealt with all its stages in a 'most cogent,
charming, lucid and competent manner.' In due course the Bill
went through the House of Lords, and received the Royal Assent.

Within months of her election, Margaret had got an important and difficult measure on to the Statute Book—and added greatly to her reputation in the process. It was, of course, sheer luck that she had come so high in the ballot; but, as she herself has often said since, you progress in politics only by seizing and making the most of chances as they come up. Margaret had seized her first chance in Parliament in a big way.

Such a Bill is quite enough for an MP to cope with in one session, particularly if it is her first, so Margaret undertook little other Parliamentary activity before the summer of 1960. But she got to know many more MPs, and naturally built upon old friendships. But, though she of course knew Edward Heath from Dartford days, she had little contact with him at that time since he had become Minister of Labour, a field in which she had little involvement.

In the following session, starting in November 1960, she decided to make Treasury affairs her main interest, particularly Chancellor Selwyn Lloyd's first Budget in the spring. Her interest in economics had begun in Oxford days, and as a tax lawyer—work which she had given up upon election—she was well qualified to speak on tax matters.

She accordingly joined in the April 1961 Budget Debate with a speech that gave ample evidence of her extensive knowledge of taxation. She began by citing legal precedents to show that the Inland Revenue already possessed considerable powers to tax capital gains which it was not using.

'It is the speculator in shares that we want to get at—the person who is making a business of buying and selling shares, not to hold them for their income-producing properties, but to live on the profit which he makes from the transactions.'

She then went on to argue against the increased tax which the Budget had imposed on companies, which she claimed would be inflationary. She welcomed the Chancellor's reduction of surtax, 'because it will help married women teachers who want to return to the profession'—but finally pointed out to him that the middle-class wife who went out to work was still taxed more harshly in Britain than in any other European country. It was an expert and impressive speech.

During her first two years as an MP her already high regard for Harold Macmillan increased enormously. 'He was the most remarkably *visionary* man,' she recalls. 'When you talked to him you realised he could see the trends going way into the future—

and this is a rare talent. He had the most wonderful gift of language, and he could write well too. His great achievement was that he seemed to bring so many things within the reach of the ordinary person. Home ownership, for example, was growing very fast. Real incomes were rising, and there was confidence in the future.'

Even now, Macmillan is the Tory Leader for whom Margaret seems to have the greatest admiration. In 1961 one was able to look back at his efforts to bring the Great Powers together, which ended in the abortive Paris Summit the previous May. 1960 saw his famous 'Wind of Change' speech to the South African Parliament in Cape Town. In March 1961 he flew to the United States to meet President Kennedy for the first time, and in the summer of that same year he was to lead his Cabinet into making the momentous decision to apply for membership of the European Community. To describe Harold Macmillan as a 'visionary man,' is no exaggeration.

But clearly her own talents had not gone unnoticed by the Prime Minister either, for in October 1961 she received a message to attend at 10 Downing Street. On that day she had arranged to meet Muriel for lunch, so the two sisters met just before Margaret left for her appointment. Two junior posts were vacant at the time, at the Ministry of Pensions and at Aviation. But Muriel recalls that in fact Margaret left hoping that she was going to be offered something quite different, and that was the humbler task of either proposing or seconding the Loyal Address in reply to the Queen's Speech opening the Parliamentary session. These two roles are awarded to promising Government backbenchers each year before the Prime Minister makes the major speech opening the debate on the programme for the session which has just been announced. But instead Margaret returned to her sister with the news that she had been offered the post of Parliamentary Secretary at the Ministry of Pensions—after only two years in the House. Muriel recalls that her sister would have preferred to have waited a little longer for promotion, until the twins were a bit bigger; but she knew that in politics 'when you're offered a job you either accept it or you're out'.

Looking back, Margaret claims with some modesty that the main reason she was chosen was that the vacancy had arisen from the resignation of another woman, Pat Hornsby-Smith, who had decided to develop her business career instead, and Macmillan wanted to maintain the female content of his team. If there is

any truth in this, then it was the first occasion on which being
a woman had worked to her positive advantage in politics. Her
first appearance at the Despatch Box was on November 6, for
Question Time on Pensions.

In her new job she was serving under John Boyd-Carpenter.
'It was a fascinating Department,' she recalls, 'because there was
a good deal of both the financial aspect and the human aspect
in it.'

One of the human aspects handled by the junior minister at
this Department were the hundreds of personal pensions and
social security cases raised by individual MPs. 'Again, I was lucky
that John was Minister at the time, for he taught me a great deal.
He was a superb debater. This was not a Department in which
sudden difficult executive decisions had to be made, so we could
spend some time on policy work for the future, which made it
very interesting.'

Margaret was three years at this Ministry, during which she
served under three separate Ministers—John Boyd-Carpenter,
Neil MacPherson and Richard Wood. 'It was interesting to sit in
on the policy meetings and see how the advice offered by the civil
service changed according to the Minister. I came to the conclusion in the end that the civil service tend not to put up advice
that they think the Minister will reject. After a Minister has been
some time in a Department, therefore, you tend to get rather
limited advice coming up.'

It is easy for Junior Ministers to feel utterly isolated in politics.
They have not the overall view of events that comes from sitting
round the Cabinet table, neither can they attend backbench party
meetings or join in all the gossip of the Commons Smoking Room.
Instead they just keep their heads down in their own Departments,
coping with all the specialised reports and case work flowing
through their hands and attending some Cabinet committees. As
Margaret puts it: 'If you're not careful you find that you're
neither fish nor flesh nor fowl.'

To counteract this the Parliamentary Secretaries of the
Macmillan Government used to meet as a group to discuss general
policy, and also had periodic meetings with Macmillan. 'He
certainly didn't keep himself aloof from us.'

By early 1962 the Government was getting into deep electoral
trouble. In response to a situation of developing wage inflation
Chancellor Selwyn Lloyd had the previous July introduced his
'Pay Pause'—an entirely voluntary measure of incomes restraint

which the Government applied rigorously to the public sector. This brought politically embarrassing groups such as the nurses into the front line of battle, but the general effect was to put a sharp brake on people's rising expectations.

One evening, on March 14, the Opposition was pressing a censure motion on pensions and social security, with their shadow spokesman Douglas Houghton leading the attack. Everyone expected John Boyd-Carpenter to reply, but instead the Government fielded Margaret Thatcher.

It was not a very enviable task, since she had to make clear that the Government had *no* plans yet for increasing pensions to meet the increased cost of living. Yet according to the next day's Press she managed to make a success of it, argued with a mass of figures that thought should be given to those who must pay for pensions as well as those who receive them. And to Labour's claim that more should be extracted from the higher income groups, she hit out against the line that 'those who choose to get on by extra effort must be publicly decried and milked as much as possible.'

It was a good defensive effort, but was swamped by the news that came in later that night from the constituency in which she lived, Orpington—that Eric Lubbock had turned a 'safe' Tory majority of 14,760 into a Liberal lead of 7,855. The middle-income groups of suburbia and elsewhere were in revolt.

'Our difficulties started with the pay pause, undoubtedly,' she recalls. 'This was the first stop to people's rising expectations, and quite a sudden and abrupt stop. But it was the right policy in the circumstances, and entirely voluntary. Householders were also getting alarmed about the rates again. The Orpington result itself contributed to the air of crisis since it showed how volatile the electorate could be' The Government also had an unlucky string of security cases, such as Blake, Lonsdale, and Vassall, and some tricky Home Office deportations. It was curious the effect that a few personal cases, and security, had on that Government.

The situation was not helped by the outbreak of personal hostilities between the Prime Minister and Fleet Street over the Vassall affair. So it was with some relish that newspapers seized on the most damaging personal case of all—that of John Profumo, a Minister at the War Office—in which he himself raised the stakes by making a personal statement in the Commons denying that a woman of easy virtue with tenuous connections at the Russian Embassy had been his mistress. Macmillan accepted his protestation in good faith, which made the blow all the harder when on June 4, 1963, Profumo admitted he had been lying and resigned.

The news came as a great shock to Margaret, as to all her colleagues. She was keenly aware of the personal tragedy involved, but the political consequences were profound too. A strong 'Macmillan Must Go' movement got under way on the Tory backbenches, and the old master seemed to be fighting defensive battles on all fronts. Though totally supporting Macmillan, Margaret had her doubts whether there was enough time left in which to recover before the next election.

Then on the very eve of the Conservative Party Conference opening that October in Blackpool, Macmillan was struck down by illness and resigned. I can remember the conference as a political correspondent, and the chaos was indescribable. Front runners for the succession were R. A. Butler, Lord Hailsham, who quickly announced that he intended to revert to being Mr. Quintin Hogg, and Reginald Maudling, and immediately the conference took on the tone of an American presidential convention.

Reginald Maudling, who has never been a fiery conference speaker, was written off after his platform speech on the economy. All the dash and drama surrounded Lord Hailsham. R. A. Butler was making the closing rally speech on the Saturday, in place of Macmillan, and great tension built up for that. But that, too, did not quite come off. Lord Home, the Foreign Secretary—and a great favourite with conference delegates—held the ring for the other contenders. But even before the conference was over a 'Draft Alec Home' bandwagon was starting to roll, and it gained impetus among MPs once they were back in London. Margaret seems to have been unaware of this at Blackpool, probably because her eyes were still fixed on R. A. Butler. In London, she held back from supporting Lord Home's candidature because of the constitutional problems she thought it raised. After renouncing his peerage he would have to fight a by-election seat—'and in the circumstances of the day I didn't think we could possibly assume the result of any by-election.'

But when Lord Home did emerge from the party's consultation process, about which there was so much bitterness later,. Margaret was 'perfectly happy. One knew that Alec was very, very good—and so easy to talk to. And Rab was marvellous about it, going straight to the Foreign Office.'

Sir Alec Douglas-Home, as he became, went on to achieve as

remarkable a feat of recovery in Tory morale in the few months available to him as Macmillan had in the three years after Suez. Following Hugh Gaitskell's death in January 1963, Harold Wilson was leading the Labour Party, and Sir Alec presented a contrast in style to him which appealed to many who had wavered or withdrawn their support from the Macmillan Government. It is amazing how, after all the disasters of 1962–3, the Conservatives recovered to such an extent that Wilson should win the 1964 election with a majority of only four.

'If only we had had two or three months left to us we'd have won it ourselves,' is Margaret's view. 'Things were moving back our way.' In Finchley, where a strong challenge had been mounted by the Liberal candidate, John Pardoe, the result was:

Margaret Thatcher (Con)	24,591
John Pardoe (Lib)	15,789
Albert Tomlinson (Lab)	12,408
Conservative majority	8,802

Thus her majority was nearly half what it was in 1959, due entirely to the growth of the Liberal vote.

'We'd planned our Pensions Bill, but we were never to get the chance to introduce it. I made a point of going into the Department to sign letters till quite near the end. But I never went back to collect anything after the election. A Department is always interested in the in-coming Minister, not the out-going one. Once you're out, you're out. And I didn't want to embarrass anyone by saying good-bye.'

For the first time in her experience Margaret Thatcher was in Opposition, with a totally different range of opportunities opening up.

CHAPTER SEVEN

What's Wrong With Politics?
1964–1969

Margaret Thatcher's immediate role in Opposition was to help
shadow her previous Ministry, but this offered very little scope
for her to shine. As promised in their manifesto, the Labour
Government brought in an immediate Bill to raise retirement
pensions, and though this, coupled with Ministers' own inflated
talk of inherited economic crisis, helped to produce a run on
sterling, there was no point in an Opposition trying to resist a
pensions increase.

Margaret was also more cautious than many in assessing the
political prospects. After becoming used to the Macmillan and
Douglas-Home Governments managing their business on a
Commons majority not far short of 100, the common judgement
was that Harold Wilson's chances of being able to hold on to
power on a majority of only four were pretty thin. This view
was strengthened when Labour lost the Leyton by-election,
which had been staged specifically to enable the Foreign
Secretary, Patrick Gordon-Walker, to get back into the Commons.

In fact, the challenge of governing on so small a majority
could almost have been designed to make the most of Wilson's
political talents. He thrived on the day-to-day drama, on the
suspense of one cliff-hanger after another. He was at the centre
of every stage. His news management, which I witnessed as a
lobby correspondent, was superb, and he had Fleet Street eating
out of his hand. All the Government's moves were essentially
short-term; as in 1974, an illusion of prosperity was created by
allowing pay increases far to outstrip real growth in production;
it was all tactics and no strategy.

On only one proposed measure was Wilson frustrated by two
rebel Labour MPs, and that was the renationalisation of the steel
industry. William Whitelaw, then Conservative Chief Whip, saw
clearly that it would be almost impossible for the Tories to bring

down the Government, and Margaret, too, could see that Wilson was setting the stage for an appeal to the country at the moment most convenient to him.

Meanwhile, the Conservatives had their own leadership difficulties. A fairly strong minority of Tory MPs began to argue that Sir Alec's image was the wrong one for defeating Wilson. But, as in the leadership situation in which Margaret featured ten years later, the discussion concentrated first on mechanics. Many in the party wanted never to see a repeat of the informal selection process by which Sir Alec had emerged in 1963, with the subsequent 'Magic Circle' allegations which it provoked.

This view was shared by Sir Alec, who set about establishing some formal machinery for electing a new leader in the event of a vacancy. In February 1965 he announced a new procedure for election by formal ballot. But it was a rather complicated one. To win on the first ballot, a contender had to secure a lead of 15 per cent of the votes cast over his nearest rival; if this was not obtained, then there would be a second ballot in which fresh candidates could enter. This was very much a formalisation of the process by which Sir Alec recalled himself becoming Leader, entering the ring only when there appeared to be no clear agreement in favour of one of the initial contenders.

With the new machinery there, pressure began to build up from a number of backbenchers for it to be used, and though Sir Alec almost certainly retained the backing of the majority of Tory MPs, he began to find his position increasingly uncomfortable. He had taken the Leadership in order to unify the party, and he had no intention of seeing it split under him. On July 22 he was due to speak to the 1922 Committee, which in Opposition is made up of all Conservative MPs, and it was made known that at this he would either announce his intention to stay and make a strong plea for unity, or announce his resignation.

The general expectation was that he would take the first course, and this is certainly what Margaret hoped he would do. But Sir Alec thought it better for the party if he went, and so surprised everyone by resigning.

'I regretted that very much,' Margaret recalls. 'I most definitely would have preferred him to carry on.'

But, once Sir Alec had made up his mind, she thought it right that the formal ballot procedure should be adopted to find a replacement.

The two obvious contenders for the vacancy were Ted Heath and Reginald Maudling, though Enoch Powell also joined in to stake his claim for the future. Margaret's first inclination was to vote for Maudling, partly on the grounds that she was personally closer to him, and partly because she greatly respected the judgements which he had made as Chancellor. But as the argument moved back and forth among Tory MPs she changed her mind, and in the end cast her vote for Heath. A common argument at the time was that his attacking qualities were more necessary if the true nature of the Wilson Government was to be exposed.

When Tory MPs went to cast their votes on July 27 Maudling was strongly tipped to win, but a secret ballot showed—not for the last time—just how wrong such common assumptions can be. The result was: Ted Heath, 150; Reginald Maudling, 133; Enoch Powell, 15. Heath had fallen short of the 15 per cent lead he needed for an automatic win, but both Maudling and Powell conceded victory, so there was no second ballot. There was a good deal of comment that, for the first time in its history, the Conservative Party had an ex-grammar school boy as its Leader.

After a highly successful launching as Leader at the party's annual October conference, Heath set about reconstructing his Front Bench team. In the second tier Margaret was moved from shadowing the Pensions Ministry to Housing and Land— the first of what was to prove a succession of different home front shadow posts before the Conservatives won the next election.

Just as, at the Bar, she had taken a succession of pupillages to give herself a broad basis of experience, so at Westminster it was as if she had a succession of 'political pupillages' to give her experience of the affairs covered by a whole range of Government Departments. In October 1965 she was appointed by Ted Heath to help shadow Housing and Land; in March 1966 she was moved to be Number Two spokesman shadowing the Treasury; in October 1967 she was promoted to the Shadow Cabinet as Shadow Minister of Power; in October 1968 she became Shadow Minister of Education.

'I was glad to be moved about so much, because it gave me such a good wide training,' she recalls. 'Changing jobs about once a year meant a fantastic amount of work catching up on what different Departments were doing, but it gave me a much

broader idea of what goes on and what the different problems
of different Departments were.'

This stood her in very good stead when she became a Cabinet
Minister. 'If you are to make a contribution to a Cabinet, you
obviously need to know about a good deal more than what goes
on in your own Department.'

Her work covering Housing and Land in the run-up to the
1966 election laid the basis for the key role she was to play in
developing Conservative housing policy between the two 1974
general elections. During this period the Wilson Government
was pushing out its plans for a Land Commission to acquire
building land and exact a development levy on the rest, for
major changes in the leasehold system, and for 'option mortgages'
at $2\frac{1}{2}$ per cent below the prevailing rate of interest for those
whose incomes were too low to allow them to get the full benefit
from tax allowances on mortgage payments. The latter proposal
was very similar to one favoured by the Conservatives, but the
Land Commission raised a fundamental point of difference
between the two parties.

It was during 1965 that Margaret was also very busy on a
case involving one of her constituents, Gerald Brooke, a lecturer
arrested in Moscow on a spying charge. A disturbing feature of
the case was the Russian authorities' refusal to allow him to be
visited by a British consul, and to state the nature of the charges
against him. Margaret maintained constant pressure on the
Foreign Office to secure access to her constituent, and organised
a protest in Parliament over the behaviour of the Russian
authorities, which eventually had its effect.

In March 1966, Harold Wilson decided to go to the country
in much the circumstances that Margaret had always imagined
he would. A by-election at Hull North at the end of January
recorded a 4 per cent swing to Labour since the 1964 election,
and this was just the signal that Wilson needed. Chancellor James
Callaghan made a rosy statement of his Budget intentions, and
the election campaign was on. Ted Heath put up an energetic
fight, trying to draw the Government on the economy and on the
Common Market, and making a list of specific Tory pledges for
action.

'But there was never any question that we could have won
that election,' Margaret recalls. 'It was loaded against us from
the very start.'

Wilson had happily allowed money incomes to race ahead of

output, thus storing up trouble for the future—but first he wanted
to cash his electoral dividend. The result of the election was to
give him a massive majority of 97. In Finchley the result was:

Margaret Thatcher (Con)	23,968
Yvonne Sieve (Lab)	14,504
Frank Davis (Lib)	13,070
Conservative majority:	9,464

That was slightly up on 1964, though her share of the poll was
almost exactly the same.

By the time the new Parliament met Margaret had already
been moved to join the shadow Treasury team under Iain
Macleod. It was a promotion from Housing, since the Government's handling of the economy was obviously going to be the
key political issue for some time to come. It also meant returning
to finance—the territory she had chosen for her first Parliamentary activity after she had got her Private Member's Bill on to
the Statute Book.

The shadow team's first task was to take apart Jim Callaghan's
post-election Budget, which among other things introduced
Selective Employment Tax. This tax had been worked out in
some haste to raise necessary revenue while appearing not to
break Labour's election pledge that there would be 'no severe
increase in taxation'.

Its introduction came as a surprise to several in the Cabinet,
and it was riddled with anomalies. The justification offered by
Callaghan was that it would help shift resources from the
service industries into manufacturing. The idea was that all
employers should pay SET of 25s. (£1.25) a week on all full-
time male employees, with lower rates for women, boys and
part-time workers. Those in manufacturing industry could reclaim the sums six months later, with an extra 7s. 6d. (£0.37½)
per employee on top. 'Neutral' industries, like agriculture, would
reclaim it but without the bonus. Service industries got nothing
back—and house-building, for the purposes of SET, was defined
as a service industry.

As a tax lawyer Margaret could hardly have asked for a richer
hunting ground, and she plunged into her task with her usual
enthusiasm. She was given her first Front Bench chance in the
Budget Debate on May 5, and it was agreed that she should tear
into the SET proposal. Happily she poured scorn on the idea of

imposing a levy of 25s. a week on thousands upon thousands of people, only to pay the same sum back six months later. Even more ridiculous, the Chancellor was proposing to take 25s. a week for thousands more, but repay their employers 32s. 6d. Why not, she asked, just pay them the balance of 7s. 6d. and have done with it? The whole SET scheme was 'sheer cock-eyed lunacy, absolute nonsense. I really think you need a woman at the Treasury!'

After poking fun at other anomalies, she went on to point out that, as proposed, SET would be an extra tax on mothers who went out to work, and who paid someone else to look after their children for part of the day. 'I doubt if this will be very good for recruitment among the teachers.'

She warned the Chancellor to expect a lot more trouble over his new tax, adding the detail that she had read every Budget Speech and every Finance Bill since 1946. Trouble he certainly got, and many amendments had to be made to the hastily conceived Selective Employment Tax before it was levied that autumn.

By July the logic of the economic situation about which the Government had been so complacent caught up with Ministers, and the pound began to slide. The Cabinet set its face against devaluation, and Chancellor Callaghan took some initial steps to dampen the economy. Harold Wilson promised a review of further measures to restrain demand and curb Government spending, and left on a trip to Moscow. By the time he returned the situation had worsened. Meanwhile the old complacent noises were coming from Downing Street suggesting that no extra measures might be necessary at all. This caused further panic.

On July 20, while George Brown let everyone know he was likely to resign as Secretary for Economic Affairs, Wilson announced to the Commons a further battery of squeeze measures—and a six-month freeze on pay and prices. There was uproar in the Labour Party, but George Brown stayed for the time being.

A Prices and Incomes Bill giving the Government very limited powers was already being considered in Committee; to this had now to be added a new Part IV giving it reserve powers to prevent any increase which breached the freeze. Thus the freeze was intended to be voluntary, but Part IV could be activated by the Cabinet if the policy was threatened. Before long it was, by a county court ruling obtained by ASSET, Clive Jenkins' union,

and so Part IV was activated. Under it, individual Orders made
to prevent pay or price rises were open to challenge in the
Commons—and challenged they were throughout the following
session, since Conservative policy at that time was totally opposed
to statutory controls over pay or prices.

As Margaret recalls: 'We fought George Brown's prices and
incomes policy, and we contested every single compulsory order
made under it. Iain Macleod was adamant that we should oppose
them; he said the statutory policy would lead to rigidity, and
that controls would get much too detailed, which they did.'

Margaret too, as one of the party's economic spokesmen at the
time, was deeply committed against a statutory pay policy.

Throughout her twenty months with him she greatly enjoyed
working with Macleod.

'He was superb at managing Parliamentary business, but
most of all one admired his capacity for oratory, and his great
knack of hitting on the really telling phrase. In the Commons
he could be very witty, and at the annual party conference his
speech usually brought the delegates to their feet.'

At this time he was conducting a major review of taxation
policy, in order to put up proposals for the party's next election
programme. As a tax expert Margaret was involved in this work,
and a big economic seminar was held at Church House,
Westminster. But before these plans reached their final stages
she had moved on again, this time promoted into the Shadow
Cabinet to handle Fuel and Power.

'This too was a very interesting portfolio to have,' she recalls.
'I was opposite Dick Marsh, who was always very pleasant. He'd
worked out a fuel policy which was keenly contested on his own
side because it was based on cheap oil and running down the
coal industry. Several important questions were coming up over
how we should exploit the natural gas deposits, and there were
some tricky problems over nuclear energy. A lot of detail to
master, but fascinating.'

But her first debate, on October 26, 1967, was one she wishes
had never been necessary—into the Aberfan disaster, in which
116 children and 28 adults were killed when a moving slag-heap
buried their school. The tragedy made a great emotional impact
on her at the time, as indeed it did on most people, but she still
cannot talk about it without appearing to relive the experience.

'I remember that mother who had sent her son off to school
after a bit of a row. It was one of those mornings when everyone

was a bit on edge, and they hadn't parted friends. Ever afterwards she'll be haunted by the thought of him going off to his
death like that . . .'

In October 1968 Margaret was moved on again, this time to
become Shadow Transport Minister. Ironically Richard Marsh,
whom she had shadowed at Power, had already been made
Transport Minister, so it seemed as if she was dogging his
footsteps. His first task had been to try to make some sense of
Barbara Castle's restrictive Transport Bill, which to some extent
he had succeeded in doing. By the time Margaret arrived on the
scene this was on the Statute Book, and the Government was
content to avoid any further major transport measures if it could.

However, though opportunities for Margaret to shine in the
Commons were limited, her new post brought a further experience
new to her : 'The striking thing about the Transport job is the
fantastic number of pressure groups for you to deal with, all of
them wanting to come to see you. There are the road hauliers,
the lorry drivers, the motoring organisations, those wanting new
roads or by-passes, the conservationist groups, and many more.
You have to meet them all—an illuminating experience.' Then
after this, exactly a year later she moved on again to cover
Education, which we shall come to in the next chapter.

It was towards the end of 1968 that she and Denis decided
that the working pressure on both of them was such that they
should leave their house at Farnborough and move back into
London. Three years earlier Denis had arranged for the Atlas
Preservative Company in Erith to be sold to Castrol, whom he
joined, only to find it taken over very soon after by Burmah Oil.
He was now on the board of Burmah, Margaret's shadow duties
were mounting, the children were away at school, and life would
obviously be easier for both of them if they could live in London.
So in 1969 they moved to 19 Flood Street, in Chelsea—almost
opposite the flat where they had begun married life together.
They were still living in this house when Margaret became
Leader of the Conservative Party.

These first two years of Shadow Cabinet office were ones of
continuing crisis for the Wilson Government. The pound was
devalued, but still came under recurring pressure, forcing the
new Chancellor, Roy Jenkins, into yet more punitive tax
measures. Labour suffered a steady stream of by-election losses,
and the Conservatives were consistently way ahead in the opinion
polls. Most Shadow Ministers recognised the going would get a

lot tougher nearer to election date, but nevertheless these were years of great hope for them as they set about preparing their policies ready for power. Their main difficulty in handling their own party sprang from Enoch Powell, whom Heath sacked from the Shadow Cabinet in April 1968 over his 'Rivers of Blood' speech in Birmingham.

In the spring of 1969 the Government announced that statutory pay controls would at last be phased out, but that immediate legislation would be introduced to curb strikes. This provoked a running rebellion in the Labour ranks, which ended in the Cabinet capitulating to the TUC in June that year—the first damaging assertion of trade union power over Cabinet policy.

It was during this period that Margaret was awarded a significant accolade : she was invited to give the annual lecture at the Conservative Political Centre's big meeting during the party's 1968 Blackpool conference. This, indeed, was a rare distinction for a newcomer to the Shadow Cabinet. CPC is the limb of the Conservative Party Organisation whose task is to stimulate and guide the party's intellectual activity across the country, and at its annual conference meeting the guest speaker is expected to make a weighty contribution. Past stars at this CPC meeting had included intellectual heavyweights like R. A. Butler, Lord Hailsham and Sir Edward Boyle, and frequently their speeches were reprinted in booklet form for sale to party workers. In accepting the offer she knew she had a high standard to reach.

In the event the title she chose was 'What's Wrong With Politics?', and the lecture she gave under it is essential reading for anyone who wishes to understand the political character of Margaret Thatcher. It is the first comprehensive statement of her own political philosophy that she ever committed to paper. Furthermore, a large part of it is as relevant to the problems of the 1970s as to those of the decade in which it was delivered. For these reasons it is reprinted as Appendix A to this book.

She began the lecture by accepting as fact that there was a deep dissatisfaction with politics and politicians. 'People have come to doubt the future of the democratic system and its institutions. They distrust the politicians and have little faith in the future. Let us try to assess how and why we have reached this pass.'

She went on to list a number of factors contributing to the

situation, and whose implications were not yet generally realised. The rapid spread of higher education had equipped people to criticise and question almost everything, but many were unable to move on to the next stage, 'which is to arrive at new beliefs or to reaffirm old ones.'

She also questioned the effect of the mandate theory—that a Government derives its authority for specific actions from pledges in its last election programme—when such programmes had become so detailed. This had led to 'a curious relationship between elector and elected. If the elector suspects the politician of making promises simply to get his vote, he despises him, but if the promises are not forthcoming he may reject him. I believe that parties and elections are about more than rival lists of miscellaneous promises—indeed, if they were not, democracy would scarcely be worth preserving.'

Then she went on to analyse where we had gone wrong. 'I believe that the great mistake of the last few years has been for the government to provide or to legislate for almost everything.' Part of this had arisen from the needs of post-war reconstruction, though in the 1950s Conservative Governments had tried to establish a framework within which people could achieve their own standards for themselves. But during the early 1960s the emphasis in politics shifted, and a high growth rate became the supreme end. 'The result was that for the time being the emphasis in political debate ceased to be about people and became about economics.'

Then came the Wilson Government, promising to plan still higher growth, and saying that if people would not conform to their plan then they should be compelled to do so. Hence, she said, 'the totally unacceptable notion that the Government shall have the power to fix which wages and salaries should increase'. Recently there had been calls for more public *participation* in government. 'But the way to get personal involvement and participation is not for people to take part in more and more Government decisions but to make the Government reduce the area of decision over which it presides and consequently leave the private citizen to "participate", if that be the fashionable word, by making more of his own decisions.' The aim should therefore be to increase the area of responsibility for individuals and families.

Developing her attack on the statutory control of incomes, she said, 'There is nothing wrong in people wanting larger

incomes. . . . What *is wrong* is that people should want more
without giving anything in return. The condition precedent to
high wages and high salaries is hard work. This is a quite
different and much more stimulating approach than one of
keeping down incomes.'

At the same time, by putting such emphasis on incomes policy
too little regard was shown for the need for the Government to
control the supply of money and to manage the general level of
demand. 'Greater attention to this role and less to the outward
detailed control would have achieved far more for the economy.
It would mean, of course, that the Government had to exercise
itself some of the disciplines on expenditure it is so anxious to
impose on others. It would mean that expenditure in the vast
public sector would not have to be greater than the amount
which could be financed out of taxation plus genuine saving.
For a number of years some expenditure has been financed by
what amounts to printing the money. There is nothing *laissez-
faire* or old-fashioned about the views I have expressed. It is a
modern view of the role the Government should play now, arising
from the mistakes of the past, the results of which we are
experiencing today.'

These words were to be echoed by many a Tory in the mid-
1970s, after another dash for growth had been tried and failed
under a Conservative Government.

She went on to list some further mistakes of current politics,
including the obsession with the idea of *size*. 'As a result people
no longer feel important in the scheme of things. They have the
impression that everything has become so big, so organised, so
standardised and governmentalised that there is no room for the
individual, his talents, his requirements or his wishes. He no
longer counts.'

Finally, she developed a criticism of the notion of 'consensus
government' which has a bearing on 1974's call for a Government of National Unity. 'The essential characteristic of the
British constitutional system is not that there is an alternative
personality but that there is an alternative *policy* and a whole
alternative *Government* ready to take office. As a result we have
always had an Opposition to act as a focus of criticism against
the Government. We have therefore not suffered the fate of
countries which have had a "consensus" or central Government,
without an Opposition. . . . There are dangers in consensus; it
could be an attempt to satisfy people holding no particular views

about anything. It seems more important to have a philosophy and policy which because they are good appeal to sufficient people to secure a majority.'

The whole lecture is a striking statement of Margaret Thatcher's political philosophy, some of which she clearly compromised as a Cabinet Minister in the Heath Government. But while the Cabinet went a different way she clung to many of its tenets, and restated them in more relevant form in the dark days of 1974. It is hard to see it as a notably Right-wing testament; rather it forms part of that central strand of Conservative thinking which seeks to expand individual responsibility and choice, and which contrasts sharply with the collectivist approach of the Left.

As a statement of political belief it would call for some revision today to make greater allowance for the monopoly power of the trade unions, though it could be argued that this itself is a defensive response to some of the factors to which she referred.

However, after the fall of the Heath Government many Conservatives were to express such ideas, little realising that they had been spelt out quite so clearly by a fairly junior Shadow Minister six long years before.

PART II

Achievement in Education

CHAPTER EIGHT

The Myth of Selsdon Man
1969–1970

When Ted Heath appointed her Shadow Education Minister in October 1969, soon after the Conservative Party conference, Margaret Thatcher did not suffer the inconvenience of having either a Right- or Left-wing label pinned to her. Throughout her time as a shadow spokesman covering successively Pensions, the Treasury, Power and Transport she was recognised by political correspondents and commentators as being within the mainstream of Tory thinking. In the context of education, the Right wing were then generally identified as being those sympathetic to the criticisms of comprehensive schools, of 'progressive' teaching methods in primary schools, and of the expansion of the universities set out in the contributions to the first 'Education Black Paper'.

The morning after her appointment the *Financial Times'* Lobby Correspondent wrote :

'The choice of Mrs. Thatcher shows that Mr. Heath has resisted the pressure from the Right to appoint a dedicated opponent of the comprehensive system. Instead he has picked an uncommitted member of the Shadow Cabinet who has won a high reputation for her grasp of complex issues in the fields of finance, social security, power and transport.'

The Political Correspondent of the *Daily Express* wrote :

By appointing Mrs. Thatcher, who is not specially identified with either side of the comprehensive controversy, Mr. Heath has ducked out of trouble with the Right wing of the Tory Party over education.

Margaret came to her new shadow job at a particularly interesting time. During the years of Labour Government the number of children of school age had been increasing, and therefore more money had to be spent to maintain existing standards. But, as one economic crisis and set of cuts succeeded another, the rate of growth in spending on education had suffered as more objectives were deferred or axed. In January 1968 fulfilment of the previous Conservative Government's pledge to raise the school leaving age to sixteen in the school year 1970–71 was postponed, the supply of free milk to secondary schoolchildren was axed, and a recommended increase in student grants halved. At the same time the school building programme was being allowed to slip back.

Margaret knew that one of her main tasks was to take charge of preparing the Conservatives' election programme on education, and that on this front the Labour Party were clearly vulnerable. This was also a period in which many of the assumptions on which educationists had worked for the previous few years were coming into question. The first 'Education Black Paper' was published in March 1969, and a second, a substantial part of which was devoted to standards within the State system, came out the following October.

But the big conflict building up was over the reorganisation of secondary education. In July 1965, when Anthony Crosland was Education Secretary, he issued his Circular 10/65 to local education authorities stating that the Government's aim was 'the complete elimination of selection and separatism in secondary education'. Labour's 1964 election manifesto commitment on this had been somewhat ambiguous :

Labour will get rid of the segregation of children into separate schools caused by 11-plus selection : secondary education will be reorganised along comprehensive lines. Within the new system, *grammar school education will be extended*; in future no child will be denied the opportunity of benefiting from it through arbitrary selection at the age of 11 . . . (my italics)

The peculiarly worded reference to grammar schools was presumably to cover Mr. Wilson's platform statement under questioning that they would be abolished 'over my dead body'. Crosland's Circular 10/65 flowed fairly naturally from this manifesto commitment. Such circulars are issued regularly by the Department of Education; they do not have the force of law, but are intended to guide local education authorities on Government thinking, and often to indicate the sort of projects likely to get Government approval and grant aid.

Circular 10/65 went on to ask education authorities to submit within one year both short-term and long-term plans for ending 11-plus selection; it also expressed a strong preference for 'all through' 11–18 comprehensives, large enough to provide a wide variety of courses at sixth form level.

But Crosland, under party pressure to stamp rather harder on many Conservative-controlled councils, was not satisfied with the response, and so on the eve of the 1966 general election issued his Circular 10/66 threatening that he would not approve any new secondary school building projects, and hence refuse grant aid, unless they could be fitted into a comprehensive pattern. Labour's 1966 manifesto commitment was also more direct :

> We shall press ahead with our plans to abolish the 11-plus—
> that barrier to educational opportunity—and reorganise
> secondary education on comprehensive lines.

When Margaret took up her appointment and Ted Short was Education Secretary, Circular 10/66 was still in force, though with very little Government money available for comprehensive reorganisation the threat contained in it did not have a great deal of force. Nevertheless, by the end of 1969 most local education authorities had submitted at least long-term plans, though eight had either not done so or had their schemes rejected by the Minister. These authorities were Bolton, Bournemouth, Bury, Kingston-upon-Thames, Richmond-upon-Thames, Rutland, Westmorland and Worcester.

Ted Short, who was far more passionately egalitarian over education than any of his predecessors, and embarrassed by decisions such as that to postpone the raising of the school leaving age, determined that he would have some achievement to show to his party. The rest of the Cabinet shared this desire, and so he proudly announced that in the 1969–70 session of Parliament he would introduce a Bill to *compel* local education authorities to submit plans for the reorganisation of secondary education along comprehensive lines.

This threatened to change significantly the balance of power over education between the Government and local councils, for though the Education Secretary had the power of veto over reorganisation schemes submitted, he did not have the power to impose his own policy from the top.

It was at this point that Margaret came on to the education scene. By this time the twins were sixteen; Mark was at Harrow, and Carol at St. Paul's School for Girls.

In fact Margaret's predecessor shadowing Education, Sir Edward Boyle, had made it clear at the Conservative Party conference just before her appointment that the Conservatives would fight Ted Short's proposed Bill. When she met the Press on her first day in her new role she renewed this commitment with relish, adding that good grammar schools which played an important role in their communities should be saved. With her own background at the Kesteven and Grantham Girls' School she clearly understood what the protesters meant.

But she went out of her way to make clear that she had nothing against comprehensive schools as such. 'Indeed, I know many parents prefer them. I certainly don't propose to un-scramble plans that are already in existence.' However, she drew a clear distinction with cases in which an 'artificial system' was imposed on a number of schools incapable of sustaining it, purely in order to claim that a comprehensive school had been created.

So the lines of battle against Short's 'Compulsory Comprehen-sives Bill' were clearly drawn, and repeated by Margaret in the Queen's Speech debate on the new session's programme. However, the Bill itself was not presented by the Government for debate until the following February.

But before then Margaret was called on to attend a unique political gathering which has since gone down in history for all the wrong reasons—the week-end conference at the Selsdon Park Hotel, near Croydon. Attending it were all members of the Shadow Cabinet and the most senior officials from Conservative Central Office and the Research Department, including Deputy Chairman Sir Michael Fraser, who had helped shape Tory policy ever since he was one of R. A. Butler's apprentices in 1945–50.

The conference began on the morning of Friday, January 30, 1970, and ended at lunch time on Sunday, February 1. Its purpose was to discuss every important field of policy, sometimes on the basis of prepared papers, and to establish the broad lines of the party's next election manifesto and programme in government. In this it was successful, though it has since come to be portrayed as the occasion of a lurch towards harsh, uncompromising and socially divisive policies.

The myth of 'Selsdon Man' was in fact invented by Harold Wilson, who with his own Government's record behind him was seeking to portray the Tories as a party of hard-faced men. Like all good myths, it has come to be accepted by many on both sides of the political argument; thus among Conservatives we have since seen the foundation of the Selsdon Group dedicated to furthering what a number of its members believe to have been a markedly Right-wing programme.

However, the myth of 'Selsdon Man' merits rather more clinical examination. It was certainly not born out of the information released immediately afterwards, which indicated priorities for the next Conservative Government. These were to set about reforming the tax system, abolishing SET and seeking to reduce the burden on individuals; to reform industrial relations along the lines of the programme already published; to give the Government greater powers to control immigration; to preserve law and order by applying existing laws with determination and if necessary strengthening them; and finally, to introduce a pension for those over eighty who were excluded from the National Insurance scheme.

The Press tended to seize on the law and order point, since the growth in crime and a series of rather violent demonstrations were causing considerable public anxiety. But only a committed Socialist could see the whole package as harsh. The Industrial Relations Act certainly did not live up to expectations, but the 1974 Wilson Governments were happy to accept the Immigration Act. Other items in the programme had a substantial welfare content. Apart from the proposed Industrial Relations Bill the proposals did not mark any break in principle from the Tory approach of 1951–64, and even the Industrial Relations Bill had been included in the 1966 election programme.

It was not until some three weeks later that Wilson made his archeological discovery of 'Selsdon Man', whom he portrayed as a relic of pre-war Toryism bent on creating a society of greater inequality. He repeated the phrase several times, inside the House of Commons and out, but with no success in arousing public fears, as the 1970 election result finally showed.

It was, in fact, not until *after* the election that the myth of 'Selsdon Man' took wings, as unemployment rose and the Tory

Government said it would refuse to bail out 'lame duck' industries. Even the 'lame duck' phrase was contorted to support the myth. As originally used by Trade and Industry Secretary John Davies it applied to *firms* who found themselves unable to compete in selling their products; Labour leaders twisted it to apply to *people* suffering misfortune or disability. It was not until this period that the myth of 'Selsdon Man' became established, to be repeated to the public at regular intervals.

Even during the 1975 Conservative leadership ballot some Labour speakers and writers sought to portray Margaret as 'Selsdon Woman'. In fact, measured by what the Selsdon conference actually achieved, she would have been proud of the title. For the discussions covered not only the immediate priorities for the next Conservative Government but also all the major fields of policy ready for the next election manifesto.

Margaret will not talk about these discussions, which she still treats as being confidential, but she has no hesitation in stating that they laid the basis for the 1970 election programme. If this is so, then it was at Selsdon Park that she won the first round of her battle to secure a major building programme to replace Victorian primary schools, to move on to an expansion of nursery education after that, and to stick by the pledge to raise the school leaving age to sixteen.

And 'Selsdon Man' can also claim the credit for laying the basis of the policies to improve benefits for the seriously ill and disabled, to pay a constant attendance allowance to the most seriously disabled, to ease the earnings rule for pensioners, and to proceed at greater speed in clearing slums—as well as to pay a pension as of right to all those over eighty. With one hand he was concerned to promote a much more vigorous and thriving economy, with greater incentives and rewards for those prepared to make the effort, and with the other to extend far more help to those people and families who were—and often still are— genuinely disadvantaged in our society. This is an approach straight in line with the Conservative tradition.

When the Shadow Cabinet met at Selsdon Park most of its members were expecting the general election to come that autumn, after summer holidays paid for from the rush of pay awards to come through after the abolition of all statutory controls. But fortunately they agreed to prepare their policies for presentation earlier if necessary, so Margaret set about the detailed work on her education policy.

First, however, came the bitter battle in the Commons with Short over his Bill to enforce comprehensive secondary education throughout England and Wales. He put his case simply : 'The Government can no longer tolerate a minority of authorities and school governors who have either ignored or openly flouted national policy as laid down by this House. The Government has decided to impose on local education authorities the need to end selection in secondary education, and to prepare plans to that end.'

Hitting back, Margaret claimed it was 'absolute tyranny' to force education authorities to go comprehensive in every area regardless of local wishes and conditions. Unless vastly more resources were provided for new school building, the Bill would certainly not achieve equality of opportunity for all pupils, as he claimed it would. A totally comprehensive system often compelled children to attend their neighbourhood school; some neighbourhoods, and some neighbourhood schools, were far better than others.

She then went on to develop an argument that was to play a major part in Conservative thinking on education over the years to come—that it is perfectly possible, and indeed desirable, to have a selective grammar school *with a very broad catchment area* co-existing alongside several comprehensives without 'creaming off' all their abler pupils. If the comprehensives were good, then many parents would choose for their children to attend them anyway. If they were poor, as in the case of some neighbourhood schools, then it was only right that brighter children should be able to attend a grammar school in order to realise their full potential.

Finally, Margaret repeated the pledge given by her predecessor, Sir Edward Boyle, that if the 'Compulsory Comprehensives' Bill became law then the next Conservative Government would repeal it. With the general election at most only a year away, that was a pledge of some significance to local education authorities.

However, the battle over the Bill in the Commons was nothing to the drama while it was being given detailed consideration in Standing Committee. For here, on April 14, the Government achieved the almost impossible feat of losing the first and most important clause of the Bill! One Labour MP on the Committee was abroad, and another had been taken ill. That reduced the Labour side to level pegging with the Opposition, but this was not serious for them since in the event of a tied vote the casting vote of the Committee Chairman is by custom used to keep the Bill in its existing form, whatever party the chairman himself is drawn from.

However, on this particular day a third Labour MP, William Price, chose the wrong moment to disappear to another part of the House, and while he was away Margaret and her Tory team surprised themselves by succeeding in throwing out the vital Clause One by a majority of one.

This put Ted Short in a very nasty spot, for without this clause he could not compel local authorities to introduce comprehensive education and abolish their grammar schools, besides which almost every subsequent clause contained some reference back to the one that had been lost. It also caused a headache for the Government's business managers, led by Fred Peart, then Leader of the House.

Eventually they decided to take the unprecedented step of holding a full Commons debate on a motion instructing the Committee to restore the clause, which they were able to carry easily with their majority. But in the end they need not have bothered; before the Bill had completed all its stages Harold Wilson decided to make a dash to the country on June 18, and so the Bill was lost.

The process by which this decision was arrived at is almost comic to recall. As statutory controls ended pay increases had begun to jump ahead of prices and production, thus creating the illusion of prosperity, just as in 1965–66. At the same time, the Tory lead in the opinion polls began to narrow, and by mid-May a couple were putting Labour ahead. Wilson was not slow to see his chance, though he was careful to insure himself against subsequent recrimination by getting every member of his Cabinet to agree to a snap poll first. By May 18 his mind was made up, and he took the plunge. If ever the timing of a general election had been determined by opinion polls, then this was it.

The Conservative manifesto, embodying all the further policy work and decisions that had followed the Selsdon Conference, was published on May 26. Margaret was well satisfied with the section on education. Indeed, its wording is very important, since it provided the bedrock of electoral justification for so many of her subsequent actions as Education Secretary. Headed simply 'Better Education', the first paragraph read :

In education above all the problem of resources is crucial. The number of children in the schools is rising. More and more are qualifying to go on to colleges, polytechnics and universities. That they should be able to develop their abilities to the full is not only right in itself but a vital national investment in the future.

Then came the valuable commitment on the primary schools, which was to prove so valuable to Margaret in her first months in office :

> Within the education budget itself, we shall shift the emphasis in favour of primary schools—the foundation on which all later education and training is built.
> We also recognise the need for expansion of nursery education. This is especially important in areas of social handicap, such as the poorer parts of our large cities, where it is so vital to give children a better start.

Next came the commitment to leave it to local education authorities to work out the pattern of secondary education most suited to their own areas :

> In secondary education, a number of different patterns have developed over the years, including many types of comprehensive school. We will maintain the existing rights of local education authorities to decide what is best for their area.
> They will take into account the general acceptance that in most cases the age of eleven is too early to make final decisions which might affect a child's whole future. Many of the most imaginative new schemes abolishing the 11-plus have been introduced by Conservative councils.

But then came the clear indication of the lines along which they must work if their reorganisation schemes were to get the necessary statutory approval from a Conservative Education Secretary.

> Local councils must ensure that the education they provide is the best for the children, taking into account the suitability of the buildings, the supply of staff, the travelling distances involved, the advice of teachers, and the wishes of local parents and electors. And they must be certain that they

provide properly for the late developer. And they will naturally be slow to make irrevocable changes to any good school unless they are sure that the alternative is better.

Thus there was a lifeline for the remaining grammar schools, provided that it was the wish of local parents and electors that they should be retained. However, a flexible approach would be necessary to enable late developers to transfer to them after the age of eleven. The section continued :

> We believe that the proper role of the central government is to satisfy itself that every local education authority provides education which will enable a child's talents and abilities to be developed to the full, at whatever age these may appear. All children must have the opportunity of getting to 'O' level and beyond if they are capable of doing so.
> We therefore believe that Labour's attempt to insist on compulsory reorganisation on rigid lines is contrary to local democracy and contrary to the best interests of the children.

The remainder of the education section contained further pledges on which Margaret was to rely to strengthen her argument in subsequent years :

> We will raise the school leaving age to 16 as planned. Opportunities should be given to some children, under the authority of their head teacher, to take advantage in their final year of the facilities available in colleges of further education.
> We will encourage the direct grant schools. Many of these schools have an excellent record and provide opportunities which may not otherwise be available for children of academic ability, regardless of their parents' income.
> Parents must have the freedom to send their children to independent schools if they wish.
> The demand for higher and further education in universities, polytechnics and other colleges will increase during the 1970s. We will expand the number of places available.
> Concern about teacher training is widespread. We will institute an inquiry into teacher training, as the Plowden Committee recommended. We wish the teaching profession

Margaret with twins Carol and Mark in 1953, when they were three weeks old. Three months later she passed her Bar Finals.

The newly-elected MP for Finchley arrives at the House of Commons in October 1959.

to have a career structure which will attract recruits of high
quality into the profession, and retain them.

This, then, was the platform on which Margaret's career as
Education Secretary was built.

The pattern of the June 1970 election campaign was even
more bizarre than the circumstances leading to it being called.
Wilson fought Labour's campaign on the general theme of 'Don't
worry, just leave it to us.' Conservatives campaigned on the issues
of strikes, high taxation and inflation. Enoch Powell conducted
a campaign of his own, going out on a limb on immigration and
the Common Market. And, as candidates trudged round canvassing in baking heat, they read in the Press of the opinion polls
giving Labour an ever bigger lead. At their peak, one poll's
figures were equivalent to a Labour majority in the Commons of
160 seats! And this after a Parliament which had seen by-election
swings of up to 22 per cent against Labour.

Some Tory leaders just did not believe them at all; Ted Heath
did not, neither did Party Chairman Tony Barber, who was
handling the special reports from the critical marginal seats,
nor did Iain Macleod. But the weight of evidence seemed so
great that many others, including Margaret, began to take a
gloomy view, even though believing that the opinion polls were
exaggerating the real situation.

'I'm not a natural optimist politically, and in those days one
tended to be influenced more by opinion polls than one would
be now,' she recalls.

During the campaign she devoted a couple of days each week
to visiting and speaking in marginal seats, including those in
Kent. In the last days of the campaign some of the opinion polls
showed Labour's lead narrowing, and on polling day itself one
suggested that the Tories might *just* win. All the pundits were
dumbfounded by the final result—a Conservative majority of
30. In Finchley the figures were:

Margaret Thatcher (Con)	25,480
Michael Freeman (Lab)	14,295
Graham Mitchell (Lib)	7,614
Conservative majority:	11,185

This represented a 2·8 per cent swing in her favour.

'Undoubtedly it was the cost of living issue that won it for us in the end. And remember there was this basis of disillusion with Labour going back two or three years,' Margaret observes. When Heath appointed his Cabinet several were switched around from their shadow jobs; but Margaret, to her great relief, was still put in charge of Education. For this, she knew, was then the area in which she could make the greatest contribution.

CHAPTER NINE

A Better Chance at School

1970-1974

It has always amazed Margaret Thatcher when the Press have described her as ruthless or highly ambitious. She is certainly not a ruthless person, and her ambition is purely that of wanting to make the very best of whatever job she has and the most of whatever opportunities present themselves.

It was in this frame of mind that she welcomed her appointment as Secretary of State for Education and Science. Having served in the Shadow Cabinet she had naturally hoped for a Cabinet post. Though given the choice she would probably have gone to the economic front, she had neither the seniority nor the experience in 1970 to be Chancellor of the Exchequer. This being so, then Education was as close to her personal interests as any other Department could be. It would still be hard to find another leading Conservative with a greater feeling and respect for education; having not had the advantage of a wealthy background, she had got where she was by climbing an educational ladder that had started in a local council school. She had gained a brief experience of teaching during her summer vacation from Oxford. And with her Science Degree she was obviously well placed to handle the Department's responsibilities in the scientific field.

The role of Education Secretary also accorded closely with her view of the purpose of politics. 'Everyone is born with some combination of talents,' she says. 'So we want a society, and an education system, that enables people to develop whatever talents they have to the full. If we don't have this, then not only do individual men and women lose out throughout their lives, but the whole of our society is poorer for it.'

But providing this was not entirely the function of the State. Parents had a very real role and responsibility in educating their children, just as her own parents had done. One also recalls her sister Muriel's observation that when the twins were young Margaret's endeavour was always to *teach* them something, and encourage them to *learn*. This respect for parental rights goes far to explain some of her subsequent decisions which so infuriated the educational Establishment. A high regard for education in its broadest sense is something that flows through Margaret Thatcher's veins.

She took office with two Junior Ministers. William van Straubenzee had understudied her shadowing Education in Opposition; he had been Parliamentary Private Secretary—a kind of political aide-de-camp—to Sir David Eccles when he had been Education Secretary, and had strong links with the Federation of Conservative Students. And Lord Belstead handled Education matters in the House of Lords. She was consulted over their appointment, and says she worked 'very happily' with them.

Margaret began her new job convinced that she could hardly do worse than her predecessor. Under the 1964–70 Labour Government growth in education had slowed; all the talk had been of greater equality, while thousands of children still began their school careers in outdated Victorian buildings and the promised raising of the school leaving age was postponed. For an incoming Minister there were great opportunities. But she also knew the strategy she was to follow, for it had all been set out in the election manifesto.

Looking back on her work in the three-and-a-half years that followed, one is amazed how she came to acquire the reputation among some sections of the public and Press of being a hard-line Right-winger. For, as we shall see, these were years of very real progress in education. However, part of the explanation lies in her very first act as Education Secretary, which was to withdraw the notorious Circular 10/66 stating that the only secondary school projects that would be approved would be those that fitted into the pattern of comprehensive education. She did this by issuing her own Circular 10/70, which we shall look at more closely when we assess her policies for secondary education in the next chapter.

However, the immediate reaction to this was a storm of protest from the National Union of Teachers, and expressions of shock from Fleet Street's education correspondents, who in those days often seemed to take their cue from the NUT. One of the main complaints was that there had been no prior consultation, yet this had been a firm commitment in the Conservative manifesto, and there would be little credibility to a Government or a Minister who on taking office began consultations on *whether* to implement election pledges. Meanwhile, in this particular case, time was pressing, as many local education authorities were anxiously awaiting new policy guidance.

Nevertheless, there can be little doubt that Margaret's prompt issuing of Circular 10/70 triggered off reactions which coloured individual judgement of many of her subsequent decisions. Those who were passionately in favour of the introduction of universal comprehensive education—as the NUT officially was—found themselves in the position of critics from the very start of her period of office, and as further issues arose it was there that they tended to stay. If only it had been possible for her to take action first on the primary school building programme, for example, then everyone in the education world would have started on a different foot.

Iain Macleod was Chancellor of the Exchequer, and one of his first decisions was that if there was to be room for the tax cuts which were part of the Conservatives' overall strategy then there had to be a substantial reduction in Government spending. Accordingly it was agreed by the Cabinet that every Minister would conduct a major review of the spending pro-grammes of his or her Department, with a view to making some economies for a package of cuts to be announced after the summer recess. But on July 20 Iain Macleod died, leaving a gap on the Government Front Bench which was never properly filled, and Anthony Barber was appointed Chancellor to continue with the same strategy.

There followed several weeks of speculation, during which a question mark was put over almost every Government spending programme. For her part Margaret set about seeing what economies could be made within her education budget, but she was determined that the essential fabric of the education service should not be cut back. Whitehall rumour had it that the Chan-cellor was looking to her to save £100 million a year on education spending. Charges for school meals would obviously have to go up again. Others suggested cuts in school building, or charges for all parents who sent their children to nursery schools. The future of the new Open University was in doubt. A proportion of student grants might take the form of a Government loan. A

charge might be made to enter London's major museums and
art galleries.

What exactly the pattern of argument over the various options
was in that Cabinet we shall never know, so long as all those who
were in it continue to respect the secrecy of its discussions. But
we do know that Margaret fought from the very start not to save
but to *obtain* a new primary school building programme, and to
honour the party's pledge to raise the school leaving age to sixteen
in the year 1972–73. Her strong belief in giving educational
opportunity to those prepared to work for it also led her to
support the Open University. And she got her priorities accepted
by her Cabinet colleagues fairly early. The final cuts package was
not announced by Tony Barber till the end of October, but by
the middle of August Margaret was able to announce the reprieve
of the Open University, which needed authorisation to enrol
students for the courses due to start on radio and television the
coming January.

In the middle of September she stood in for Ted Heath at
the NUT's centenary dinner, and was able to tell the teachers
that the Government would still give priority to replacing and
improving out-dated primary schools, and that the raising of the
school leaving age would go ahead as planned. Early in October
she told the Conservative Party conference in Blackpool that after
the Chancellor had announced his package of spending cuts she
would announce a primary school building programme to start
in 1972–73.

'I can promise you that the drive to get rid of our inadequate
schools will be resumed in earnest,' she said. 'When the programme is announced I am sure that you will be pleased with
it, and I am sure that the local authorities, and the churches
with their responsibilities for voluntary schools, will seize the
opportunities that we are giving them. By this means we hope to
give children a better start, because their progress in primary
school can and does affect their whole future. Later perhaps we
shall be able to turn to the needs of nursery education—but for
the time being I have put our top priority on the primary
schools.' The message could hardly have been more clear.

The background to the Cabinet's decision was serious, for by
then some 7,500 primary schools in England and Wales needed
to be pulled down and rebuilt or to have substantial improvements. Altogether some 1,300,000 children attended these schools,
and one out of every seven children in primary school had to

study in a Victorian building. But the effect did not stop there. As Margaret explains :

'A lot of these very old buildings were in areas where the children tended to have a poor home background. Then you often found that these bad school buildings also had bad equipment, and that it was very difficult to get teachers to go there. So these children suffered a triple deprivation, lacking a decent home, proper school buildings and enough good teachers. If only you could give them a good school then this gave them some experience of a nice building and good conditions. Then where the children came from a modern council estate to a bad school building you had a further set of problems, because their first experience of school was such a bad one.'

Priority for the primary schools was confirmed in the Queen's Speech setting out the newly-elected Government's programme for the following sixteen months. Then on October 27 Chancellor Anthony Barber made his long-awaited announcement of a package of cuts designed to reduce Government spending by £330 million in the following financial year, and by nearly £1,600 million by 1974–75. At the same time, he promised to take sixpence (2½p) in the pound off the standard rate of income tax in his next spring Budget. Details of the cuts, and of the spending programme on education, were set out in a White Paper.

Soon afterwards Margaret commented from her Department in Curzon Street : 'In the Queen's Speech we said we would give priority to the primary schools, where the foundations for all later education and training are laid. The White Paper shows how we are beginning to honour that pledge.' In 1972–73 the value of the schools improvement programme would go up to £38.5 million. 'This is the highest sum ever to be allocated in one year solely for the betterment of our schools. This is a major step forward in getting rid of poor schools. Virtually the whole of the £38.5 million will go to the replacement and improvement of old primary schools built before 1903.' But, she concluded, 'this is only a beginning. No decision has yet been taken on the size of the improvement programmes in later years, but it will certainly be large. My hope is that over a period of five years, of which 1972–73 will be the first, we shall really break the back of this problem of bringing the old schools up to date.' Meanwhile, among secondary schools, the £50 million building programme to provide for the raising of the school leaving age was going ahead.

One can understand her feeling of jubilation. A policy which had received outline acceptance at the Selsdon Park conference, and which had been spelt out as a firm commitment in the election manifesto, had survived intact from a very critical review of Government spending programmes. This was in part due to her own tenacity in Cabinet, but she had valuable support from some colleagues. Ted Heath, himself the product of a Church of England primary school and later a grammar school, was said to be particularly anxious that the party should honour its commitments on primary education, even though economies were being made in other areas. But for Cabinet success on this scale a certain price has to be paid; Margaret had to show that her Department was willing to accept some economy measures. And so it was that the cuts package included an end to the provision of free school milk for children of eight to eleven, higher charges for school meals, and the imposition of charges at some London museums and art galleries to which entry had hitherto been free.

Over the coming months these cuts were to cause her no end of political trouble, but looking back now she has few regrets.

'On the whole I got what I wanted,' she says. 'I got the primary school building programme, and there was no further postponement of the date for raising the school leaving age. Every Department had to make some cuts, but I was determined that I wasn't going to make mine in education itself. School milk and meals aren't *education* as such. I took the view that most parents are able to pay for the milk for their children, and that the job of the Government was to provide such things in education which they couldn't pay for, like new primary schools. The previous Labour Government had stopped free milk in the secondary schools, and though some on their own side objected there was no great storm over that. The important thing was to protect *education,* and that's what we did. Indeed, we expanded it.'

Altogether she had certainly done very well. On the credit side was a school building programme of some £186 million, including £38 million for primary schools; on the debit side, a saving of £20 million on school meals and milk, rising to £38 million and £9 million respectively.

This judgement was echoed the day after the announcement, when Margaret went to address the annual conference of the Association of Education Committees, where she was welcomed as a heroine who had kept education itself totally free of cuts. The cuts on milk and meals they saw as peripheral. As she told them in her speech : 'The important fact which emerges from the review of public expenditure is that the education budget will continue to grow at a considerable rate, and that educational opportunity will continue to expand. ... Our emphasis on primary schooling derives basically from the fact that it is the foundation on which all later education and training are built. There is a wealth of evidence to show that the impact of the first few years of schooling can make a decisive difference to a child's subsequent progress.'

Then, turning to the cuts, she stressed that free milk would continue to be supplied in special schools, and to all children aged eight to eleven for whom it was medically necessary. And, though the charge for school meals was being raised, so were the income limits for free meals, which meant that more children would qualify for these.

'We think the indiscriminate type of subsidy no longer represents a good use of taxpayers' and ratepayers' money,' she said, 'but we have been at pains to see that children who are vulnerable will not suffer.'

This was more than the Labour Government had been when withdrawing free milk in secondary schools nearly three years before, though that did not deter the Labour critics.

Margaret's political difficulty was that, unlike some Ministers who were able to implement their cuts by a simple statutory Order, she had to introduce a Bill to stop local authorities giving milk to those aged eight to eleven and to give them legal authority to sell milk in schools instead. The same applied to the museum charges, which caused trouble out of all proportion to the potential saving of £1 million—money which in the end the museums were told they could keep anyway. As a result, both issues were kept running long after discussion of other items in the cuts package had died.

However, looking at all the education elements in the October package, one cannot see what substance they give to the myth of Margaret the hard-faced Right-winger. Rather they were the product of a mind which rates giving all children a good start in their school careers as a higher priority than giving all those aged eight to eleven a third of a pint of milk free each day, especially when Labour's withdrawal of milk from the over-elevens could be seen to have had no adverse effects on their nutrition. As she pointed out in the debate on her Education (Milk) Bill, it is a peculiar sense of priorities which allows you to go on spending twice as much on milk in primary schools than on books.

Another example of her determination to advance the ideal of educational opportunity was her vigorous defence of the proposal to raise the school leaving age to sixteen in the school year 1972–73—a matter on which she faced considerable opposition within the Conservative Party. Throughout this period Labour leaders suffered from a guilty conscience over their Government's decision in 1968 to postpone 'ROSLA', as it came to be known in teaching circles, for yet another two years.

However, many Conservatives were far less emotionally committed to the proposal, and voiced their criticisms on ground of cost, the difficulty in handling reluctant pupils for a year in which they would rather be earning money, and the kind of school work many of these pupils were likely to be given in their final year. But Margaret was committed to ROSLA just as deeply and sincerely as she was to improving conditions in the old primary schools. For her it meant promoting equality of opportunity at the other end of the progression through school. In March 1971 she told a conference on the implications of the extra year in London that the decision to raise the leaving age in 1972–73 was 'inviolate'. Under questioning in the House from backbenchers she stuck to her guns.

There was further criticism in October 1971 from delegates to the Conservative Party conference in Brighton. But in her speech Margaret hit back by pointing out that there had been criticism of raising the school leaving age ever since 1893, when the Privy Council said they hoped that in fixing it at eleven they had not fixed it too high. It had been Sir Edward Boyle, Education Secretary in the 1959–64 Conservative Government, who had proposed raising it from fifteen to sixteen in the school year 1970–71. Subsequently the Labour Government postponed it two years.

'I believe that fifteen is still too young and too immature an age to put some of our children out into the complex world and into the complex industry which they meet,' she told delegates. 'It would be far better if they had an extra year in which to mature, and far more guidance could be given to them during that year at school. We have put a lot of effort and money into extra buildings, extra teachers and a proper curriculum. I believe it is time for it to go up, and I believe it will be of great benefit to the average child when it does go up.' From this position she would not be moved.

Another argument was the one she put in the Commons in an education debate in April earlier that year :

'If there is one thing that really helps the regions, and the teachers in the regions, it is raising the school leaving age. The children who have suffered most under the compulsory school leaving age of fifteen have been those whose parents have insisted that they left school at the earliest possible opportunity to go out and earn for themselves. The proportions of children in some of the regions, in the Northern region and elsewhere, who have left school early have been far higher than in other areas. So the effect of the programme to raise the school leaving age is directly to benefit the regions, to reduce inequalities, and to provide greater opportunity for those who would not otherwise have it.'

On January 14, 1972, she signed the Order to raise the school leaving age to sixteen that September—further proof that the deeds of a Conservative Minister deeply concerned in education were worth far more than all the Labour Party's words promising this advance over the years. And further proof that Margaret, in pursuing the policies she believed necessary to increase opportunity in education, was quite prepared to stand up to pressure from the Right wing of her party.

Here, again, she was acting in the *true* spirit of Selsdon Man. As she told the 1971 Conservative conference : 'Our object is to give those who have had a bad start a better start and a better chance, and for the rest to go on steadily improving. It is a policy of levelling up.'

Another question loosely related to ROSLA was the educational opportunity available to girls, in which Margaret took a close interest. In a speech to the Electrical Association for Women in London in May 1971, she stressed the need to encourage girls to make much fuller use of the educational opportunities available to them. Fewer girls stayed at school beyond the compulsory leaving age than boys. At sixth form level, and at university entrance, there were far more boys than girls.

'There are also signs that girls do not set their sights as high as boys of comparable abilities,' she said. But she gave a good insight into her attitude towards Women's Lib by adding that she was 'not entirely convinced that it is always in the interests of girls and women to press our interests so exclusively that the sense of being *different* and *special* is reinforced, when what we really want to emphasise is the *equality* of ability and talent, justifying equality of opportunity'. Young girls at work should be encouraged to make much more use of day release courses.

Then, taking up the sentiments she expressed nineteen years before in her newspaper article 'Wake Up Women', she predicted: 'I believe the whole trend in employment will be towards greater opportunities for women to return to work when their families no longer need quite so much attention. And there is no doubt that those opportunities will be greater the better educated you are, and the more you have been able to keep in touch during the intervening years.'

Another theme running strongly through Margaret's years at this Department was her deep concern to protect and promote *quality* in education. An Education Secretary is under constant pressure to embrace all manner of fashionable fads which are seen by their advocates as the answer to society's ills, but paying too close attention to these can easily undermine standards of literacy, numeracy and academic attainment in schools.

As Margaret remarked in her somewhat philosophical paper to the North of England Education Conference in 1971 (part of which is reprinted in Appendix B), 'fortunately the fashions in educations doctrines tend to wear themselves out long before they have done too much damage'. A good Education Secretary must endeavour to stand back from these, bearing in mind the constant need to maintain and improve the quality of learning in the education system.

Right at the start of her period in office Margaret told the 1970 Conservative conference that hitherto Governments had been engaged in trying to cope with the *numbers* entering the different levels of the education system; but now these were falling off she hoped that 'a theme for the 1970s will be increasing concentration on the quality of what the pupil and the student receive from the education service'.

The first area in which her concern for quality was applied was that of the teaching profession itself. The 1970 election manifesto had promised an inquiry into teacher training, and in December that year Margaret appointed a committee under Lord James of Rusholme to consider this. Its report, published in January 1972, made a number of recommendations, including regular in-service training for established teachers, and progress towards an all-graduate profession. Margaret warmly endorsed most of these recommendations, which after further discussions were incorporated in her December 1972 White Paper.

Next came the question of reading standards in schools. In March 1972 a disturbing report from the National Foundation for Educational Research indicated that in an average class of thirty to thirty-five children leaving primary school in 1970, five would be considered only semi-literate by 1938 standards. Furthermore, of these one would still be only semi-literate when he or she finally left school four years later. Several of those who had contributed to the Black Papers claimed that this only bore out their own warnings of the effect of so-called 'progressive' teaching methods in primary schools.

Soon after this report came out Margaret decided to appoint a committee under Sir Allan Bullock, Vice-Chancellor of Oxford University, to investigate the teaching of reading and the use of the English language. However, this committee was unable to complete its report until after she had left the Department.

Meanwhile there was growing disquiet, both among teachers and parents, over a number of cases of violence in school, particularly in some of the very large city comprehensives in which it seemed possible for a number of pupils to terrorise teachers and fellow-pupils alike.

Had Margaret been the reactionary Education Secretary she was sometimes portrayed she would have seized on this in order to attack those education practices most strongly criticised by a section of her party. Instead, in a speech to the National Association of Schoolmasters in April 1972, she stressed that the first need was to establish the facts.

'We must first talk together before deciding whether any further action is possible and desirable, and if so what form it ought to take,' she said. 'If there is agreement, among those really able to observe what is happening, that there is a problem of violence in schools, let us be honest and say so. I am not in favour of sweeping it under the mat.' But she went on to warn : 'Let us not run the risk of turning relatively isolated incidents into a more general pattern of behaviour if there is a better way of handling them.'

Thus her response to this highly emotional issue was purely pragmatic; establish the facts first, then work out what action is called for. Soon afterwards she called a meeting of representatives from teachers' organisations and local authorities to discuss the problem, and at this it was agreed that a questionnaire should be sent to all Chief Education Officers asking for details of serious incidents in 1971-72, and whether the number of such incidents was rising or falling compared with previous years. Such detailed information took some time to collect, and was being studied in her Department when the February 1974 election overtook it.

A further aspect of Margaret's concern for quality in education was her deliberate support for the direct grant schools. These schools provided at least 25 per cent of their places free to children from local authority primary schools, while the Education Secretary paid a grant direct to them so that the fees paid by the parents of other children attending them were determined by what they could afford. The majority of these schools were of high academic excellence, and, as Margaret told the 1970 Conservative conference, 'they are unique the world over and I shall do everything I can to encourage them. They are the bridge between the completely independent system and the State system.' Accordingly during her two-and-a-half years she made two increases in grants and improved the parental income scale.

With the programme for replacing or improving the older primary schools well under way, Margaret turned her attention to working out her priorities in education over the coming years, and from them a blueprint for the future allocation of resources. The result of this study was her White Paper 'Education: A Framework for Expansion', published in December 1972. This covered the future pattern of school building, staffing standards in schools, teacher training following the James Report, and extending opportunities in higher education. But above all it enabled her to launch an ambitious programme to bring free nursery schooling to 50 per cent of three-year-olds and 90 per cent of four-year-olds within the following ten years. The programme would start in 1974, and initially priority would be given to deprived areas. Indeed, within the first two years more than half the new nursery places would go to areas of social need, not only in the inner city areas but also some rural areas and new housing estates.

This was a programme about which Margaret felt as deeply as she had about the replacement of Victorian primary schools. 'I sent my two children to a nursery school, just a couple of hours each morning, and this is something that should be available to all who want it. It educates them ready for full-time school, and teaches them how to mix properly with other children. But nursery schools were especially needed in the deprived areas. You found that, by the time children came to school at the age of five, a lot of them were already behind because they came from homes where no interest was taken in the children, where the parents didn't talk to them. But it's very important to talk to them. You would find sometimes that they were just sat in front of the television, and weren't able to communicate at all. That put them at a great disadvantage from the start.

'So we wanted to get them to school at an earlier age, so that they learned to talk and communicate properly with other children. Of course, the State can never take the place of good parents—I mean ones who take an intense interest in their children. But it can help redress the balance for those born unlucky.'

She stresses that hers was a purely *educational* programme, and not a social one. 'I was talking about nursery *schools*, not about day nurseries. For educational purposes you need the youngsters for only half a day. Of course that takes some stress off the mother, but doesn't enable her to go out to work full time. And it doesn't meet the need where housing conditions are very bad, where the mother has so much difficulty just trying to cope that the children drive her up the wall and she is snappy the whole time. In cases like this you need a nursery school working in conjunction with a day nursery, which is something very different.'

However, once a nursery school was located in a deprived area she did not want its intake restricted to deprived children. 'If you put all the deprived children together then you get a lot of non-communicators together. You have to mix them up with other children. It's also very interesting how children from different backgrounds need different things. Children who have had very little notice taken of them at home benefit most by going into a fairly disciplined atmosphere; whereas those who have been a bit over-disciplined respond to greater freedom. You just have to leave it to the nursery school teachers to judge.'

These again are the words of a woman deeply committed to giving every child an equal chance to make the most of his or her abilities, rather than of the hard Right-winger of popular Press legend.

The White Paper also provided for a programme of improvement for secondary schools, better teacher training, more teachers and better staffing standards in schools, and more places in higher education. It added up to a programme of expansion over several fields, yet it came under political attack for not doing enough.

Margaret hit back against these criticisms when she told a meeting of the Schools Council in March 1973; 'When the Education White Paper talked about expansion it meant expansion, and not contraction. For many education will start earlier, and for more than in the past it will go on longer. That is an expansion of the service—at both ends. There will be more teachers, and we hope they will be better trained. That is expansion. Taking altogether the policies outlined in the White Paper, covering three-quarters of the service, annual expenditure could rise by nearly half—£960 million—over the decade.'

By June 1973 she was able to report an enthusiastic response from local education authorities to her nursery school proposals, and a good start towards implementing the programme. However, by December she suffered a setback from Chancellor Barber's cuts in public spending in particular response to the energy crisis and the new high cost of fuel. The great pressure on the construction industry had led to much higher building costs, and one result of this was the decision to defer the school building programme for three months. However, after this deferment the full nursery school programme was retained. There were also cuts in the higher education programme, though the effects of these would not be as severe as might be expected for the simple reason that the number of young people wishing to become students had fallen off over the previous year on a scale that no one had foreseen.

Despite this setback, however, there can still be no doubt that the two-and-a-half years starting in June 1970 were ones of real advance in education. A record programme for replacing outdated primary schools was under way, an ambitious nursery education programme started, the long-delayed raising of the school leaving age accomplished, a start made on providing a more highly trained and qualified teaching profession, and more resources devoted to an increased number of students in higher and further education.

It is a record of which any Education Secretary, from any party, could justifiably have been proud. It was not equalled in the years immediately before Margaret took over the Department of Education and Science, and to the time of writing it has not been equalled since. How was it, then, that she came to acquire a reputation for 'hard-faced Toryism' among substantial sections of the Press and public? That is the mystery that we must now seek to unravel.

First, we must take note of the Labour leaders who were shadowing her. For the first two years she was shadowed by her predecessor at the Department, Ted Short, bitter that his own period there had been so unproductive and that his Bill to make comprehensive secondary education compulsory had never reached the Statute Book. To say that his views on education were egalitarian would be an understatement; they were positively collectivist. He made no secret of his belief that the purpose of education was to change the whole basis of society. He was on record as opposing any kind of selection by ability, and even to separating children according to their different abilities once they are in a comprehensive school. He was against examinations of any kind, and would have liked to see the non-selective, comprehensive principle extended to universities too. He also, needless to say, looked forward to the day when all forms of private education were abolished.

Thus between him and Margaret there was almost no common ground, and his attacks on her across the floor of the Commons took on a very bitter tone. He accused her of 'injecting her own hard Tory philosophy into the running of our education system', and the charge was repeated regularly. When Ted Short was succeeded by Roy Hattersley one might have expected a more civilised tone to prevail, but in fact the up-and-coming Hattersley seemed to demonstrate that he was even more egalitarian than his predecessor.

'Competitive education which allows the few to leap further and further ahead ensures that the less fortunate fall further and further behind,' he declared. 'That is why *the pursuit of equality of opportunity has to be replaced by the pursuit of equality itself.*' Hold children back to make sure no one does better than anyone else—the philosophy of the social engineer in education could hardly have been more eloquently expressed.

Thus one can readily see how, with Margaret faced by these two in succession across the floor on the House, differences came to be magnified and essentially moderate policies portrayed as being extreme.

The first really effective Labour attack on Margaret personally sprang from the decision to withdraw free school milk from the majority of children aged eight to eleven. This was not mounted in earnest immediately the cut was announced, since in the context of the far more generous programme to replace out-dated primary schools it appeared to most people to be quite reasonable. In the first instance Labour leaders concentrated on the increased charges for school meals, and the number of pupils whom it was claimed would switch to eating sandwiches or nothing at all. In fact, though there was an immediate drop in the numbers taking school meals, the total soon built up to normal again.

The brunt of the attack over school milk came later, and inflicted more lasting damage. As we have seen, to implement the milk cut Margaret needed to get a special Bill through Parliament. This had the effect not only of spinning out the controversy over a relatively minor measure, but also of enabling it to be viewed and attacked in isolation.

And so the picture of Margaret snatching the milk from infants' mouths was steadily built up. Someone in the Labour ranks with an ear for a catchy phrase thought up the slogan 'Margaret Thatcher, Milk Snatcher'. It was printed on posters, chanted at demonstrations, and conveniently fitted the developing myth of hard-face Selsdon Man. It was effective, too, since the 'milk snatcher' tag clung to her long after the school meals issue had been forgotten—and, indeed, after another Labour Government had raised their price again. Meanwhile, Labour MPs mounted a furious campaign alleging that her policies were undermining the health of the nation's children.

However, the 'milk snatcher' campaign also affected Margaret herself. It was such an unfair representation of what she had actually achieved in the Cabinet discussions through the summer of 1970 that it hurt her deeply. It was made worse by the fact that the campaign was echoed by a handful of MPs on the Tory benches. As a lobby correspondent at the time I can clearly remember some of the younger members of the 1970 intake who cultivated a 'with-it' image starting a 'Shift Thatcher' campaign, and on several occasions the Press carried reports that she was about to be moved to make way for someone more acceptable to her critics. But Margaret stayed.

This was the first time she had been under such sustained personal attack, but that old streak of sheer determination saw her through.

Once, after another wounding incident, Denis Thatcher said to her, 'To hell with all this, why not pack it up?'

To which the reply came straight back, 'Not likely'.

It must also have been galling to her after 1972, when contemplating the damage her political reputation had suffered over an effort to save £8 million, to see the Cabinet authorising the expenditure of vastly larger sums in various directions to stimulate economic growth. The final irony—and vindication of her position—was not to come till three years later, when the subsequent Labour Government decided not to restore free milk for pupils aged eight to eleven, after a Departmental survey had shown that its withdrawal had no effect whatsoever on children's health.

The Right-wing image was strengthened by a number of conflicts with bodies of teachers and students. Her relationship with the teachers' organisations varied considerably. With what is called the 'Joint Four'—the headmasters, headmistresses and their assistants—relations were consistently good. But the rank-and-file National Union of Teachers was rather more difficult. It began by opposing her Circular 10/70, and this campaign continued. There has always been a strong Left-wing element in the NUT, and they made much not only of the comprehensive schools issue but the school milk issue too. However, a body like the NUT works on several different levels at once. On one level it might be hitting at Margaret over Circular 10/70, on another pressing its members' latest pay claim quite militantly, while on yet a third co-operating with the Department on a number of studies and investigations.

Whatever was being said in public, Margaret always found she had a reasonable relationship with NUT leaders when they met in a conference room at Curzon Street. Once, when she was invited to speak to the NUT's 1972 annual conference, around a hundred teachers boycotted the meeting in protest over the comprehensive issue, while another hundred staged a noisy walk-out as she rose to speak. But the eighteen hundred delegates left immediately dissociated themselves from this action by applauding her warmly.

The following year she was to find NUT spokesmen strongly critical of her White Paper, after the extreme Left-wing Max Morris had succeeded Harry Allison as NUT president. However, looking back on those two-and-a-half years, one can fairly say that her relations with the teachers' leaders were probably as good as those of any other recent Education Secretary. The NUT is an efficient pressure group, and its pressure is applied continuously upon whoever holds that office.

Rather less happy, and certainly more damaging, were the running attacks on her from students, including the traditionally Left-wing leaders of the National Union of Students. Soon after she took office the NUS president, Jack Straw—later to become a political adviser to Barbara Castle at the Department of Health and Social Security—was telling students to get ready for a fight with the Government. 'When a High Tory Government meets an organised student movement a clash seems certain,' he declared at the NUS half-yearly conference in Margate.

However, this could easily be dismissed as so much conference hot air; what was rather more worrying was the growth of Left-wing intolerance at a number of universities and polytechnics, which sought to deny any Conservative speaker even a hearing.

One such demonstration greeted Margaret when she went to present the designation document to the Liverpool Polytechnic at a ceremony in the city's Philharmonic Hall in June 1971. Her speech was drowned by shouts of 'What about school milk?' and 'Tories out', while paper darts whizzed across the hall. According to the London *Evening Standard*, when a vote of thanks to her was proposed 'a loud burp was heard'. To avoid further demonstrations Margaret left by a side door. The audience had barely heard a word of her speech, but then at this time listening was rather out of fashion in some of the newer seats of learning.

Such demonstrations were generally the work of minorities, who might have continued as such had Margaret herself not presented them with a splendid campaigning issue. Over a period of months there had been growing concern over the uses to which student union funds at some universities were being put. Cases had come to light of court fines imposed on students being paid out of union funds, and of payments to certain African freedom movements. This might have been acceptable had not the subscriptions to many of these unions been compulsory, and in consequence paid by the students' sponsoring local authorities —and hence by the ratepayers and taxpayers. A Tory backbencher, Sir Gilbert Longden, introduced a Private Member's Bill seeking to establish a Registrar of student unions.

In this situation Margaret decided to seek a reform herself in November 1971 by publishing a consultative document in which she suggested that the university or polytechnic authorities might themselves take over responsibility for financing student unions. This had the students up in arms. She was mobbed when later that month she went to the Queen Elizabeth Hall in London to present another designation document to the South Bank Polytechnic, and most of the students due to receive awards refused to come forward to accept them. The following month a crowd of chanting students tried to waylay her in the City, and in a day of protest students throughout the country joined in boycotts and demonstrations.

By January 1972 it was clear that not only students but also the university vice-chancellors, lecturers, and local authority associations were against her proposals, so Margaret announced she would shelve her plans for a year. In fact, they were never resurrected.

Looking back, she still regrets that she could not get an agreed reform of the student unions, to cover not only their finances but also to guarantee democratic voting procedures. 'It's the old problem of trying to ensure that the moderate majority assume their responsibilities, and don't leave it to the militant minority,' she says.

But in retrospect the exercise appears to be the only obviously unwise political move in her years at Education, for she was taking the battle on to the Left-wing students' home ground without ensuring that she had effective allies first. The ultimate effect was to harden the image which the Left had already sought to give her on other issues.

So it was that a Minister whose policies brought real advances to education, and a far better chance to those children who had hitherto been disadvantaged, came to be given the reputation among a sizeable section of the Press and public as a hard-line Right-winger. At the same time, running like a thread through all these events, was the argument over the reorganisation of secondary education—which we come to in the next chapter.

CHAPTER TEN

Pragmatism and Parental Rights
1970–1974

When an angry deputation from the National Union of Teachers arrived at the Department of Education in Curzon Street on July 13, 1970, to protest to Margaret Thatcher over her decision to leave local authorities to propose whatever kind of secondary school organisation they wished, they found an Education Secretary who refused to accept that any one pattern of schooling was either possible or desirable for everyone.

Six months later her broad approach was well expressed in her address to the North of England Education Conference on the theme of 'Education and Society'.

In this she gave her view that 'the strongest and most generous education system is one whose organisation and institutions are as various and different from each other as the needs of the people they serve and the people who serve in them. From time to time there are pressures on the education service to embrace some one method of organisation whose advocates deem it to be so obviously right and just and so plainly of universal application that any conscientious Education Secretary must try to impose it, and all conscientious local authorities and teachers must welcome its imposition. Fortunately the fashions in educational doctrines tend to wear themselves out long before they have done too much damage. One theoretical truth succeeds another. Meanwhile, in an illogical and untidy pattern, real schools, real colleges and real universities get on with the real work of education.'

The true Conservative view of fashions in educational thinking could hardly have been better expressed. Education, like society itself, was constantly developing in an organic manner, rather than attaining perfection in some single form of static organisation. The paper to the Conference gives a revealing insight to her thinking, and an extract is reprinted in Appendix B.

When Margaret became Education Secretary the conventional wisdom in the world of education was undoubtedly to favour comprehensive secondary schools for children of all abilities in place of a selective system for allocating children between different types of school, including grammar schools. This did not necessarily spring from egalitarian motives such as those expressed by Ted Short and Roy Hattersley. There was a genuine dislike of the eleven-plus examination among many parents, and there was a general recognition that this was too early an age at which to make a final decision about what kind of education a child should receive. Many of the best schemes for reorganisation along comprehensive lines had in fact come from Conservative-controlled local authorities. And Margaret's own words and actions showed clearly that she too approved of comprehensive schemes that were soundly based. But in any reorganisation scheme the first geographical areas to be tackled are inevitably the easiest ones, and the more difficult and complex ones left till later. When Margaret arrived at the Department a number of the more difficult and controversial schemes were starting to come forward. In a number of parts of the country there was no general desire to move to a comprehensive system at all. Feelings ran high on both sides of the controversy, and it was clear that any Education Secretary exercising his or her powers here was treading on a minefield.

However, before examining how Margaret handled this issue we need to be clear what her powers and duties were. These sprang from the 1944 Education Act, a bi-partisan measure, which gave the Minister the general responsibility of promoting education and ensuring that local authorities provided 'a varied and comprehensive educational service in every area'. The word 'comprehensive' is used here in the sense of being broad, and does not refer to a particular kind of school. Indeed, the Act laid down no set organisational pattern; if it had, it would probably have been the three-tier grammar, technical and secondary modern school system generally favoured at that time.

However, the Act did establish a set procedure for changing the character of any existing maintained school, and this is spelt out in its Section 13. Under this, any local authority wishing to change the character of a school—its age range, for example, or from being selective to being non-selective—must first put the proposal to the Education Secretary, and post notices where parents and others can read them giving details of the proposals.

These notices must be on display for two months, during which time any group of parents or electors have the right to lodge their objections with the Education Secretary, who is then under an obligation to make a decision on the proposal in the light of the objections received.

It is thus his or her statutory duty to act as a kind of court of appeal for any parents or electors who disagree with an education authority's proposal for a particular school. If the Education Secretary then concludes that a proposal is not well-founded, would not be in the best interests of the children concerned or does not accord with local wishes, it is his or her duty to reject it.

This is the famous 'Section 13 procedure' through which any local authority wishing to change the character of a school from that of a grammar, bilateral or secondary modern to being a comprehensive or part of a larger comprehensive must go. It was this procedure that Labour Education Secretaries had bent to meet their own purpose by refusing permission for any change that did not make up part of a comprehensive pattern. This was backed up by the power to refuse to sanction any secondary school building programme which did not fit into a comprehensive pattern—the threat contained in the notorious Circular 10/66. But the Act gave them no power actually to order a local authority to undertake something different from what it proposed; neither did it give them power to force a local authority to submit reorganisation proposals in the first place.

It was to obtain these extra powers that Ted Short had introduced his abortive Education Bill in 1970. The effect of this would have been not only to rob local authorities of the freedom to put up those proposals they considered best for their areas, but also to rob parents who objected to a particular school becoming a comprehensive of their existing right of appeal. It was to guarantee this freedom, and this right, that Margaret issued her Circular 10/70 soon after taking office.

We have already seen how this raised the wrath of the NUT, and the indignation of education correspondents, because she had gone through the procedure of consulting the local authority and teachers' organisations first. But we have also seen how this was a clear pledge in the Conservative election manifesto, and, as Margaret said subsequently in the Commons, 'I could not be influenced to go back on an election promise.'

The promise and the policy had also been clear since long

before the general election. Her predecessor as Shadow Education Secretary, Sir Edward Boyle, had stated on several occasions that a Conservative Government would not impose a particular pattern of educational organisation on local authorities. It was in this spirit that the Tories had fought Ted Short's Bill. But even more to the point was the statement by Ted Heath the previous October in a letter to the National Education Association that also appeared in the Press, which stated clearly: 'You will have seen that in recent statements Sir Edward [Boyle] and I have been very specific both about the repeal of legislation enforcing comprehensive education and the need for continued variety. *Certainly a Conservative Secretary of State would not continue to operate Circulars 10/65 and 10/66.*'

The effect of Circular 10/70 was simply to withdraw these two, as promised. And in February that year Margaret had even gone to the lengths of spelling out from the Opposition Front Bench the criteria by which she believed any reorganisation scheme should be judged.

So there was no justification for the hands that were suddenly raised in horror when her circular was issued. The NUT must have been aware of this long-standing commitment, and was probably pressing its protest in order to make sure the union was consulted on future policy matters. But it is surprising that education correspondents were not more aware of Conservative education policy, and the manifesto commitment. Perhaps, given Labour's long lead in the election opinion polls, they had taken a Labour victory for granted—and so been surprised to discover subsequently what the new Government's policy was.

On the day of her circular Margaret told BBC radio listeners: 'We are saying that local education authorities, and parents, and electors, have some right to a say in the sort of schools they shall have locally, and that we are not having any sanctions on them by holding up schools from being built. We have increased the freedom of local authorities, either to go comprehensive, or if they think they have got a very good system of education as it is now then they can continue with it. If people want a fully comprehensive system, and it commands local support, then they can go ahead just as well under this circular as before.'

Meanwhile she showed that she had no bias against comprehensive schools as such by approving a scheme submitted by the Leeds education authority, which had attracted no significant objections from parents or teachers.

A week after her circular she outlined her approach in the House of Commons : 'A rigid system is the enemy of advance. Almost every practical educationist advises one to have policies which are flexible so that one can stand ready to take advantage of new methods and new research.' And she warned MPs that she would look especially carefully at any proposals which involved the abolition of grammar schools of proven academic worth.

'I believe there is still a place for certain selective schools of excellence. Other nations with largely comprehensive systems have found the necessity to have them. I believe it is wrong to exclude them from our future plans.'

Neither was the retention of a number of good grammar schools incompatible with a comprehensive system alongside. This would not be possible in a small rural area, 'but in some of the very large areas it is possible, because the grammar school or direct grant school have quite different catchment areas from the comprehensive schools.'

As Labour MPs shouted 'Impossible' she went on to cite the example of Tulse Hill, one of London's best comprehensives, which thrived in an area where there were good grammar and direct grant schools too.

So the policy promised for so long in Opposition was clearly established. On July 13, a week after the Commons debate, the NUT arrived at Curzon Street to make its protest. But on July 22 Margaret received valuable backing from the 'Joint Four' associations representing more than 55,000 headmasters, head-mistresses and their assistants. After their meeting with her at her Department they issued a statement warmly endorsing Circular 10/70, welcoming the principle of greater freedom for local authorities, and rejecting any idea of a single pattern for secondary education.

A separate, though related issue was that of the direct grant schools, and it was brought to a head by the Labour-controlled Inner London Education Authority. This body had decided, in furtherance of Labour policy not to allow any selection by ability, not to take up the places available to it in London's direct grant schools after the following year. But Margaret effectively blocked this move when she told the 1970 Conservative conference :

'Local authorities are free to take up places in direct grant schools or not, as they choose. If they do not choose to do so I shall attempt, by arrangement with the direct grant schools, to enable pupils from that area to go by direct application to the direct grant school. I think it is right to keep open some choice to parents who would otherwise have none.'

Margaret was frequently to justify the continued existence of these schools. 'They are unique the world over . . . a bridge between the completely independent system and the State system,' she told the 1970 conference. 'They offer opportunities to pupils regardless of their parents' income or background, and I am particularly concerned that these opportunities should remain open.'

And again in 1972 : 'The attack on direct grant schools has come, not because they are bad, but because they are very good. What a terrible philosophy to try to hold back a good school while the others catch up!'

Accordingly she reviewed the direct grant regularly, and improved the income scale governing parents' contributions to help those of more modest means.

Throughout her period in office, Margaret was under sustained attack over the flexible approach she was adopting towards secondary reorganisation schemes. A picture was painted by Labour spokesmen and some teachers of an Education Secretary hell-bent on preserving the eleven-plus examination and indeed extending it.

The reality was very different. When in February 1973 the Opposition mounted a full-day Commons attack on her policy, she was able to reveal that since taking office she had approved 2,650 proposals from local authorities to change the character of secondary schools, and rejected only 115—approximately 4 per cent.

'These figures reduce to proportions the very limited scale of those contentious cases which receive a great deal of publicity,' she commented.

The biggest battles were naturally over proposals to abolish grammar schools with enduring reputations for academic excellence. These were particularly sharp in cases where the alternative proposed was for a number of 'neighbourhood' comprehensives, since the general standard achieved by these would vary so much according to the neighbourhood, thus creating inequality of opportunity through many children's whole school career.

Other frequent objections were to 'botched up' schemes which involved basing a so-called comprehensive on two or more school buildings some distance apart, and to the sheer size of some of the schools proposed. At one point Margaret had to turn down a scheme from Wiltshire to put four different schools in Trowbridge together and call them one comprehensive consisting of 2,700 pupils.

Other local authorities ran into protests when they tried to redraw catchment areas in such a way as to exclude pupils from attending good grammar schools which had hitherto been open to them. A bad offender here was Surrey, and on one occasion Margaret had to take the extreme step of using the power given her by the Education Act of issuing a directive to its county council not to rob pupils of their existing rights by erecting a 'ring fence' round a particular school.

'There is no basis in law for a strict catchment area,' she has pointed out. 'There is no basis in law for an education authority saying that if you live on the wrong side of the road you can't go to a particular school.' Much of her influence was exercised to encourage local authorities to keep their catchment areas flexible.

It was not long before some local authorities began to complain that they were being forced to proceed by trial and error, and that they had no clear guidance on the criteria which the Education Secretary was adopting in judging their proposals. Circular 10/70 spoke simply of educational considerations in general, local needs and wishes in particular, and the wise use of resources.

Margaret had spelt out criteria when in Opposition, but did all these still apply two years later? So she took the opportunity presented by her speech to the NUT's 1972 annual conference— the one where she faced a walk-out by a hundred teachers— to give more details of the factors she took into account when considering Section 13 proposals. Where these had been thought out carefully, and were 'matched by the ability to implement them in reasonable conditions' she invariably considered them sympathetically, she said. Proposals involving split premises she looked at more critically.

'Comprehensive education has sometimes been introduced in existing buildings which were not designed for the needs of the full-ability range. I give careful attention to any plan for a school on two or more sets of premises. Comprehensive schools in split premises do create problems of administration and communication, and they can often impose severe strain on the staff.'

She also 'looked twice' at proposals for two-tier secondary

schools, in which pupils moved from one to the other at the age of thirteen or even fourteen. 'In looking at such proposals I have found myself worrying a good deal about the continuity of education between separate schools, and in general I am reluctant to see the introduction of arrangements on this basis.' Thus she covered the main arguments against the 'botched-up' comprehensives.

Equally important in this speech, she went on to guide local authorities away from proposing new very large comprehensive schools. In speaking thus to teachers she had a sympathetic audience, as there had been growing concern within the profession and outside it over the problems of communication and discipline in a number of existing very large comprehensives, particularly in inner city areas. Until a short while before such schools had been looked on with favour in the education world, and indeed been encouraged in Labour's Circular 10/65, on the grounds that a large annual intake of pupils was necessary to sustain a wide variety of courses at sixth-form level.

Now Margaret was pushing the argument the other way. 'Not enough attention has been paid to the advantages of smaller comprehensive schools,' she declared.

A number of such schools of 750 pupils or less already existed —'and have given ample proof of their ability to survive and succeed'. In them the numbers choosing to stay on for sixth-form education were 'well above the national average, and many of them have developed strong sixth forms offering a good range of "A"-level options. They may not offer the breadth of opportunity at *all* levels which is available in a larger school. But there may come a point when increasing the size of a school merely to provide variety of courses becomes counter-productive. Many children benefit and prosper within the atmosphere of a smaller community. This can be more important than providing ever widening course options.'

One recalls her argument against creating too large and impersonal institutions in her paper to the Conservative Political Centre in 1968.

To the teachers she concluded : 'There is increasing evidence that the very large schools which were once seen as the norm for comprehensive organisations are no longer so regarded.' Already there were more than a hundred such schools, with rolls building up to fifteen hundred pupils or more. 'We have not yet solved the problems of organisation which such schools pose,' she observed.

Subsequently, in response to parental pressure, even the Inner London Education Authority—who had led the way in building very large comprehensives—was to reverse its policy.

One of the difficulties in considering Section 13 proposals was that local authorities would frequently submit a scheme covering a whole range of schools, sometimes all the secondary schools in a city, whereas it was Margaret's duty to consider the proposals as they affected each school in turn. Parents' and electors' objections were often lodged in defence of one school out of a number involved, and again it was her duty to satisfy herself that pupils in a school that was already working well did not suffer as a result of reorganisation. However, this frequently led to accusations that she had wrecked a whole scheme by refusing to allow the changes proposed for one or two schools in it.

A classic case of the amazing lengths to which a local authority would go to present a so-called comprehensive reorganisation scheme in haste and with almost blind disregard for the problems created came from Birmingham, whose application Margaret had to consider in the first half of 1973. Here the plan was to take more than ninety secondary schools in the city and group them into consortia bringing together a number of schools in each area. Pupils would stay in their own school for the first three years, and teachers from other schools in the consortium or peripatetic teachers would move to teach them as necessary. But after this the pupils would themselves travel between schools for different classes. The local education authority was able to provide very little detail on how the consortia arrangements would affect pupils and staff in individual schools —yet the whole scheme was due to be implemented that September!

Parents were up in arms. In January a van delivered a protest petition containing 1,300,000 signatures of local parents and electors to the Department of Education in Curzon Street. Against this the supporters of the scheme managed to muster 24,000. In both cases there was probably a degree of duplication. But, quite apart from the strength of the protests, the scheme was clearly built on a number of fragile assumptions, and on June 28 Margaret rejected the proposals for all but two of the proposed consortia.

The reasons for her decision were set out in the letter from her Department to Birmingham's education authority, and the chief of these was the 'sense of rootlessness' which such arrangements would create among pupils. 'The situation could arise where pupils from several schools converged on another school for a whole morning or afternoon session', the letter stated:

> Most pupils would have to use public transport or walk. Some children would lack that sense of identity in belonging to a school which can sometimes compensate for the adverse social conditions in which they live. The arrangements involved would, in the view of the Secretary of State, tend to disrupt studies, add to the amount of time in the day spent on travelling, with its attendant hazards, create a sense of rootlessness and increase the rate of truancy among the pupils concerned.

The proposed scheme would also create considerable difficulties for teaching staff, since many would have to move frequently from one school to another. 'Severe problems of administration and time-tabling will arise', said the letter, and there would be no clear accountability between the schools and parents. Margaret also doubted whether the education authority had allowed enough time to prepare for such a major change in organisation, and indicated that it would be better for it to gain some practical experience of running consortia on a limited scale first.

The effect of her decision was to save eighteen selective schools from being swallowed up in such a chaotic arrangement. One could hardly find a better example of a scheme devised to abolish selection at almost any price. One wonders whether even Ted Short would ever have allowed it through.

A more typical example of the kind of conflict that arose between an education authority and local parents and electors came from Epsom that same year. On Surrey County Council an alliance of a number of Conservatives with Socialists and one or two others was seeking to force through a policy of moving to comprehensive education throughout the county. The proposal for Epsom was to absorb boys' and girls' grammar schools which had high academic reputations, and drew pupils from a broad area around, into a comprehensive system. This brought protests from 24,000 parents and electors (Epsom's electorate was 80,000), and this was the conclusive factor leading Margaret to reject the proposals. As the letter from her Department stated:

She has had regard to the desirability of preserving, wherever possible, existing opportunities open to parents and children. In her view the balance of educational advantage lies in enabling these schools to continue to make their contribution to the provision available in the area.

Later, after suggestions had been made that the two grammar schools might be squeezed by tightening their catchment area, Margaret wrote to the Surrey education authority indicating that the two schools should still recruit to their existing capacity, remain open to pupils whose homes were reasonably accessible, and draw from their traditional areas. It was a favourite tactic of some authorities to use various administrative devices to further the very ends that had been frustrated by a Section 13 decision that had gone against them.

Margaret was frequently attacked after decisions such as that on the Epsom case, on the grounds that the Conservative election manifesto had promised to retain the 'rights of local education authorities to decide what is best for their area'. But the manifesto had also said that in doing so they should take into account 'the wishes of parents and local electors', and it was clear that, in cases such as Epsom's, this proviso just had not been met.

On both the examples we have chosen Margaret gave her decision in 1973. But some time before that there was growing evidence of disquiet, to say the least, among sizeable groups of parents over the direction that secondary school development was taking. Though some comprehensive schools were reaching very high standards, there were others clearly failing to live up to their high promise. Again, many parents who had initially been persuaded to support reorganisation schemes on the grounds that they would 'get rid of the 11-plus' were dismayed to find that in their case reorganisation meant they could no longer choose between single-sex and co-educational schools, or that some school which they had fondly imagined would still be open to their children was put beyond their reach.

Even among a number of educationists—quite apart from the Black Paper critics—the former glad confidence in comprehensive education and the benefits it would bring was beginning to wane. The first manifestation of this was a shift in public discussion away from the rigours of the 11-plus examination—and quite a range of more flexible forms of selection were being practised by

Margaret reading a nature book to twins Carol and Mark.

On holiday with friends at Seaview, Isle of Wight. Denis Thatcher is on the extreme left.

Margaret boating with son Mark off the Isle of Wight in 1964.

Picnicking with the twins on the same holiday.

local authorities—to concern about how *parental choice* could be preserved or even extended in any reorganised system.

This was reinforced by the feeling among many parents of remoteness from the education authorities who were making the decisions about what kind of education their children should have, and by a growing anxiety among poorer as well as better-off parents about the standards of literacy and numeracy being reached in many schools.

Neither were these anxieties confined to those areas whose councils were under Labour control; it was also noted that a number of education committee chairmen on Conservative authorities seemed more open to pressure from their chief education officers than from the electors whom they were supposed to represent.

Margaret's answer was in part that good grammar schools should be retained with very broad catchment areas, thus happily co-existing with comprehensives while offering the parents of brighter children a choice between two different kinds of institution. Voluntary selection procedures could embrace teachers' reports and tests conducted at the grammar schools for those pupils whose parents felt strongly enough or encouraged enough to enter their children for them. In such situations, as she said, there were a number of parents who would choose a comprehensive if it happened to be a good one. But many local authorities, including some Conservative ones, were reluctant to embark on this kind of organisation, particularly where the grammar school buildings in a particular town were needed as part of a comprehensive complex. She also did her utmost to secure for parents a reasonable choice between comprehensives, and was throughout opposed to rigid zoning systems. But in many parts of the country the sheer physical limitations to parental choice were very real; there was the local comprehensive, or nothing.

As a result of all this, there began to grow within the Conservative Party a demand for a more positive education policy than simply weighing up local authority proposals against educational considerations in general and local needs and wishes in particular. But the Tory dilemma here was a very real one. Local education authorities, including those under Conservative control, were under constant pressure from the Labour Party and pro-comprehensive groups to move towards that system, but there was no counter-balancing pressure from the other end of the political spectrum to move towards something else. So frequently Conservatives and groups of parents would end up in a purely defensive position.

This Conservative view was well expressed by the mover of the education resolution at the 1973 Conservative conference in Blackpool, Mr. J. Stansfield, when he said, 'The Labour Party does have an educational philosophy, however wrong-headed it may be. We have policies, certainly, but not a philosophy .... Diversity of choice is, we are told, one of the cornerstones of modern Conservatism. But there has been little real, positive effort to put it into practice in education. The provision of choice for all should be our basic philosophy. Many parents are far from satisfied with the educational system which is forced upon them ... They have witnessed the wanton destruction of good schools in the cause of comprehensive education, on occasions helped by members of our own party.'

There were many in the Tory ranks who would agree with this. But, just as the Socialist ideal of abolishing all independent schools was rendered impossible by the sheer cost to the State, so too was any meaningful development of the Tory ideal of increased parental choice in the maintained sector.

One suggestion pressed on Margaret very hard from 1972 onwards was that she should re-open the list of direct grant schools, and the pressure came within the House of Commons and outside. The idea was that a more evenly spread pattern of such schools across the country would help fill the gap where grammar schools had been abolished, and provide a guaranteed avenue of opportunity for the most able children. There was also the suggestion that some of the voluntary aided grammar schools —those whose governors still had considerable discretion over their future—could preserve their existing identity simply by being admitted as direct grant schools.

But, though Margaret had great sympathy with the proposal, she put off any action on it throughout her period in office. The main reason was its cost; there were many other contenders for whatever public funds were available, such as new nursery schools. Furthermore, the 1970 manifesto had promised to expand nursery education; direct grant schools were to be encouraged, but there was no mention of re-opening the direct grant list, so those urging her to do so were disappointed.

A far more radical proposal being pushed by a section of the Tory Party was that the party should move towards introducing

a 'voucher system' in education, designed to give far more freedom and powers to parents. As explained by Dr. Rhodes Boyson,
then headmaster of a London comprehensive school, in a CPC
booklet *Battle Lines in Education* published in 1973.

> Every parent would be given for each school child a voucher
> which can be spent only on education. Its value would be
> equivalent to the cost of State education, which in 1972
> was £110 per annum in primary schools, £205 in secondary
> schools for those aged 11–16, and some £300 in
> sixth forms. These vouchers, which could be supplemented
> by the parent, would then be 'spent' at the State or in-
> dependent schools which parents chose for their sons and
> daughters. The schools would cash the vouchers with the
> Government. Schools that were then unresponsive to parental
> demand might decline and might ultimately close, in which
> case their buildings would be let or sold to some other
> private or voluntary or State body which was prepared to
> try harder to meet local or special demands. The parents
> and not the politicians would then be in charge of the schools
> they pay for through their rates and taxes.

It was suggested that one local authority should be encouraged
to run a pilot voucher scheme. However, the idea was opposed
by others in the party, who asked what a headmaster was supposed to do if two hundred parents came offering him their
vouchers to fill ninety vacant places. Would it be 'first come,
first served', with the less sophisticated parents losing out? It
would also be expensive, since it involved giving to parents of
children at independent schools the equivalent to the cost of a
State education which they were not already receiving.

Margaret herself gave no encouragement to the advocates of
the voucher scheme, many of them drawn from the Right wing of
the party. Speaking at the 1973 Conservative conference in
Blackpool, she said she saw real practical difficulties.

'The real problem at the moment is that we have too many
schools which still need bringing up to standard, and we should
do that in justice to the parents of the children who go there
before we contemplate a voucher system.'

So the true picture of Margaret Thatcher's record in handling
the complex issue of secondary school reorganisation becomes
much more clear. Far from being a dedicated opponent of com-

prehensive schooling as her critics would have us believe, as
Education Secretary she steered what was essentially a pragmatic
course between the strong and sharply contrasting pressures being
applied to her. She stood up vigorously to those on the Left who
sought to introduce comprehensive schools regardless of local
circumstances, wishes and consequences, she approved the
majority of schemes, and at the same time fended off contrasting
policies that were proferred from within her own party. At a time
of growing doubt and uncertainty among parents and educationists, she refused to accept that one pattern of secondary
education offered a final solution, and used her power to retain
what was best in the system she inherited.

Fashions change in the world of education, as they do any-
where else, and they were starting to change then. Her job, as
she saw it, was to implement the policies set out in the 1970
manifesto, for primary and nursery schools, raising the school
leaving age, raising standards and restoring some flexibility to
the organisation of secondary education.

That was a programme for one Parliament. After that, as she
confided to the North of England Education Conference only
seven months after taking office, she would have liked to
strengthen the legal rights of parents 'in the exercise of the choice
of schools their child should attend' (see Appendix B). In fact,
this was to form the basis for subsequent Conservative education
policy. But that was for a further manifesto, and a further Parliament—and the sudden election in February 1974, after only
three-and-a-half years in office, overtook such plans. Meanwhile,
in several fields of education policy, Margaret's achievement was
to open doors that had been slammed shut.

PART III
The Making of a Leader

CHAPTER ELEVEN

The Lessons of Defeat
1970–1974

'We were returned to office to change the course of history of this nation—nothing less,' Prime Minister Heath declared from the platform in the Winter Gardens Ballroom in Blackpool on October 10, 1970.

In a speech to the party conference that rang with confidence, he held out the promise of a free and responsible society—'free from intervention, free from interference, but responsible; free to make your own decisions, but responsible also for your mistakes; free to enjoy the rewards of enterprise, but responsible for making sure that those rewards are justly and fairly earned; free to create for yourselves and your families that better tomorrow which we all want, but responsible for those who, through no fault of their own, cannot create it for themselves.' This task, he said, called for 'a revolution so quiet and yet so total that it will go beyond the programme for a Parliament'.

It was an inspiring speech, putting flesh on the bare bones of the Tories' election manifesto. Greater freedom of choice and action, and responsibility towards one's fellow men—Ted Heath had restated and developed a theme that runs through the history of the Conservative Party.

Less than two-and-a-half years later, as the lights went out and Britain worked a three-day week, he appealed to the country to strengthen his Government and its counter-inflation policy against the industrial might of the National Union of Mineworkers. But the country declined to do so, sending the Conservatives back to Westminster five seats behind Labour, together with larger contingents of Liberals and Welsh and Scottish Nationalists. The course of history had indeed been changed—but what had gone wrong with the quiet revolution over the intervening forty months?

In a biography such as this we cannot attempt to analyse all the judgements and actions of the Heath Government from June 1970 to February 1974. However, if we are to understand the events within the Conservative Party in the year that followed, culminating in Margaret Thatcher's election as party leader, we must at least try to answer the crucial question 'What went wrong?' And, since Margaret was a member of that Government, we must also look at her position in relation to its failings.

To do this is not to embark on an exercise in recrimination. The vast majority of Conservative MPs in the 1970–74 Parliament either supported the Government's measures with enthusiasm or at least acquiesced in them, and in politics acquiescence means support. The same is true of the majority of party workers in the country. Responsibility is shared. But, after that defeat in February 1974 had been followed by another in October, no Tory politician could afford the luxury of not looking back with humility on the events of those years and learning some lessons from them.

Such an examination should not detract, either, from the very real achievements of those years. The most historic was certainly Ted Heath's success in leading Britain into the European Community. Better social provision was made for those in need, such as the chronic sick and the seriously disabled. Retirement pensions increased in real value, and legislation was passed reforming pension arrangements for the future. An impressive hospital building programme was carried out. Taxes were reduced, and one rate of VAT was an advance on the jumble of different Purchase Tax rates and Selective Employment Tax. Much greater protection was provided for the consumer. Immigration control became far more effective. The police were strengthened. Council house rents were rationalised, and help provided where needed in the form of rent rebates and allowances. This list is not exhaustive, and to it we must add the real advances in education which were to Margaret's credit, and which we have already examined.

But still the question remains, what went wrong? For at some point in those two-and-a-half years the glad confident message in Heath's Winter Gardens speech was lost, and the Tory Government found itself travelling along a road it had never intended. The decisive turning point, or 'U-turn', as these switches came to be called, was undoubtedly the Cabinet's decision, announced on November 6, 1972, to take statutory powers to control all increases in pay, prices, dividends and rents.

This certainly reflected the conventional wisdom of the day, as expressed by various economists, commentators and sections of the Press, but it left most party supporters in the country utterly bewildered. After all, they had been led to expect less Government intervention in the economy, not more. And all Ministers freely admitted that the new policy was in direct contradiction to their stand while in Opposition and the party's manifesto commitment.

It was also clear that this was not to be a short sharp 'freeze', but a prop for all the Government's other economic policies for a long time to come. Indeed, once a Government has started running on the track of statutory controls over pay and prices it is very hard to get off it. The first stage, of a freeze or control, is easy to administer and almost invariably successful; the second stage, of partial thaw, can achieve apparent success too, provided it is kept short; it is in the final stage, as shackles are shaken off, that the real price for such a policy has to be paid. For by then such pressure has built up that the incomes dam begins to burst, and as each jet comes surging through broader and broader channels have to be provided to try to disguise the obvious fact that the dam is breaking up completely.

So it was with the Heath Government's counter-inflation policy; Stage One was acclaimed as a success, Stage Two won broad acceptance from trade union members, but Stage Three brought pressures that were impossible to resist. Admittedly the Government was unlucky in that Stages Two and Three coincided with an explosion in world food and commodity prices, though this in itself was a reflection of the fact that all Western industrial countries were striving for economic growth at the same time.

The effect of this, however, was to dispel public support for the policy before it faced its most damaging challenge from the miners' union. And the effect of the whole statutory approach was to involve the Government in a collectivist apparatus of control and intervention in every corner of the nation's economic life, while holding back the enterprising in the vain hope of winning the approval of the mass.

But it is not enough simply to criticise the Cabinet for its decision in November 1972 to rely on a statutory prices and incomes policy, for by that time its freedom of manoeuvre had been heavily circumscribed. At its very birth it inherited a situation of wage inflation, and its continuing attempt to bring this under control brought it into periodic conflict with powerful unions. In 1971 Chancellor Anthony Barber dangled the carrot of increased take-home pay through tax cuts, and later tried to work through prices by lower purchase tax and getting the CBI to recommend a voluntary 5 per cent ceiling on price rises to its members. The Government promised to match this in the nationalised industries, which set it on the path of heavy subsidy payments—the first, gentle U-turn on manifesto commitments.

It had long been part of the Conservative strategy, certainly since the Selsdon Park conference, to budget for economic growth, though in its first year of office the argument was that wage inflation should be restrained first. Judgements of when to start reflating, and by what amounts, and when to slow down are always very difficult, and in November 1971 Barber began to reflate by accelerating Government spending.

But that winter turned out to be a bad one, with the unemployment figures reaching one million, and the Cabinet came under strong pressure to start reflating heavily. On the Tory benches, too, nerves became rather frayed, as a number of MPs called for speedy action. In January the miners went on strike, in February a State of Emergency was declared and at the end of the month, after a bitter war of attrition in which power stations were picketed, often violently, the Government was forced to capitulate.

Meanwhile, Government spending programmes were being extended on all sides; £35 million of aid was promised to the regrouped Govan Shipbuilders on the Upper Clyde, less than a year after Margaret had been arguing through her Bill to save £8 million on school milk. In March Barber brought in an expansionary Budget, with massive tax cuts, aimed at getting the economy on a growth rate of 5 per cent a year by early 1973.

It was this dash for growth, with its associated increase in Government spending *while the underlying wage inflation continued*, that was the most significant U-turn, and which made recourse to strict pay controls inevitable. When the TUC, after long discussions, could not guarantee a voluntary system, then there was little choice left to the Cabinet but to take statutory powers.

We are reminded of Margaret's warning to the CPC meeting in Blackpool in 1968 of the dangers of making economic growth the supreme end in politics—'hence compulsion on prices and incomes policy'. And of her claim that if governments exercised more control over their own spending than over other people's incomes, and stopped financing their expenditure by printing money, the whole body politic would be much more healthy.

But, looking back on this whole period, one can see that the mistake of going for growth before all else, and the consequent acquisition of statutory controls over pay, prices, dividends and rents, were simply the most gross examples of a more fundamental fault of the 1970–74 Government, which was that it had more faith in managerial solutions to Britain's problems than in the efficacy of the politics of persuasion.

Part of this was the result of bringing into office some policies which had been worked out in too great detail while in Opposition—notably the plan to reform industrial relations. But there was also a certain assumption that, if only the right policy could be formulated at the top and put into legislative effect, then the logic and virtues of it would be clear for all to see. It was a managerial approach, for example, that dictated that local government would be more efficient if the whole country was regrouped into larger authorities; a more politically sensitive approach would have been to single out the anomalies for action while leaving the majority of citizens with the smaller councils they knew and understood.

But probably the worst example of political insensitivity was in the field of housing. The reform of the structure of council house rents, and the introduction of rent rebates and allowances, was a most valuable measure, and long overdue. But no politically sensitive Conservative Government would have allowed its overall economic policies to have the spin-off effect that this one's did on the private housing market and on the hopes of thousands upon thousands of couples of ever acquiring a home of their own, as house prices rocketed and mortgage rates soared. This is perhaps the classic example of how the 1970–74 Government, preoccupied with the problems of entering the European Community, curbing wage inflation and expanding the economy, got out of touch with the needs and aspirations of a large cross-section of the British public, many of them its natural supporters.

This fault was compounded, in the latter year or two in government, by the psychological error of stressing all the time the *moderation* of Conservative men and measures, in the mistaken belief that this would win support from the centre of the political spectrum. This is not to say that moderation is an unworthy quality in politics; it most certainly is not. But it is a mistake to imagine that proclaiming it will arouse the enthusiasm of that elusive figure, the ordinary voter. For, though he would regard himself as being moderate too, he at the same time feels passionately about these things closest to him—perhaps the fact that his married son cannot afford to buy a house, or conditions at his youngest child's school, the lorries parking in his street, or his own environment at work. And he will be inspired, not by a Government professing moderation in all things, but by a Government which he believes will fight and fight hard for those things closest to his heart. A Government which puts too much stress on its moderation risks forfeiting any clear identity on those issues that concern ordinary people most.

So, looking back, one can see how the seeds of defeat were sown long before the challenge of the miners' strike in February 1974. It is quite possible that, without this challenge, the Heath Government would have gone on to win a general election eight or sixteen months afterwards. However, by either of those dates it would have had to make up a lot of ground to be able to claim that it had begun to secure a 'quiet revolution' for greater freedom and responsibility in the nation's life. All politicians are human, and make errors; but from these errors they and other politicians must learn.

Having now levelled these criticisms with all the wisdom of hindsight, we must next ask what Margaret herself was doing while the Cabinet of which she was a member set off in pursuit of economic growth before all else, and got trapped on the road to more collectivist control over individual economic activities. Surely, given the precise expression of her own views on such matters as making economic expansion the supreme end in politics, the repugnance of statutory pay controls, and the need for strict control over the Government's own spending, as set out in her 1968 CPC lecture, she should have been aware of the dangers inherent in some of the steps the Cabinet was taking?

This is very true, though we must exempt her from one of the criticisms levelled above; in her Department of Education she certainly did not lose contact with the needs and values of ordinary citizens so far as schools and schooling were concerned. She was throughout her period there deeply involved in providing better school buildings, better teachers, higher standards, and as much choice for parents as possible, often in opposition to the bureaucratic designs of local authority planners. In education, as in the field of pensions, the 1970–74 Government never lost touch.

Margaret has never sought to duck her share of the blame for the misjudgements of the Heath Government. 'For past errors, in Government and Opposition, I accept my full share of collective responsibility,' she said during the subsequent leadership contest. And she does not dispute that, in the circumstances of November 1972, she thought it right to impose a statutory freeze on pay, prices, dividends and rents. But, as we have seen, the Cabinet by then had little option unless it chose to jettison the targets for expansion set out by Tony Barber in his Budget the previous spring.

In fact, though the major U-turns may have looked like spectacular sweeps at the time, they were made up of a series of movements, each of which seemed to lead naturally into the next.

But to understand Margaret's position in this period we need also to understand how modern Cabinet Government works. The broad lines of economic policy are really sorted out between Prime Minister and Chancellor of the Exchequer, and are rarely the subject of general and free-ranging discussion round the Cabinet table. Next, most of the detailed application is worked out within an economic policy committee of the Cabinet. Such a committee would of course include the Treasury Ministers, and the Secretary for Trade and Industry—but not the Education Secretary.

Thus most of the detail on which often fine judgements were based would never have come before Margaret anyway—besides which, in any Cabinet, one's natural inclination is to accept the judgements of colleagues in their own fields of responsibility. Similarly the Foreign Secretary, for example, would accept collective responsibility for Margaret's policies at Education, but he would be unlikely to query her judgements of priorities within an overall spending programme.

As we have seen, too, many of the judgements we would now dispute were ones of how soon to start reflating the economy in a situation of growing unemployment, by how much, what growth target it was feasible to aim for, and how soon to start easing off. All these involve careful study and analysis of a number of economic indicators, which no Minister in a non-economic Department could possibly undertake.

We must remember, too, that Education and Science was a very busy Department, with plenty of difficult controversies of its own. At the time the Government was making its U-turn on public spending in the winter and spring of 1971–72, Margaret was involved in her own troubles over the financing of university student unions, in preparing the further guidance she should give to local authorities on the reorganisation of secondary education, and in setting up an inquiry into the teaching of reading in schools.

When she agreed in Cabinet that the Government should take statutory powers to control pay and prices she was deep in preparing her crucial White Paper for publication the following month on priorities in the education service over the next ten years. All this hardly left her any time in which to conduct her own analysis of the Government's economic strategy. In the complex circumstances of modern government, Ministers have enough to do keeping their own corner, without seeking to manage those of their colleagues as well.

However, it would seem that Margaret participated fairly fully in the Cabinet discussions which did precede these and other decisions, at least to the extent of posing some critical questions and seeking responses to her own point of view. She still refuses to talk of the discussions that went on in Cabinet at that time, since she is bound by the rule of confidentiality.

However, as one who was a lobby correspondent at the time, I can well recall two alternative versions of her Cabinet role which were current among Tory MPs from 1972 onwards. One, among friends, was that she was one of the few Ministers who was prepared to question in Cabinet a number of the assumptions on which Prime Minister Heath and some of his closest colleagues were proceeding. The other, from less friendly sources, was that she tended to hold up progress in Cabinet by making spirited contributions to discussion of the policies of Departments far removed from her own.

Which version one accepts hardly matters; but both would seem to indicate that she was no automatic 'yes-woman', and that she sought to subject the policies of other Departments to at least passing critical scrutiny.

In the autumn of 1973 the effects of a number of separate events began to converge in a tragic pattern that was to lead to the Government's downfall. On October 8, at a Press conference called in London's Lancaster House, Ted Heath announced the complicated formulae for Stage Three of the counter-inflation policy, with continuing rigid controls over prices but a range of extra pay provisions covering anomalies from Stages One and Two, efficiency deals, unsocial hours and cost-of-living thresholds.

In fact, the package had deliberately been devised in such a way as to allow a substantial rise for the miners. But the miners wanted a 31 per cent increase, and turned down the Coal Board's Stage Three offer.

On October 6 Egypt and Syria attacked Israel; the war raged on till October 22, while the Arab states cut back oil supplies to the Western nations in a bid to deny Israel military and diplomatic support. Meanwhile, oil prices were rocketing.

On November 12 the miners began a ban on overtime, including safety work. Next day the Government declared a State of Emergency and restricted the use of electricity. Motorists began to scramble for petrol, and on November 29 the Government began issuing petrol ration coupons as a precautionary measure. On December 12 train drivers began a ban on overtime and Sunday working, thus inflicting considerable hardship on commuters into London and some other cities. On December 17 Chancellor Barber announced a £1,200 million package of Government spending cuts and re-imposed hire purchase controls. Finally, on January 1, 1974, the major part of British industry moved on to working a three-day week. One could hardly imagine a less auspicious run-up to a general election campaign.

In early January more and more pits closed as the overtime ban on safety work took its toll, coal stocks dwindled, talks with the miners were still at deadlock, and they had yet to decide whether to call an all-out strike. Meanwhile Laurence Daly, general secretary of the National Union of Mineworkers, and Mick McGahey, its Communist vice-chairman, boasted openly that their industrial action could break the Tory Government. Indeed, the political motive behind the dispute was becoming only too obvious.

It was in response to this that pressure built up among Tory MPs for a snap election on the issue 'Who governs Britain?' This pressure was very evident when the Commons was recalled for an emergency debate on January 9 and 10, and a number of Ministers very close to Heath favoured this course. Their argument was that, with a demonstration of popular backing at the polls, the Government would have all the authority it needed to take counter-measures, that the miners would be isolated from the rest of the TUC, and indeed that such a demonstration of popular feeling might deter the miners from intensifying their action before negotiating on the pattern of a settlement within Stage Three. The alternative was seen as capitulation, as in

1972, and the collapse of any policy to curb wage inflation as every other union jumped into the breach.

In fact, despite the hardships of the time, this was quite a plausible argument. There were strong indications that public opinion was much more inclined to support the Government than the miners, and many Labour MPs feared their party would be slaughtered in any election on the issue 'Who governs Britain— the Government or Mick McGahey?' Regional reports and opinion surveys reaching Central Office confirmed this pattern, and so under its Chairman, Lord Carrington, the Conservative Party machine began to clear the decks for action.

Anyone visiting Central Office at the start of this third week of January found the place like a battle HQ, with extra telephones being installed everywhere and special new offices set up. The strategic plan was that Heath would move quickly to announce that Thursday, January 17, that the election would be held a bare three weeks later, on February 7. Lord Carrington, a very close colleague of the Prime Minister was convinced of it, and if Heath did not actually order these preparations he certainly did nothing to stop them. In the middle of that week Sir Michael Fraser, Deputy Chairman of the Party, and Sir Richard Webster, Director of Organisation, went to him to report that all was ready and morale was high. They returned to Central Office crestfallen; Heath had heard them in stoney silence, then told them he had decided to make one more effort to reach a settlement with the miners before going to the country. There would be no election on February 7.

Many since have seen this as the first of a series of bad tactical decisions by Heath that were eventually to cost him the party leadership. For it turned out to be a gamble that failed. The final meeting with the miners' leaders proved abortive, and on February 5, backed by a majority of miners' votes in a ballot, the NUM called a national strike, to start in five days' time. The Government had no room for manoeuvre left. On February 7— the day on which he could have been holding the general election —Heath announced that polling day would be on February 28.

In fairness one should make clear that the Cabinet had not been united in favouring a poll on February 7, and neither had Tory MPs. William Whitelaw in particular, who had been made Employment Secretary the previous month, believed there was scope for one final negotiating effort. But, *if he was to call an election at all*, it is clear now that Heath should have struck while the iron was hot. Delaying it three weeks risked losing the initiative—as, indeed, the Conservatives did in the final week of the campaign.

To keep public attention focused on the one issue of 'Who governs Britain?' for three weeks was expecting a lot, but in effect the Government was hoping to keep it so focused for six. But again, the platform was only pulled from under the Government in that final week as a result of another bad tactical decision. For on the day he called the election Heath also announced he was asking the Pay Board to examine how miners' pay stood in relation to wages paid in other broadly comparable industries.

To have this Pay Board inquiry going on *in public* while the election was on made the Tories vulnerable to any presentation of evidence at it. And sure enough, just a week before polling, the newspapers were suddenly full of news that a mistake had been made in calculating relative pay rates, and that the miners probably deserved as much as they had been asking for in the first place. Further inquiry revealed that these Press reports sprang from a briefing given by Derek Robinson, deputy chairman of the Pay Board—and a strong Labour supporter who had helped prepare the party's nationalisation plans.

In vain did Heath protest that all that had happened was that the NUM had changed the basis of their claim. The heart had been taken out of the battle, and public attention was diverted to other issues, such as the inflated price of private housing, mortgage rates and the cost of living. So the seeds of defeat, sown long before the miners' pay claim was ever presented, grew and blossomed. The final, unintended blow came from Campbell Adamson, director-general of the CBI, who was reported as saying that the Industrial Relations Act had sullied all relations between employers and unions, and should be repealed.

So the election which was called on such a clear-cut issue ended in confusion. And this confusion was well reflected in the result :

> Labour, 301 seats;
> Conservatives, 296;
> Liberals, 14;
> United Ulster Unionists, 11;
> Scottish Nationalists, 7;
> Welsh Nationalists, 2;
> Others, 3;

Thus the February 1974 election produced no clear winners. In terms of percentages of the total vote, the position of the three main parties was: Conservatives 38 per cent, Labour 37.2 per cent, Liberals 19.3 per cent.

In Finchley, now a much smaller constituency with changed boundaries, the figures were:

Margaret Thatcher (Con)	18,180
Martin O'Connor (Lab)	12,202
Laurence Brass (Lib)	11,221
Conservative majority:	5,978

Looking back on the campaign, Margaret's view is that 'we went to the country on a point of principle, and all the signs at the start were that the country was with us on it. But that report from the Pay Board inquiry into relative pay rates pulled that point of principle from under us. From then on, I think, we were on the defensive.'

Back in Downing Street, Heath was facing an agonising decision. What should he do in a situation in which there were no clear winners? The Conservatives were just five seats behind Labour, but at the same time Labour was thirty-two seats behind everyone else combined. More to the point, Labour had gained only 37 per cent of national support; the policies of the Conservative and Liberal Parties were closer to each other than either was to Labour, together they commanded 57 per cent of national support, and in the new House of Commons their combined strength put them nine ahead of Labour. True, this did not give them an overall majority, but if a Government could be formed on this basis would it not reflect the will of the people more closely than any other?

So on March 1 he summoned his Cabinet and put this view to them. Several Ministers were sceptical of the idea of a 'Con-Lib' Coalition, but there was no point in accepting or rejecting it until they knew its possible terms. Accordingly Heath was authorised to open talks with Jeremy Thorpe, the Liberal leader, to see if there was any basis for agreement. On March 4, as the Liberal MPs met at the Commons to discuss his offer, the Cabinet was again summoned to await the reply. It was 'No', so the issue was closed. Heath left for Buckingham Palace to resign, and by that evening Harold Wilson was again Prime Minister.

What the reaction of different members of the Conservative

Cabinet would have been if Jeremy Thorpe had answered 'Perhaps', and gone on to drive a really hard bargain (which, it could well be argued, would have been the Liberals' wisest response), is a matter for fascinating conjecture. It is certainly doubtful whether Heath could have carried all his colleagues with him in making anything more than minimal concessions to the Liberals.

Furthermore, in the process of opening discussions with them he made one mistake—he made no provision for simultaneous consultation with his own backbenchers. Immediately the alarm was sounded by some senior Tories, and while the coalition offer to the Liberals was still open Edward du Cann, chairman of the Tory backbench 1922 Committee, sent telegrams summoning members to an early meeting.

By the time this took place the Coalition proposal was dead, but from subsequent conversations I am certain that a sizeable number of Tory MPs were ready to fight it. Indeed, if Heath had succeeded in forming a Coalition with Jeremy Thorpe in March 1974 he would in all probability have lost more votes from his own followers than he gained from the Liberals. Nevertheless, the Coalition idea lived on—with damaging consequences to the Tory Party and to Edward Heath himself.

CHAPTER TWELVE

Avoiding the Coalition Trap
February–October 1974

In the painful inquest that followed the February 1974 defeat one conclusion emerged on which almost all Tories were agreed: their Government's overall record on housing and home-ownership had cost it votes among those very people on whom it could normally depend for support. Housing, in fact, has been a crucial issue in most general elections since the war. The Tory pledge to get 300,000 new homes built each year played an important part in the 1951 election campaign, and in 1955 the party could point to this as a promise kept. Part of the basis for its 1959 steamroller victory was the growth in home ownership under the Macmillan Government. In 1964 Labour won votes on George Brown's pledge of very cheap mortgages, and in 1966 on the promise to build 500,000 now homes a year by 1970. But come 1970 the house-building programme was running down—a failure which Ted Heath and the Tories exploited to the full.

However, by 1974 these roles were reversed. To its credit the party could point to the reform of council house rents and to the new system of rent rebates and allowances, which ensured that no family could lose their home through inability to pay the rent. But after an early surge the house-building programme was declining again and there was a feeling of disillusion among those owning their homes and young couples wishing to do so.

One result of lifting credit control at a time of strong inflationary pressure was that investment funds had flooded into property, including houses and land. A new word, 'gazumping', entered everyday language, and almost every intending home-buyer could tell a story of inspecting a house one day and returning the next to find that its price had risen a couple of hundred pounds.

The effect of this was to put a home of their own beyond the reach of many young couples who hitherto might have been able to afford the deposit and subsequent mortgage payments. Meanwhile, existing home-owners got little comfort from seeing the value of their homes increase when mortgage interest rates were climbing up.

In 1973 a temporary Government subsidy was paid to the building societies to keep the rate below 10 per cent, but this hardly added up to a coherent strategy. Annual rates bills, too, reflected the steep rise in local councils' labour costs, and became a heavy burden on those families and retired people whose incomes were not keeping pace with such rises in their housing costs.

Many householders and would-be householders who could hitherto have been counted as Conservative supporters began to feel that their Government was deserting them, more interested in trying to appear 'moderate' to trade union leaders than in protecting the interests of people such as themselves. And so, in England at least many began to turn in protest to the Liberals, giving them spectacular by-election victories in Sutton and Cheam, Ripon and the Isle of Ely, and putting Liberal candidates a good second in many Tory seats in the general election.

After the election was over Heath knew that the party's housing policies needed to be reassessed by someone who had no previous record in this field to defend, and who also had a keen understanding of the problems of finance involved. Margaret Thatcher fitted this specification admirably, so he appointed her Shadow Environment Minister with the specific task of re-creating a genuine Conservative housing policy, in line with the party's historic commitment to the ideal of a property-owning democracy.

This was a massive policy area to have to tackle. Time was short, no one knew just how long the minority Labour Government would last, so Margaret knew she would have to start by establishing some priorities and concentrating her efforts on them. One area crying out for a really penetrating review was the tangle of laws on private rents and on relationships between landlord and tenant—to which the Labour Government was now adding security of tenure for all those in private furnished accommodation as well. However, this was far too big a job for the likely time available, and would have to be postponed till later.

Instead, she decided her priorities would be to devise some protection for home-owners against steeply rising mortgage interest rates, to bring some hope to those couples willing to work and save to buy a home of their own, and ideally to extend opportunities for home ownership to council tenants too. The Heath Government had always encouraged local councils to sell homes to those tenants willing and able to buy, but Labour-controlled councils had refused to do so, and some Tory councils had not been keen.

Finally, if there was time, Margaret wanted to work out a policy to bring some relief to domestic ratepayers. To get through this policy review programme as quickly and efficiently as possible she enlisted the help of a number of Tory MPs, who worked in liaison with the backbench committees. Of particular help to her were two of the new intake of MPs: Michael Latham, who from 1967 onwards had worked for the National Federation of Building Trades Employees, and from 1971–73 had been director of the House Builders' Federation; and John Stanley, an investment analyst who was keenly interested in housing finance. These and others worked with her flat out through the spring and summer, ready for the election which almost everyone by then expected to break that autumn.

Meanwhile, in the Commons, Margaret was leading the Tory attack on the Government's Bill extending security of tenure to the tenants of private rented furnished accommodation. The burden of their criticism was that this would cause injustice to many who had let flats or houses furnished on the understanding they would be able to recover them for use later, and it would have the effect of drying up the supply of such accommodation—a warning that proved amply justified.

As Margaret declared during the Second Reading debate: 'The supply of new lettings will be severely affected and may even cease.... There are many empty rooms, cottages and flats which could be made available by owner-occupiers, but these people are afraid to take such a step.' Viewing the situation more broadly, she observed: 'We do not seem to have approached landlord and tenant law on any basis other than the expediency of the moment. We should try an approach on the basis of fairness between landlord and tenant. We have done much to help the deserving tenant but comparatively little to help the deserving landlord, or to encourage him to let empty houses or vacant rooms.'

By July Margaret had a comprehensive housing policy covering all her priority areas ready to put to the Shadow Cabinet, where it went through some very critical scrutiny. However, when

Heath threw his weight behind it the package was finally agreed.

This had five main elements. First, mortgage interest rates for home-buyers would be held at no more than 9½ per cent by varying the rate of tax paid by the building societies. This protection would apply to existing home-owners as well as to new ones. Secondly, for those willing to save regularly over two years to buy their own home the Government would pay a grant of £1 for every £2 saved, up to a given ceiling. Thirdly, every council house tenant who had been in his home for three years or more would be given the *right* to buy it from his council at a price one-third below its market value. He could do this on a 100 per cent council mortgage, with no deposit. If he resold the house within five years an appropriate proportion of his capital gain would have to be repaid to the council. Fourthly, to ease the rates burden the entire cost of teachers' salaries and a larger proportion of the cost of police and fire services would be taken over and paid by the Government. And fifthly—the boldest proposal of all—domestic rates would be abolished entirely and the burden shifted to the taxation system.

One can easily see how this fitted in with the Conservative ideal of a property-owning democracy; its effect over a period of years would be to increase greatly the number of families owning the homes in which they lived, and to break down the rigid divide between council and privately-owned estates.

However, this did not guarantee her proposals an easy passage through the Shadow Cabinet. Some of her colleagues doubted the wisdom of offering further subsidies to any group of people when the obvious need was for greater financial stringency. To them Margaret paraded the figures given in January by the independent Housing Research Foundation, showing that tax relief on an average mortgage cost public funds some £280 a year, whereas the average cost of subsidising a family in a council house was nearer £900 a year. Council housing was becoming increasingly expensive to provide; so, she argued, it made economic sense to help families to buy their own homes. As one Shadow Minister remarked afterwards: 'Why is it Margaret always gets away with a spending programme when everyone else has to cut back—education in 1970, housing in 1975 . . . ?' But she was very firm that a strict limit had to be set to the commitment.

Some six months later, during the leadership campaign, it was claimed by some of her Press critics that in the Shadow Cabinet discussions she had fought against mortgage subsidies, and had to be dragged 'angry and protesting' to accept the $9\frac{1}{2}$ per cent ceiling. This was untrue; what happened was that she refused to accept Heath's proposal to set the limit *lower* than $9\frac{1}{2}$ per cent because of the heavy extra burden this would impose on the Exchequer.

There was less discussion of her proposal to help first-time buyers, since the grants which would start to be paid out two years after the necessary legislation was passed were tied directly to personal savings in an approved scheme in the interval. But the proposal that did provoke lively discussion was that to abolish domestic rates. After all, a Green Paper produced by the Heath Government three years before had stated that exhaustive studies had led to 'the almost universal conclusion' that a property tax such as the rates 'must remain the principal source of local revenue'. Some Shadow Ministers were not happy with the idea of shifting the burden direct to the Exchequer; could not other broadly-based taxes be devised?

Finally it was agreed to accept the commitment, but for implementation towards the end of a five-year Parliament, thus allowing reasonable time to work out the details. This Margaret was happy to accept.

With the new policies on housing and rates agreed, Margaret set off for two weeks' holiday she had arranged in the country, fully expecting to unveil them during the election campaign.

However, Conservative Central Office had other ideas, and rang her no less than five times on the first day of her holiday. Their point was that, with the election expected in October, some political pressure should be maintained from the Tory side through the summer; the Conservatives had a party political broadcast coming up on television in August, and they wanted to use it to project the new policies for existing and prospective home-owners.

So on the second day of her planned holiday she was back in London to help prepare the film, drum up those who had been working with her on the policies to appear on it too, and prepare for a formal Press conference to make the full details public.

This took place at the end of August, and got a mixed reception. The popular Press reacted with either enthusiasm or scorn, according to political commitment though the 'quality' papers seemed to find so many details hard to digest at once. But Labour Party leaders knew that the proposals were likely to have more appeal than their own to take all building land into public ownership, and they hit out at them straight away. 'Margaret's Midsummer Madness,' said Environment Secretary Anthony Crosland, claiming that her housing proposals alone would cost £570 million a year. But Margaret put the cost of reducing mortgage rates from their current 11 per cent to 9½ per cent at not more than £200 million a year, which could be obtained straight away by stopping the money the Wilson Government was allocating to local councils to buy up private houses. There was some further argument over projected figures, but there the matter rested until the October election campaign got under way.

The campaign for the general election of October 10, 1974, in fact began on March 12, the day the new Parliament was opened. The Wilson Government increased pensions, introduced a wide range of food subsidies, brought in Bills designed to consolidate Labour support, such as by helping trade unions and the tenants of furnished homes, yet obviously was keeping back its planned nationalisation measures, which were electorally unpopular.

It was, in a number of ways, a phoney Parliament; no one on the Opposition wanted to give Wilson an excuse to hold an election in June, which the country did not want and for which the Opposition would have been blamed. Consequently there was an air of unreality to Parliament's proceedings; the price of a minority Government seemed to be a hamstrung Opposition.

However, once the threat of a summer election was out of the way Tories, Liberals and some others were able to combine to defeat the Government a number of times in June and July, notably on the retrospective cancellation of £10 million taxes paid by trade unions, rates and the closed shop provisions of the Trade Union and Labour Relations Bill.

Meanwhile a number of trade unions followed the miners in getting pay awards well ahead of price rises, and it was clear that Wilson was fostering an illusion of prosperity just as he had in 1964–66. Chancellor Denis Healey's July Budget reducing VAT was the final pointer; everything was being set up for an October poll.

However, throughout this phoney Parliament there was keen discussion in Press, political and academic circles about whether this pattern in which no one party could command an overall majority was not likely to repeat itself after yet a further election. Was the hitherto accepted structure of political life in Britain, whereby a winning party took all and provided stable Government for some four or five years, undergoing a fundamental change?

It was suggested in *The Times* and elsewhere that the two-party system was breaking down, and that Liberals and Nationalists were more likely to grow in strength at the expense of the two big parties which had exchanged office regularly since the war. If this was so, many went on to argue, should there not be some realignment of political forces to produce a Government more in line with the concensus of opinion in the country, a Centre grouping which would exclude the harsh men of the Right and the neo-Marxists of the Left?

So the idea was peddled, not only that some form of Coalition Government might be desirable, but also that it might become a necessity if the country was to have majority Government at all. And one of the most fascinating political phenomena of the seven months between the two general elections of 1974 is the way such thinking appeared to influence Edward Heath himself.

His efforts to form a Coalition with the Liberals that February had been a considered response to a confused and wholly unexpected situation, and it can be argued that he had a constitutional duty in that situation at least to make the effort. But he went on believing that such a Coalition would have been the best and most proper response to that indecisive electoral verdict. Then, as winter turned into spring, the message came through more and more clearly from some of his trusted colleagues, and from reports of his remarks to at least one private luncheon gathering, that Heath did not believe the next election was likely to produce any more conclusive result than the last. In other words, a situation in which he had to discuss the possibility of a Coalition with the Liberals was more than likely to arise again.

One could see the basis for his reasoning in the fragmented groups on the Opposition benches. Due to his Government's commitment to power sharing in Northern Ireland, and the Sunningdale Agreement to set up a Council of Ireland, eleven independent United Ulster Unionists sat on the benches where formerly orthodox Ulster Unionists had received the Tory Whip. They were unlikely to disappear at the next election, which gave him a handicap of eleven before even starting to form a Government. Then in Scotland it was assumed that the resurgent Nationalists would make their next inroads into the Labour vote —but that would not produce any more Tory MPs from

Scotland. Such calculations suggested that Heath would have to make an alliance with someone if he was to move back to Downing Street after the next election.

But there was another dimension to the argument which was also important. The fact that the Liberals increased their share of the national vote in February by nearly 12 per cent over their 1970 figure was interpreted by many as evidence of a shift in public opinion towards the Centre. Heath himself believed strongly in the 'politics of moderation', and wanted to put the Tories in a position to win more Centre support.

On June 25 Jeremy Thorpe said in a broadcast interview that if there were another situation of stalemate, the leaders of all the major political parties might find that their duty lay 'in a degree of co-operation which we have not seen since time of war'.

The following day, in a speech which was widely interpreted as an overture to the Liberals, Heath warned of the danger of runaway inflation and severe unemployment. To tackle these problems the country needed a programme of national unity, he said, which the majority of people would see as sensible. Each political party would have to give up some of its favourite policies which were unacceptable to the others, and to this end the Conservatives had decided not to reintroduce the Industrial Relations Act.

Wilson scorned any Coalition idea as 'feeble and flabby compromise' which would be bound to lead to weak government —and many backbench Tories privately agreed. But by this time Heath was firmly set on the rails to proposing Coalition government, not merely as a response to a stalemate situation, but as something desirable in itself.

There was considerable discussion on this among Shadow Ministers, but no agreement. Most conceded that another inconclusive election result might make some arrangement between a major and a minor party necessary, but by no means all shared Heath's own belief that a call for Coalition would of itself attract much extra support in the country. However, Heath and some of his colleagues were adamant, so to cover both points of view the following passage was included in the election manifesto :

It is our objective to win a clear majority in the House of Commons in this election. But we will use that majority above all to unite the nation. We will not govern in a nar-

row partisan spirit. After the election we will *consult and
confer* with the leaders of other parties and with the leaders
of the great interests in the nation, in order to secure for the
Government's policies the consent and support of all men
and women of goodwill. We will invite people from outside
the ranks of our party to *join with us* in overcoming
Britain's difficulties. The nation's crisis should transcend
party differences. [My italics]

When the contents of the manifesto were prematurely leaked
from the printers on September 9, then promptly issued in full
by Party Chairman William Whitelaw, it was obvious that this
passage was capable of more than one interpretation.

The promise to 'consult and confer' with the leaders of other
parties could mean no more than an attempt to secure bi-
partisan agreement on an economic policy in much the same way
as it had been secured before on Northern Ireland or on foreign
policy. The promise to 'consult and confer' with the leaders of
'the great interests in the nation' could simply mean another
round of discussions with the TUC, CBI and other bodies. The
invitation to 'people from outside the ranks of our party to join
with us' could be taken to refer to Liberal and Labour MPs, or
it could refer to individuals outside politics, perhaps in industry.
Furthermore, it was not clear precisely what they would be
invited to join—the Cabinet, or a vamped-up National Economic
Development Council? We know that Heath intended the
passage to refer to a Government of National Unity. But in the
manifesto there was no mention of this, or of the word 'Coalition',
in the interest of maintaining Shadow Cabinet unity.

However, there was no difficulty over the central theme of
the manifesto, and of the subsequent Conservative campaign
—that the country was in dire economic straits, with inflation
quickening and unemployment rising, that restraint and even
sacrifice were necessary all round, and that there was no room
for early improvement of living standards. This was repeated by
Heath and other Shadow Ministers throughout the election, as
Chancellor Denis Healey claimed he had brought the inflation
rate down to 8·4 per cent.

No means of fighting inflation were ruled out, which clearly
left the door open to the further use of statutory powers. But
those of Heath's colleagues still inclined to take this approach
were embarrassed by a speech delivered by Sir Keith Joseph in

Preston on September 5, in which he squarely blamed his own Government's expansionist policies for the current inflation, and said that statutory curbs on wages were no cure for it.

'Our inflation has been the result of the creation of new money, and the consequent deficit financing, out of proportion to the additional goods and services available,' he said.

The Tory Government had known all the arguments against statutory controls—'we had used them in Opposition in 1966–70. Why, then, did we try incomes policy again? I suppose that we desperately wanted to believe in it because we were so apprehensive about the alternative : sound money policies. . . . We were dominated by the fear of unemployment.'

Sir Keith's new diagnosis was widely quoted in the 'heavy' Press, and Heath was not pleased; but there is little evidence that it had much influence in the election campaign.

On September 12 all Tory MPs and prospective candidates were summoned to a meeting under the auspices of the 1922 Committee in London's Europa Hotel, in Grosvenor Square, to hear Heath's call to battle in the election which still had not yet been announced. The speech was typical of the man, a thorough exposition of all the main areas of Conservative policy, stressing the sheer *reasonableness* of the party's platform rather than its inspiration. Significantly the pledge to 'consult and confer' was presented almost in the words of the manifesto; there was no attempt to expound its meaning. In front of me I noticed one Shadow Minister nodding off to sleep. As we emerged into the sunlight another ex-Minister remarked to me that 'Ted will need more fire than that when the election gets going.' The next time Tory MPs were summoned to the Europa Hotel was five months later, with Tory peers and the National Union of Conservative and Unionist Associations—to confirm Margaret Thatcher as Party Leader.

The following week Wilson announced that, as expected, polling would be on October 10. The election campaign that had begun in March was reaching its climax. But the excitement felt in the parties' headquarters barely communicated itself to the voters, as the party leaders spent the first week of the campaign in argument over what the rate of inflation really was. Not until 'D minus 13', September 27, did the Conservative campaign come to life, when Margaret was called in to take the daily Central Office Press conference.

She had made considerable preparations for this; since the

Press conference which unveiled her housing and rates policies at the end of August she had been able to study the reactions to her proposals from a number of expert sources, and therefore to refine much of the detail. Reports from the constituencies also indicated the great electoral potential of her plan for 9½ per cent mortgages.

However, whenever she expounded the policy the inevitable reaction was for people to say: 'That's splendid—but when?' She knew she would be asked that question at the election Press conference too, so that week she consulted Heath and Shadow Chancellor Robert Carr to check that the necessary changes to building society taxation could be implemented in the first few weeks in office. Accordingly she opened her Press conference by making an announcement: 'I intend to make it absolutely clear that our plans for a 9½ per cent mortgage are unshakeable, *and will be introduced by Christmas.*'

The effect was immediate. The Press headlined 'Margaret's Christmas Box' or 'Christmas Cracker', and the public's imagination was caught. Here was a Tory politician presenting a policy of immediate relevance to the household budget, and with a time scale for its implementation attached. In vain did Wilson protest about 'election bribes', in view of his own Government's pre-election offers, and Margaret's demonstration how the cost would be covered by savings from other economies. In reply to the question why the Tory Government had not implemented this and her other home-ownership policies before, she replied honestly that they had learned from their mistakes.

In a general election few candidates are aware of the subtleties of Press conferences, leaders' platform speeches or party political broadcasts; they are too busy with their heads down in their own constituencies. In my own constituency of Reigate and Banstead I made the pledge to 'consult and confer' part of my election platform, but it aroused little enthusiasm. Some of my active supporters were strongly critical of it, others thought it would mean no more than bringing in a couple of the more reasonable Liberals, while the vast majority of voters were utterly indifferent to it.

By contrast, I was asked about the party's policies for home-owners, young couples wanting their own home, and council tenants in almost every road and street I was in, and this experience was common among Tory candidates across the country.

Meanwhile, Heath was still convinced that the Coalition card would appeal to 'moderate' voters, but he did not want to play it yet. Questioned about what the manifesto commitment really meant, he suggested expanding the National Economic Development Council to include farmers, housewives and a whole range of other groups, who would meet in London and other regional centres to discuss the economy, all linked up by television. But after this he began in speeches and Press conferences to build up the idea of a National Government, making comparison with the Churchill Cabinet that saw Britain through the war.

In this he was encouraged by a number of Shadow Ministers, but by no means all. One of those who disagreed profoundly was Margaret Thatcher. Elections were won, she believed, by putting forward clear policies that met the real, everyday needs of ordinary voters—as, indeed, her policies on housing and rates did. What was the point, she asked herself, of spending half her time working out detailed policies such as these if they were to be traded off against some unacceptable Labour or Liberal policy in a Coalition Cabinet held together by its lowest common denominator? For it is relevant to note that her proposals, particularly for 9½ per cent mortgages, had been attacked by the entire Labour Cabinet *and by the Liberals*, and so were unlikely to survive any Coalition deal. It also seemed to her to be dishonest to campaign on a policy which you promised to implement by a certain date, yet at the same time admit that you might compromise it in order to secure some Government of National Unity.

For Margaret the crunch came on October 1, when she was called back to share the Central Office Press conference platform with William Whitelaw and Sir Geoffrey Howe, to help keep up the momentum of the party's housing appeal. Several very close to her claim that this was the moment at which she pinned her colours to the mast, and accepted publicly that she might have to part company with Ted Heath and go her own way after the election.

After a number of questions on Heath's National Government proposal and the compromises it might entail had been answered by Whitelaw, another journalist asked, 'Mrs. Thatcher, are the Conservatives prepared to compromise on housing policy after the election?'

Margaret had asked herself the same question many times, and she knew her own answer. 'No,' she replied, 'my policies are *not negotiable.*'

Already she knew that she would not and could not serve in any Cabinet, Coalition or otherwise, which did not have as part of its programme the introduction of $9\frac{1}{2}$ per cent mortgages by Christmas. In a Coalition situation there would need to be some leading Tories who were uncompromised, and who would keep distinctive Conservative policies alive from the backbenches.

On the week-end before polling day Heath played what he regarded as his trump card. In a special message to all Conservative candidates he repeated his warnings of the dire economic crisis facing the country, then went on to assert: 'I have no doubt that the real hope of the British people in this situation is that a National Coalition Government *involving all the parties* could be formed, and that party differences could be put aside until the crisis is mastered.... When the Conservatives obtain a majority at this election I will immediately set out, with this majority, to establish a Government that can transcend party divisions, a Government representing men and women of good will *of all parties* and of none.' [My italics].

So the objective of an all-party Coalition, going much further than the manifesto commitment, was formally written into the Conservative election programme. Heath put it there on his own authority as Party Leader; agreement from the whole Shadow Cabinet was neither sought nor obtained.

The evidence suggests that this initiative had little effect either way on the closing stages of the campaign. Those Tories opposed to the idea were glad it had not been pushed earlier, since it tended to undermine the credibility of the party's own distinctive policies. I can recall a couple of voters asking, if I was the Coalition candidate, then who was the Conservative? But that was all. The appeal itself lacked credibility, since all Labour leaders said consistently that they would have nothing to do with it, while the Liberals said they would not join such a Cabinet exclusively with the Tories. To take it seriously one had to believe that a number of Labour and Liberal leaders would change their minds in the event of a Conservative victory or the Conservatives emerging as the largest single party.

In the event such speculation proved irrelevant. The election resulted in Labour winning 319 seats; Conservatives, 276; Nationalists, 14; Liberals, 13; United Ulster Unionists, 10; and others, 3. Labour had a majority of only three, though given the

Margaret as Education Secretary in 1971, after dedicating a new school in St. John's Wood, London.

A surprise kiss from William Whitelaw during the leadership election of February 1975. A fellow contestant, he later became Margaret's Deputy in the Shadow Cabinet.

fragmented state of the Opposition, Wilson's majority worked out in practice to be something over 20.

In Finchley the result was :

Margaret Thatcher (Con)	16,498
Martin O'Connor (Lab)	12,587
Laurence Brass (Lib)	7,387
Janet Godfrey (Nat Front)	993
Conservative majority :	3,911

This was a fairly typical pattern in Tory-held seats in the South. Margaret's majority was down on a lower poll, but her share of the poll increased. But Labour's increased far more, at the expense of the Liberals, who were pushed right back.

Looking back on the campaign, her view is that 'we just couldn't beat down the idea that Labour were offering a quieter life than we were. People just weren't in a mood to accept the nature of the crisis that faced us.' It was not many months before the enormity of the crisis was to become apparent. But before that the Conservative Party had a crisis of its own to settle first.

CHAPTER THIRTEEN

Why Ted Heath Had To Go
October–December 1974

The first act in the tragedy of Ted Heath's decline and fall began with the Cabinet's decision in November 1972 to take statutory controls over pay, prices, dividends and rents. The second was when he missed his chance at the start of 1974 to appeal to the country earlier in the miners' dispute. The third began when he publicly espoused the cause of all-party Coalition—and lost.

The final three chapters in this book are very much one Tory backbencher's observation of the subsequent events that led to Margaret Thatcher's election as Leader of the Conservative Party in February 1975. I write them as one who supported Heath personally and most of the policies of his Government from 1970–74, and indeed who still admires his achievements, notably in leading Britain into the European Community. I won my Reigate seat on the issues as he presented them in February 1974, and again in October, campaigning mainly on his warnings of the economic plight facing the country and on the party's policies for homes and education. It is therefore with no pleasure that I describe the rot that began to eat away at the Conservative Party in the two months that followed.

The fact that the Wilson Government technically had an overall majority of only three tended to disguise just how shattering the Conservative Party's defeat had been. Not only was it now forty-three seats behind Labour, but its hold in the big towns and cities was weaker than at any time since 1945. In the five English cities of Manchester, Birmingham, Liverpool, Newcastle and Bristol the Tories held only six seats, compared with Labour's twenty-nine; even in the dark days of 1966 the party had managed to muster a total of ten. Of the seventy-one Scottish seats the Tories held only sixteen—only just ahead of the Scottish Nationalists' eleven. In Wales the party held eight seats out of thirty-six. And any link with Northern Ireland had gone completely. The awful picture was of a party largely driven back into England to defend the final bastions of the suburbs and the shires. In the South outside London the party had done rather better, pushing back the Liberal challenge, but that was scant consolation for the losses suffered elsewhere.

A party in this situation obviously had to take a long and very critical look not only at its methods and individual policies, but also what it really stood for.

For Heath the first backlash from his second successive election defeat came quickly, and it came from his friends. Close colleagues such as Lord Carrington and James Prior correctly anticipated the opposition likely to build up in the party, and advised him to resign in dignity forthwith.

There was also a feeling among some of his friends that a quick leadership election would enable someone like William Whitelaw who shared their own views on such matters as the management of the economy to step into his shoes, before back-bench support had time to muster around someone less sympathetic to their own position. After all, they already had the warning signal from Sir Keith Joseph's Preston speech in September, which had been welcomed by a number on the backbenches.

But Heath was not the sort of Leader to give up that easily. He believed that he had fought the election on the right policies, that once the disappointment of defeat had passed those policies would be seen still to be right, and that he should be ready to respond to the needs of the nation when the inevitable economic crisis broke upon it. So he would stay.

After such a defeat a party needs a little time for mature reflection; decisions reached on the rebound are as dangerous in politics as in love. But it could be argued that in his own interests Heath's best course would have been to resign and then offer himself immediately for re-election, thus flushing out his critics before that reflection bore its fruit.

However, in rejecting his friends' advice Heath also set his face against seeking any kind of vote of confidence in his continued leadership from the Parliamentary Party. And this led him to make his first major blunder, by getting involved in a confrontation with the Executive of the 1922 Committee. Aware of the anxiety within the party, these senior backbenchers felt they should meet to talk over the situation, so the 1922 chairman,

Edward du Cann, called a meeting on October 14 at his home in Lord North Street, almost opposite that of Harold Wilson.

At this strong feelings were expressed that before long the party would at least want to review the leadership question, and that the most sensible course would be to hold a fresh ballot, in which Heath himself would be a candidate. Furthermore, it was agreed that du Cann should call on Heath at his home in Wilton Street and convey this advice.

This du Cann promptly did but Heath reacted strongly, claiming that the 1922 Executive was acting outside its responsibility. In order to report back what Heath had said, du Cann had arranged another Executive meeting the following day within the discreet walls of Keyser Ullman's, the merchant bank in the City of which he was chairman. The choice of venue proved to be unfortunate, but it was the one which that day was most convenient to a majority of Executive members.

At this further meeting Executive members were amazed by Heath's hostile response, and decided to put their point to him again more formally in a letter. Meanwhile the Press had been tipped off that a plot was being hatched within the walls of Keyser Ullmann's, and as the MPs began to leave by the front door they came face to face with a photographer. So they retreated into the building, and rather unwisely made instead for the rear fire exit in Milk Street. But the photographer anticipated their move and was waiting there too, with the result that three Executive members were pictured making a furtive exit past the dustbins. 'Milk Street Mafia' proclaimed the headline in London's *Evening Standard*.

Most backbenchers treated the incident as something of a joke, but a number in the Heath camp were furious, accusing du Cann of plotting against the Leader—even, it was suggested, in order that he should inherit the crown himself. When Heath replied to the Executive's letter it was to say curtly that he was prepared to talk to them *after* they had been re-elected in the new Parliament. Meanwhile his aides claimed that the Executive had no authority, since it had been elected in the previous Parliament —and that anyway there would have to be a clean sweep to remove these 'plotters' when the elections were held.

Several Executive members were threatened directly that they would be voted out of office if they persisted in trying to raise the leadership issue. The incident did not augur well for brotherly love on the Tory benches in the sesison that was about to begin.

The following week, after many of us had been to the Commons to take the Oath of Allegiance before the Speaker, one of the younger backbenchers held a party in his flat. At this I was surprised by the extent of the criticism among MPs from the 1974 intake of the leadership in the election campaign, while more senior colleagues predicted the party would have a new Leader before the coming session was through. However, no one seemed at all clear who that new Leader should be.

This confusion was understandable. At that time the only Front Bench Tory to have argued publicly against the assumptions on which the Heath Government's policies had come to be based was Keith Joseph, in his Preston speech early in September. Meanwhile, before the October election, he and Margaret had set up an independent Centre for Policy Studies, the aim of which was to undertake research 'with particular attention to social market policies'. Many saw this as a counterweight to the orthodox Conservative Research Department in the evolution of future Tory policies, though this was denied by its sponsors. These two factors together tended to focus attention on Keith Joseph as a possible alternative to Heath as Leader, particularly if the purpose of change was to secure a general reappraisal of policy.

However, any such thoughts were quickly upset by Keith Joseph himself, in a speech on October 19 to Edgbaston Conservatives, the effects of which were to change the whole leadership situation. For in this speech he chose to turn from economics to give his view of the Conservative Party's proper role in a permissive society. Indeed, he claimed that the party had lost by concentrating its arguments too much on economics, rather than on the restoration of those moral values which made a healthy society. But unfortunately he went on to present an argument which led to considerable misunderstanding and very hostile publicity.

A rising proportion of children, he claimed, were being born to mothers 'in socio-economic classes four and five' who as a result of their own deprivation were least fitted to bring up children. This presented a dilemma, in that these people affected by the permissive climate made less use of birth control techniques. Thus 'the balance of our population, our human stock, is threatened'. Even before extracts from his speech were in the papers there were howls of rage from all directions. He was accused of advocating 'master race' theories, and wanting 'pills for the proles'. For a full week afterwards he had to issue successive denials and clarifications of what he meant, and altogether the speech proved to be a somewhat counter-productive political exercise.

Back at Westminster the speech had a number of important political effects. In conversation it became clear that a number of MPs who had been inclined to regard him as a possible alternative Leader now asked themselves whether the merits of his undoubted intellect were not in part offset by occasional but dangerous lapses in judgement. But, at the same time, backbenchers also noted the glee with which one or two of Heath's closest supporters watched this Shadow Minister in trouble, while protesting loudly what great harm they thought he was inflicting on the party. Any potential leadership challenger was clearly going to be vulnerable to calculated denigration by a number of Parliamentary colleagues the moment he—or she—put a foot wrong.

Finally there was the effect of the experience on Keith Joseph himself. It gave a taste of what life could be like for those who were seen as leadership contenders or indeed who eventually lead parties—and he did not like it.

In this prevailing atmosphere it seemed to me that the leadership question was going to have a paralysing effect on the party, acting to stultify any expressions of original thought on the policy appraisal the party should be making. Following Keith Joseph's experience every Shadow Minister knew that if he made any public comment which appeared to question the wisdom of the Heath Government's actions he would be labelled as a leadership contender, and therefore become vulnerable to attacks from within his own party.

On October 25, in a speech in my constituency, I gave my view that, though it was right to avoid rushed judgements in the aftermath of defeat, a ballot on the leadership should take place before the winter was out so that the issue could be closed and the party unite behind Heath or whoever else might be elected.

With Keith Joseph ruled out as a possible alternative leader for the moment at least, Heath appeared to be in a rather more secure position when the new Parliament opened on October 29. And indeed it looked as if he intended to dig in and defy his critics to come out into the open. Had he decided there and then to put the criticisms of his leadership to the test in a ballot, he

would most probably have emerged the victor, since no alternative
Leader was immediately apparent.

However, at this stage Heath began to receive what proved to
be bad advice from those around him, and their assessment was
that time would tell in his favour, that the criticisms were nothing
more than a reflex response to defeat, and that after further
demonstrations of his leadership from the Front Bench his critics
would be reduced to an embittered backbench rump. They also
looked to national events to prove the correctness of his judgement. In the election Heath had warned the country of the
looming economic crisis, the argument ran, and it was only a
matter of time before he would be proved right. There was
therefore no need to embark on any fundamental rethinking of
economic policy. Indeed, there was no need to undertake
fundamental rethinking at all. The Conservative's October
election platform was still the one most relevant to the country's
situation, as would be proved by events.

From conversations in the Members' Dining Room, Smoking
Room and elsewhere in the Palace of Westminster where Tory
MPs congregate it was obvious that many felt this approach fell
far short of the party's need. The party had become severed
from its popular roots and separated from so many of its
natural supporters, and something more than honest economic
forecasting would be needed to win them back.

The key event that Tories awaited in that opening week of
Parliament was the first meeting of their backbench 1922
Committee on November 1. This body gets its name from the
famous meeting of Tory MPs in the Carlton Club that year,
which instructed those Tory Ministers serving under Lloyd
George to quit the Coalition and return to base. After that it was
decided there should be regular meetings of backbenchers, under
their own chairman and served by an Executive, to ensure that
their views were taken properly into account by the party
leadership.

When the party is in Opposition it is open to all Tory MPs
and peers who receive the Tory Whip to attend its meetings.
The Party Leader, however, attends only by prior arrangement.
While Parliament is sitting it meets every Thursday evening in
Committee Room 14, and begins by hearing the whipping
arrangements for the following week. Then, after any special
reports from other party committees have been heard, it is open
to any backbencher to raise any topic, though usually prior

notice of this is given to the chairman. No formal votes are taken, but the sense of the meeting is quick to emerge, and is always conveyed to the Chief Whip, if he is not present, and then if necessary to the Party Leader. The discussion is supposed to be confidential, though when anything up to two hundred MPs are present news of what has happened soon spreads, and occasionally the chairman will issue an official statement.

There have been times in the past when the 1922 Committee has gone through moribund periods. However, in the three months following the October 1974 defeat it performed its function of giving expression to backbenchers' views perfectly, thanks very largely to the open style of chairmanship adopted by Edward du Cann. I attended all its meetings in these weeks, and am bound by its rule of confidentiality. However, well-informed accounts of its proceedings appeared in the Press.

The 1922 Committee meeting of November 1 proved to be a crucial one in the leadership saga that autumn and winter. First, it demonstrated that a number of Tory MPs were determined on a change of leadership. Heath had invited his critics to 'stand up and be counted', and this meeting established that they were not afraid to do so, even knowing that versions of their remarks would leak to the Press. Next morning *The Daily Telegraph* reported :

> When Mr. Heath receives candid accounts of last night's meeting of the 1922 Committee he will be left in no doubt about the predominant feeling of Conservative MPs that the time has come for a change of leadership.

Only two of the twenty-odd who joined in the discussion spoke in his favour, the rest being either hostile or neutral. But second, and equally important, the meeting established that there would have to be a leadership ballot, and that in order to secure one the election rules would have to be changed.

As the situation stood, under the 1965 rules introduced by Sir Alec Douglas-Home there could be a ballot only after the post of Leader became vacant; Heath had no intention of resigning, so there could be no ballot. According to the Press Kenneth Lewis, who initiated the discussion, asked whether the Party Leadership should not be held on a 'leasehold' rather than 'freehold' basis.

His point was echoed by others, and there was agreement all

round that the rules should be changed to provide for a new leadership election within a specified period of a general election defeat, and possibly at further intervals thereafter.

These two factors together dictated a change in Heath's strategy. Until then some of his closest supporters had argued that in due course a fresh ballot would be unnecessary; now they had to accept that Heath could not remain as Leader without the clearly demonstrated backing of the majority of Tory MPs. They were still confident he would get this backing, especially if the ballot took place after the expected economic crisis had come to a head. Meanwhile, they argued, the revision of the rules should not be rushed; in particular, the party should take care not to be caught in an internal contest in the country's moment of crisis.

It was also claimed that those who were making the running in criticism were those older Members on the Right of the party who had been privately critical of Heath since the day he was elected Leader ten years before, and certainly the critics contained a number of such people. At the same time, Heath's friends and many in the Press assumed that when it came to a crunch he would be able to count on the support of nearly all the younger Tory MPs.

However, the more conversations I had with my contemporaries the more convinced I became that this just was not so. Those younger Members from the 1970 intake—several of whom had now lost their seats—tended to be as strongly committed to Heath as they were to the proposition that 'growth first' should be the main objective of economic policy. They were also much more inclined to support the idea of a Coalition with Liberals and Right-wing Socialists as a desirable objective. But the 1974 intake were of a different character; its members took a far more detached view of the history of the 1970–74 Government, and were far stronger in the opinion that the Conservative Party needed to rediscover its fundamental beliefs if its policies were to be more appealing and more relevant to the needs of ordinary voters, and that if Heath's leadership stood in the way of this then it was he who had to go.

Of course this view was not unanimous, but it was far more general among the new generation of Tory MPs than Heath's close supporters allowed. Furthermore, the 1974 intake was numerically very strong; of the 54 first elected in February 53 remained, and to them had been added another eight in October.

We were thus not far short of making up a quarter of the total Tory strength of 276. I well recall remarking to a much older colleague in November that if Heath were defeated it would be the 1974 intake that tipped the scales against him.

But anxiety over how the party could regain its identity was not confined to the 1974 intake. During November three more senior backbenchers, Reginald Eyre, Keith Speed and Fergus Montgomery, arranged a meeting to discuss the party's lost appeal among urban voters which was heavily attended. Significantly all three had represented Midlands seats in the 1970–74 Parliament. The upshot of the meeting was that it was agreed the three organisers should collect evidence and comments from a range of party agents and others in urban seats to see what general pattern of dissatisfaction with the party and its policies could be established. The Tories' survival instinct was at work. But it is significant that the initiative was taken by three backbenchers, and did not spring from any decision of the Leader.

Further evidence of the state of backbencher opinion came on November 7, when du Cann and all the other 1922 Executive members of the so-called 'Milk Street Mafia' were re-elected *en bloc*. No challenger to du Cann had ever emerged, and those who unsuccessfully contested the other offices had not done so on an openly pro-Heath ticket. Of the two new men elected to the Executive one, Sir Paul Bryan, was on record as believing the time had come for a change of Leader. The writing was on the wall.

By this time Heath had recognised his need to cover his weak flank. He indicated he was willing to attend the following week's meeting of the 1922 Committee, and at the same time he made efforts to broaden the base of his Shadow Cabinet by inviting both du Cann and Maudling to join it. But both declined; du Cann, having been denied Front Bench rank in Government and Opposition for eight years, preferred to continue as 1922 chairman. So the two vacant places went to Nicholas Scott, one of Heath's most fervent supporters, and Timothy Raison. But more significant was Margaret's move from Environment to serve under Shadow Chancellor Robert Carr. As the official announcement put it :

'In Treasury and economic affairs Mr. Carr will be assisted by Mrs. Thatcher, who will have particular responsibility for financial legislation and public expenditure.' This was not really a demotion, but an attempt by Heath to bring together two rather different approaches to economic matters on his Front Bench. Indeed, it turned out to give Margaret a golden opportunity to shine immediately before the leadership election.

At this time I did not count myself in anyone's camp on the leadership issue, other than with those who believed it was imperative for the health of the party that a ballot should take place before the end of the winter, and that everyone should then unite behind whoever won it. But in early November it was far from clear what the choice offered in a ballot would be. A number of backbenchers were still rooting for Keith Joseph, but he had undoubtedly damaged himself by his Edgbaston speech, and no one knew whether he would agree to stand.

Others wanted to draft du Cann, but he had made their task difficult by accepting office for a further year as 1922 chairman, one of whose duties was to act as returning officer. He was also unacceptable to many because of his coolness over membership of the European Community.

Margaret's name was mentioned by several, but apparently she was not willing to stand against Keith Joseph. My own view, stated at the time, was that of these three she would be by far the strongest candidate. William Whitelaw was seen as a strong contender only if Heath stood down or was badly mauled in a first ballot. A few yearned to bring Sir Christopher Soames back from the European Commission in Brussels, though the obstacles to this were insuperable. Enoch Powell, who had been on everyone's lips as a leadership challenger if the Tories had lost the 1970 election, was no longer even in the party.

Then there was the suggestion that, if no one of weight was willing to risk his neck in the first ballot, a respected backbencher would stand as a straight protest candidate, in the hope of opening up the field in the second.

Meanwhile, I decided to start my own consultation process in my constituency. After the 1922 Committee meeting on November 7 I attended the quarterly meeting of my own Association's Executive Council in Redhill, at which I asked all branch representatives to conduct their own consultations and then write to me in confidence telling me whether they thought we should fight the next election under Heath's leadership or not, and why. I made it clear I would not regard the majority view as an instruction, but that it would weigh very heavily with me when I came to cast my vote.

On November 14 Heath attended the 1922 Committee and announced that he was willing to make immediate arrangements for the leadership election rules to be reviewed. He would therefore have discussions with Edward du Cann, representing Tory backbenchers, Party Chairman William Whitelaw, Lord Carrington representing Tory peers, and Sir John Taylor for the National Union of Conservative and Unionist Associations. According to the Press the two hundred present gave him a 'warm and courteous' welcome. A couple of weeks before there had been ideas for broadening the franchise to embrace a few peers and even some area representatives of constituency associations, but since then opinion had swung heavily in favour of keeping the ballot to Tory MPs. Since any Tory Leader's power derived from his support in the Commons, then that was where he should be elected. Several at the meeting stressed it was more important to have the ballot soon than to devise any fancy franchises. But the significance of the meeting was that Heath had now accepted that there would be a ballot. And it was therefore now open to anyone to state that he or she was willing to stand for election in it.

I remember after this meeting reflecting rather sadly on the position in which Heath found himself. Here was the man who, after June 1970, exercised undisputed power over his Cabinet and party, still not really aware how the ground was moving from under his feet. He had many achievements to his credit, was dedicated to his objectives, and yet was so boxed in by the planks of his October election platform that he could not move to give the Tory Party the lead it needed in reassessing from basic principles its policy objectives. If only he could have made that move and admitted the need to rebuild again from base. But it seemed he could not, and indeed was being advised by those closest to him that he had no need to do so. He was, it seemed, being insulated from the true nature of the feeling on his own backbenches.

After that November 14 meeting of the 1922 Committee the pace of events quickened. That very night there was at least one private gathering away from the Commons to discuss who should run in an election against Heath, and many present were in favour of persuading du Cann.

Independently of this another highly respected senior backbencher, Airey Neave, was sounding out colleagues on the need

for a change of leadership if the Conservative Party was to re-
capture its appeal and vigour. As time went on Neave was to play
a more and more crucial role. He had been in the House since
1953, and had served as a Junior Minister under Macmillan
from 1957–59, when he had to withdraw from office due to an
illness from which he subsequently recovered. He was always
described in the Press as the man who was the first to escape
from Colditz, and who returned to Britain via Switzerland and
Gibraltar in 1942 to organise the escapes of other prisoners of
war. He was a familiar figure among backbenchers, and had
gone out of his way to get to know the new MPs from the
February 1974 intake soon after their arrival. He had the quality
of being a good listener as well as talker—and over these weeks
Neave was listening very hard.

Meanwhile another senior colleague, Sir Frederic Bennet, told
me he was formally asking Keith Joseph if he intended to stand,
and promising him wide support if he did. My own view was
that Margaret would have broader appeal. However, Keith
Joseph replied that he would not stand. Bennet then saw
Margaret, and the following day he told me of her reply. She
had made the fateful decision to contest the leadership.

In fact, Margaret had been pressed by a number of colleagues,
particularly by Fergus Montgomery, who had been her Parliamentary Private Secretary at Education after November 1973.
When he had lost his seat in the February election she had been
on the phone to him by 8 am the next morning offering
condolences—before she went to her own count in Finchley.
Soon after he was returned for Anthony Barber's former seat at
Altrincham in October he told Margaret she should run for
Leader, but she would not so long as Sir Keith was seen as a
challenger. If he stood she would support him, since she admired
the lead he had given in re-examining the party's past performance and policies to see where they had gone wrong. But as
soon as he told her he would not stand then she knew straight
away that she must do so, just as at that October election Press
conference she knew that her housing policies were 'not negotiable', whatever happened to Heath's dream of a Coalition
Government.

However, she was by no means convinced that she could win
against Heath; she simply knew that, if the leadership ballot was
to mean anything at all, then she had to stand on behalf of those
who wanted to make a clean admission of past mistakes and a

start on reconstructing a distinctive Conservative platform which would win back those natural supporters whom over the years the party had lost. But some candid advice came from her husband Denis : 'Obviously your friends will be disappointed if you don't stand, but you should make sure you're able to make a good showing. If you go down badly then you'll be slaughtered afterwards, that's for sure.' However, her friends assured her that she could make a good showing, though they could certainly not guarantee her victory.

So, reassuring herself that the party clearly wanted a contest and that you could not have one without contestants, Margaret threw her hat into the ring. Her first move was to go to Heath and tell him of her decision.

The news of her decision soon spread on the Tory benches, and within a week was reported in the Press. From that moment on she was a marked woman by some of Heath's most fervent supporters. Every move she made and action she took was scrutinised in search of ammunition with which to shoot her down—which brings us to the saga of the so-called 'food hoarding interview'.

Back in the summer Margaret had given an interview to a new magazine caller *Pre-Retirement Choice* whose objective was to give advice and help to those approaching retirement. She had been chosen as the personality for interview in its first issue because Denis was due to retire the following year. The interviewer, John Kemp, asked for advice on how people could make some practical provision for the time they retired, and he got it. With inflation running at its present rate, said Margaret, a wise thing to do was over a period of years to buy a tin a week of high-protein food like ham, tongue or sardines and put them into store. Indeed, she herself had done this, knowing full well that the cost of such food was bound to rise.

The interview duly appeared in the first issue of the magazine, which came out in mid-November. But immediately this was seized on as the gaffe that her opponents had been seeking. In no time at all reports appeared in the Press saying that Margaret Thatcher was encouraging food hoarding and, even worse, panic buying. In the Commons a Labour MP helped the campaign by accusing her of 'filching little tins of salmon from supermarkets and taking them out of pensioners' mouths'. In vain did Margaret issue a statement saying that in keeping a stock of food at home she was guilty of nothing worse than prudent housekeeping. The incident was a gift to cartoonists, while those who feared most from a defeat of Heath protested loudly that this just showed how out of touch she was with ordinary people who could not afford to stockpile salmon as a hedge against inflation.

The crescendo reached its peak in a hard-hitting article by the late Derek Marks, a strong Heath supporter, in which he described her action as 'the political equivalent of an officer having a meal before first ensuring that his men have been fed'. It showed she was 'totally out of touch with anybody but carefully corseted, middle class, middle aged ladies ... She has not only harmed herself, she has harmed the whole Tory Party just as Sir Keith Joseph did by his call for birth control for the working class.'

One cannot believe that Heath himself can have given any sanction to this campaign of attempted character assassination. But there is no doubt that some of his strongest supporters who were not MPs were actively promoting Press interest in the story, and that others in the House were trying to capitalise on it. By the start of December they, and sections of the Press, felt satisfied it had put paid to Margaret's leadership chances, just as Keith Joseph's Edgbaston speech appeared to have put paid to his. But the whole exercise boomeranged, for three quite separate reasons.

First, the spectacle of some in the Heath camp pushing such a campaign of character assassination against a Shadow Cabinet colleague caused more offence among Tory MPs than it won support. If this was to be the pattern under Heath's leadership, some said, then the sooner it was ended the better. Second, the publishers of *Pre-Retirement Choice* very kindly sent a copy of their first issue to every MP for interest—and on reading the interview Tories discovered that Margaret had not been advocating at all what had been alleged. Her advice had been to buy such foods 'over a period of years', perhaps one tin a week, while making the most of any special offers in supermarkets. 'Don't buy in huge amounts,' she had cautioned.

Finally, the critics failed to allow for the effect of their attack on Margaret herself. Her first reaction was one of disappointment, a feeling that perhaps she had let her own supporters down by saying something which could be so distorted. But as the campaign against her mounted and it became clear who was pushing it, the effect on her was quite different. For she had been through all this before over the 'milk snatcher' smear—and it made her

doubly determined to stand up to those who were resorting to
such techniques against her.

Meanwhile Heath had, as promised, appointed a body to
review the election rules. Lord Home, who had fathered the
existing procedures, accepted the chairmanship, and under him
were representatives of MPs, peers, the Party Organisation and
the National Union. Apart from Home, the leading participants
were du Cann and Whitelaw. It was obvious that they had to
make provision for a ballot within a certain period after the start
of a new Parliament, and possibly annually thereafter. They also
had to decide on the composition of the 'electoral college', and
whether it should be broadened from MPs to include some peers
and National Union representatives. The final sensitive question
was whether the existing provision enabling fresh candidates to
enter in a second ballot should be retained. There were some in
the party who felt that every contestant should be obliged to
stake his or her claim from the very start. However, the most
pressing requirement urged upon them was speed, so the review
body worked hard to get their report out before Christmas.

As MPs waited through December for the report no new
challengers came forward. Margaret remained the only committed candidate apart from Heath himself for more than a
month—a fact which surprised her slightly, but which undoubtedly worked in her favour once the election campaign
really began. From the end of November a group of MPs began
to meet periodically under the chairmanship of Sir Nigel Fisher,
another senior backbencher with a rather liberal record, to keep
under review the possibility of drafting du Cann. During these
weeks there was some discussion, particularly among older backbenchers, over whether the party and the country would really
accept a woman as Leader.

Meanwhile there was a round of speculation that revived
many memories of the past election campaign. Reports came in
from many close to the City that an economic collapse was fast
approaching, quite possibly in January, that would rock the very
foundations of the Wilson Government and call for measures
which could never be made acceptable to its Left wing. In all
probability another pay freeze of sorts would be necessary, it was
said. And so the old chimera of Coalition was revived, a National
Government of Labour 'moderates', Liberals and those Tories
who had been leading members of the 1970–74 Government.

This view of the likely pattern of events was sincerely held by some of Heath's closest supporters, and there were suggestions that the Great Crash might even overtake the leadership ballot arrangements. But the notion of getting back into Government this way found little favour among the majority of backbenchers; the Coalition idea represented to them the very policy dead end from which they wanted to escape.

Of rather more interest was the Parliamentary performance of the only declared leadership challenger. During this period Margaret had carefully kept herself out of the general political controversy, concentrating instead on marshalling her detailed attack on Chancellor Denis Healey's November Budget proposals. These included a totally new tax on capital transfers, which as put together hastily within the Treasury posed a direct threat to family firms, farms and charities, among others.

In her new Shadow role Margaret's task was to lead the Tory attack on the Finance Bill implementing these proposals, which gave her the same scope to exploit her old mastery of tax matters as Callaghan's Selective Employment Tax had eight years before. On December 17 Tory MPs filled the benches to hear her sweeping attack on the Bill, and on the Capital Transfer Tax in particular. They were not disappointed. She paraded detailed arguments with her usual skill, and put Healey firmly in his place when he tried to taunt her over food hoarding. She was rewarded with warm applause from the Tory benches when she sat down.

By coincidence on the same day the Home review body published their proposed changes to the election rules. Under these the main structure of the existing system would remain intact, with the additional requirement that a leadership ballot should be held between three and six months after a new Parliament had assembled. Thereafter there should be annual elections within twenty-eight days of the start of each new session. There were to be more formalised arrangements for consulting all constituency associations through the machinery of the National Union, and peers, but the 'electoral college' would remain confined to MPs.

There was one other small change which greatly annoyed the Heath supporters. To win outright in the first ballot a candidate would need a lead not merely of 15 per cent of the votes cast, but of 15 per cent of the total electorate. This, in fact, made an abstention into an effective vote *against* the leading candidate. Most backbenchers saw Heath as a certain leader in the first round, and there were dark murmurs about the rules being rigged against him. In the end, of course, it made no difference.

Just before this a somewhat bizarre meeting had taken place in Heath's room. Neave, who had by this time taken very wide soundings of opinion on the Tory benches, had come to the conclusion that Heath was unlikely to win a leadership ballot. Accordingly he arranged to see Heath, and told him in as friendly a manner as he could that his evidence was that he would be defeated, and suggesting to Heath that it would be in his own interests to retire gracefully and so avoid the bitterness which a contest would cause.

Heath apparently listened patiently, but was unconvinced. All the soundings relayed to him by his circle of friends indicated that he had nothing to worry about. It was on this assumption, clearly, that he was preparing to enter the coming contest. In fairness, too, one should say that Heath and his supporters were not the only ones to think thus. The Press saw him at this time as a certain winner in a second ballot, if not in the first.

However, others knew that peculiar things could happen once the election went to a second ballot. Whitelaw felt honour bound, as Party Chairman appointed by Heath, not to join himself in the first round, but whether he entered in a second would depend very much on how far Heath was from an outright win on the first.

And so, in the midst of such speculation, MPs broke up for their Christmas recess. As soon as Christmas was over I settled down to analysing the letters I had received in response to my request to my constituency association's Executive Council stating whether they wanted to fight the next election under Heath's leadership or not, and why. They took some analysing, since some answered on the basis of talking to a couple of branch officers, while others had initiated a full branch committee discussion ending in a vote. The replies also came in over a period of three weeks, during which the national context had changed.

However, whichever way I broke them down, the broad pattern was the same. Some 40 per cent thought Heath should quit if the party was to have any chance of winning the next election. More than 50 per cent came down in Heath's favour,

but so many with reservations ('provided he changes his style' . . .
provided he changes some of his policies' . . .) as to make enthusiastic support far less. The balance, dodging the question I had
put, thought he should stay on until a successor emerged more
clearly. Whichever way you looked at it, if this pattern were
repeated across the country it would hardly indicate any basis
for the revival of Tory morale and support under Heath's continued leadership.

CHAPTER FOURTEEN

Offering Leadership that Listens
January–February 1975

Margaret Thatcher returned to Westminster in the third week of January 1975, knowing that she was soon likely to face the most severe test yet in her political career. Some five days earlier she had entertained Airey Neave, an old friend from twenty years back, to lunch at her home in Flood Street, and he had outlined the leadership situation as he saw it. This was, first, that anxiety over the deteriorating state of the party ran deep on the Tory benches, and whoever stood against Ted Heath was guaranteed a substantial following; second, that while she had a great many supporters there were also some forty backbenchers who wanted Edward du Cann to run; and third, that it was still not clear whether du Cann was willing to be drafted or not.

Margaret's response was that it would be best if those wanting a change of leadership could all rally behind one candidate. She did not commit herself to standing down if du Cann wanted to run, as she had in the case of Keith Joseph, but obviously the situation should be clarified before she made any public announcement of her intention. Neave promised to keep her in touch.

Margaret then spent the latter days of the Christmas recess with Denis at their cottage in Lamberhurst, where on walks across the Kent countryside she turned over and over in her mind the crying needs of the Conservative Party, and how if given the chance she would set about meeting them. But she did not commit any thoughts or programmes to paper. Furthermore, when Parliament resumed on January 13 she still did not have any organisation behind her that could remotely be called a campaign machine. Fergus Montgomery, her former Parliamentary Private Secretary, and William Shelton, an old ally from her days at Education, were willing to organise one, but at this stage it was not yet in being.

By contrast, Heath's machine was already in existence, having evolved naturally from the circle of intimate colleagues who had together been arguing in his defence among backbenchers from the very start of the Parliament. Chief among them was Peter Walker, a senior Minister throughout the 1970–74 Government, who had successfully organised Heath's first leadership campaign back in 1965. There were his two Parliamentary Private Secretaries, Kenneth Baker and Sir Tim Kitson, and Nicholas Scott, who the previous November had been promoted to the Shadow Cabinet. As a group they worked well together, and were to be serviced in the leadership campaign by the secretariat in the Leader of the Opposition's Private Office.

However, there was also another rather more loosely-knit organisation at work, and that was the group who had been meeting regularly under Nigel Fisher since the end of November in the hope that they could organise a campaign in support of du Cann. Thus du Cann had a machine waiting ready, while Margaret did not. Neave was a member of this group, though he had told them before Christmas that in his view Margaret was the stronger candidate and would appeal to a broader spread of backbenchers. Those in the group had been sympathetic, but several had doubted whether the Tory Party could ever be induced to follow a woman Leader.

However, on January 13, just two days after Parliament resumed, Fisher called another meeting of his group, and at this the message was imparted that du Cann had made a firm decision not to stand—and that he personally would be casting his vote for Margaret. With only a handful of exceptions the twenty-five to thirty MPs present agreed to throw their weight behind her too, and told Neave he should be the campaign manager.

Later that evening Neave had a meeting with Shelton, and told him that an embryo campaign machine was now at Margaret's disposal. It was then agreed between them that Neave should direct the campaign, and that the more junior Shelton should be his deputy. Montgomery, believing that the ballot would not come before the end of February, had accepted an invitation to join a Parliamentary delegation to South Africa. Neave and Shelton then drafted a note to about ten backbenchers, including the leading members of the Fisher group, inviting them to what was to prove the first of a series of Thatcher campaign committee meetings the following Monday.

The next day Margaret was told of these developments, which

she naturally greeted with some enthusiasm. She was now in no doubt that it was her duty at least to offer the party an alternative course to the downhill road along which it was travelling. However, her habitual caution led her to take a somewhat pessimistic view of her chances. At this stage she felt she would do well to collect 100 votes out of the total of 276.

Later that evening the 1922 Committee had its first meeting to consider the proposals from Lord Home's review body for amending the leadership election rules. Though some MPs had reservations over one or two provisions, notably the one for annual elections, the message emerging from the meeting could not have been clearer : the party wanted a ballot as soon as possible, and was therefore prepared to accept the amendments as they stood. Meanwhile Sir John Taylor reported the National Union's more critical view to Heath. Besides objecting to their exclusion from the 'electoral college', they saw no reason why new candidates should be allowed to enter in the second ballot. However, to have accepted their advice would have meant delaying the ballot several more weeks, and by now it was clear to Heath that he would only do himself damage by refusing to meet the almost unanimous demand of his own backbenchers. Few doubted that the following week he would set the new machinery in motion.

At this stage Margaret herself was not called on to perform any campaigning role. Her most important task was leading the Tory attack on the Finance Bill, which was now in its Committee Stage—the first part of which, in the case of Finance Bills, is taken on the floor of the full House.

However, quite apart from those already involved on the Thatcher campaign committee, a number of backbenchers began to go direct to her to offer their help and support. I was one of them. Had Heath offered himself for re-election before mid-November I would in all probability have voted for him, but the evidence of disintegration and fratricide in the party since had been too much. One had also had time to think more deeply on the 1970–74 Government's performance and where it had gone wrong, and on the Coalition stance adopted in the October election. A substantial reappraisal of policy was clearly necessary, but by January it was obvious it would not come without a change of leadership. There was also the evidence from my own constituency soundings and from conversations with those who had lost marginal seats. Finally, there was the important factor of the personality of Margaret herself, whose values and courage in advocating them I had long admired. And so I offered my help, particularly in handling relations with the Press, of which as a political correspondent for thirteen years I had some knowledge.

In fact Margaret had an important engagement with the Press very soon. On January 21 she was due to speak to a private luncheon club of a number of leading national and provincial political correspondents, to which some Fleet Street editors and MPs were usually invited. The occasion was an important one to her, since until then the Press had tended to dismiss her as the representative of a largely Right-wing faction, whose most important function was to open up the field to another candidate such as William Whitelaw in the second ballot. Margaret had to show them that she was a more serious contender than this. Fortunately I had been invited to the lunch too, which so far as I was concerned was her first election campaign engagement.

In fact she handled it with great skill, giving a serious account of her political beliefs and purpose in standing, then answering questions with humour and vivacity. She also deployed her old skill of condensing a complicated economic argument into plain man's language; those journalists present would dearly have loved to be able to explain the concept of negative fiscal drag to their readers in five hundred words as clearly as Margaret did to them that day.

From impressing political correspondents Margaret moved on to the next opportunity in the Commons, in the continuing Committee Stage debate on the Finance Bill. For the crucial clauses on the Capital Transfer Tax had now been reached, and she was due to sum up the Opposition's case. Late that night Tories packed the benches to hear what proved to be a massive onslaught on CTT as conceived by Chancellor Healey. All the facts and arguments were at her fingertips; in vain did Labour MPs intervene to try to trip her up. Then finally came the commitment the Tories were waiting for—that the next Conservative Government would repeal the tax. It was a virtuoso Parliamentary performance, for which she was loudly cheered. From that moment on her stature as a potential Party Leader began to grow.

It was about this time that a third MP, Hugh Fraser, made it known that he would probably enter the leadership contest. A senior backbencher of some standing and independence of mind,

Fraser was seen as providing a first ballot haven for those Tories opposed to Heath but who also objected to a woman as Leader, and who could then move to supporting someone else at second ballot stage.

Meanwhile, though the election had not yet been formally announced, the canvassing of backbench opinions by the two main campaign groups was well under way. A number of my 1974 intake contemporaries were surprised, and in some cases embarrassed, to receive invitations to lunch or dinner at the homes of some of Heath's closest supporters, at which it was indicated the Leader would be present. At the same time Shelton and his aides had begun their canvass. Both sides knew what they had to aim to get. To win outright on the first ballot Heath needed a clear majority, which meant at least 139 votes, but also a 15 per cent majority of all available votes, which meant a lead of 42 votes over Margaret. In other words, if Heath were to win with 139 votes, then she had to get no more than 97. If he got 150, then she had to get no more than 108, and so on.

On January 21, before Margaret made her notable Finance Bill speech, Shelton's returns showed 69 pledged to vote for her, and 43 for Heath. A day later showed 95 for Margaret, 64 for Heath, and nine for Fraser. Thus, *even before the election was announced*, Neave and Shelton knew they were within a very short distance of denying Heath the 15 per cent lead he needed to win in the first ballot. When these figures were reported to Margaret she was amazed. 'In that case,' she said, 'let's really go.' Said Neave: 'You can only go forward. You can't turn back.'

On January 23 Heath went to the 1922 Committee and announced that he had decided to accept the Home proposals on the ballot rules for the time being at least, and to set the new election machinery in motion. He received a friendly reception, but the news he brought was what everyone had expected. Nominations would close the following Thursday, and the first and perhaps only ballot would be held the Tuesday after, on February 4. So now the leadership election campaign was formally under way.

On Friday Neave told the Press he was confident that Margaret would not be eliminated in the first ballot, but he refused to make any prediction of the voting figures. There were still too many backbenchers uncanvassed, or who had not yet made up their minds, to make forecasting possible. On Heath's side, however, Walker and Baker were talking of an outright victory. In the Shadow Cabinet Keith Joseph was the only one backing Margaret. The rest were supporting Heath, though Whitelaw and Jim Prior were saying they might stand themselves if there was a second ballot.

On Saturday, January 26, Heath was in Liverpool and at a Press conference outlined the platform on which he was fighting. 'Any time after losing a general election is a difficult time,' he said, 'particularly when you believe you have been fighting the election on policies which are right and that you told the country the truth. Now it is becoming more evident that we were right.' This was the argument that backbenchers had heard so often in the weeks before Christmas, and which seemed to rule out any substantial reappraisal of policy. Meanwhile Margaret was being hostess to Prior at a dinner in her constituency that had been arranged weeks beforehand.

Every Sunday evening during the campaign Neave and Shelton went to Margaret's home in Flood Street to review the situation and strategy for the coming week. Keith Joseph was also present as a senior adviser. Throughout the campaign these were the only four to see the figures emerging from the canvass of back-benchers. On January 26 they agreed that these were most encouraging, and that the aim should be to canvass everyone except those who had declared themselves publicly for Heath. On the following evening Margaret should attend a meeting of her campaign committee to explain her approach and answer questions, so that the campaigners could honestly answer the questions that were being put to them. In between sessions fighting the Finance Bill, now in a smaller Committee upstairs, she should be available to meet any backbenchers who had not yet made up their minds. Finally, at the end of the week she should make a speech in Finchley and issue a statement which together would constitute her 'manifesto' in the campaign. This should help to focus interest on her over the week-end before the ballot.

The week opened with the Heath campaigners stepping up their criticism of Margaret and what they claimed she repre-sented. A victory for her, they suggested, would mean a lurch to the Right, spelling electoral death in the country. Her advocacy of 'middle-class values' might appeal to those who were already Tory supporters, but would alienate uncommitted voters of the Centre. By electing her as Leader the Tories would also be relegating themselves to being a party of the South-East, with little support north of Watford.

Meanwhile those of us campaigning for Margaret asked if backbenchers really wanted the party to go on in its existing state, tied rigidly to policies and a platform which had twice been rejected by the electors. As for the regional argument, had not the retreat to the South and the shires taken place under Heath's own leadership? Both sides made the most of their candidate's personal qualities—in Heath's case, his honesty in putting the true facts of the economic situation to the country, in Margaret's her willingness to admit past mistakes and courage in putting herself forward while many men in the Shadow Cabinet held back.

Meanwhile a sharp contrast was presented by the administrative organisations of the two campaigns. Heath had the obvious advantage here with his own speech-writing and secretarial staff in the Leader of the Opposition's Private Office. Margaret's were almost worthy of Heath Robinson. Her own office, with its filing cabinets, was just about large enough to accommodate two people seated and one standing. Her secretary, Susan Shields, worked at the end of a large room with many other secretaries off Westminster Hall. Neave's office, no larger than Margaret's, was almost ten minutes' walk away from hers up stairs and lifts at the other end of the building. In it, with one telephone at her disposal, worked Joan Hall, a former MP, who made virtually all the administrative arrangements for the Thatcher campaign. She was under immense pressure from within the campaign committee and from people outside the Commons wanting interviews, pictures and details of Margaret's arrangements, and her phone was rarely unengaged. At weekends she shifted her office into Flood Street, and frequently drove Margaret to appointments. Meanwhile Shelton made his base in the Commons Library, a central point at which he could receive canvassing reports and any other details. Neave spent his time moving between these and other places where MPs congregated, and was the hardest one of all to find.

There was also a contrast in style between the two main candidates in their contact with backbench voters. A number whom Walker and Baker judged to be doubtful were invited to lunch or dinner at the London homes of Heath supporters such as Scott or Anthony Berry, formerly Walker's Parliamentary

Private Secretary. The account of one of these ocassions by an MP from the February 1974 intake was instructive :

'I met my Leader for the first time over lunch yesterday. He seemed slightly uncomfortable, and spoke for twenty minutes justifying the way he handled the miners' strike a year ago. He seemed convinced he had been totally right, both then and in October. Any doubts I'd had about whether to support him were certainly dispelled. I came away determined to vote for Margaret.'

Heath was clearly not at ease wooing voters in this way—something he had never had to do before as Party Leader. Margaret, at her meetings with interested backbenchers, was able to be far more relaxed. These took place in the room of Robin Cooke, an authority on the arts and the fabric of the Palace of Westminster, and the emphasis was on answering questions rather than offering statements. Again Margaret impressed many with her talent for compressing a complicated argument. The sole hospitality offered, by Cooke, was a glass of very agreeable claret.

The previous Thursday Harold Wilson had announced that the Government had decided to hold a national referendum on the question of Britain's continued membership of the European Community, and this had a certain fall-out effect on the Tory leadership campaign. The majority of Tory MPs, particularly among the 1974 intake, were strongly pro-European, and naturally wanted the party to give a strong lead in persuading the British people to vote to stay in the Community. Heath's European commitment was obvious; after all, it was his great achievement that Britain was in the Community at all. Margaret's was less obvious, since in Government her Department had been involved only marginally in Community matters. As a strong pro-European myself I had naturally satisfied myself on her total commitment to Community membership, but a number of the backbenchers who came to see her raised precisely the same point.

In this connection a good opportunity came Heath's way on January 28, when he had been invited to brief members of the Conservative Group for Europe, of which I was an active member, in St. Stephen's Club on our role in the referendum argument. The meeting had of course been arranged weeks before the leadership contest, and wisely Heath did not refer to it in his speech. Instead he gave a stirring call to battle in defence of

Communty membership, which would obviously have impressed the strongest pro-Europeans on the Tory benches. The suggestion peddled that Margaret was 'cool on Europe' was one we were unable to kill until almost the end of the campaign.

Since the end of the previous week the *Daily Telegraph* had been printing an instructive series of articles by leading Conservatives on the theme 'My kind of Tory Party'. Margaret's turn came on Thursday, January 30, and it was her first chance to spell out in print to party supporters outside the Commons what it was she stood for. Looking back on two election defeats, she wrote :

> 'To deny that we failed the people is futile, as well as arrogant. Successful Governments win elections. So do parties with broadly acceptable policies. We lost.

She admitted her share of collective responsibility for past mistakes, adding that two lessons emerged :

> 'The first is that in the long run rapid inflation is the worst enemy, and must at almost all costs be brought under control. The second is that we must never again allow a preoccupation with macro-economics and industrial growth to blind us to the day-to-day problems of ordinary people, in all walks of life.'

Then she hit back at the accusation that she represented only 'middle-class values' :

> 'If "middle-class values" include the encouragement of variety and individual choice, the provision of fair incentives and rewards for skill and hard work, the maintenance of effective barriers against the excessive power of the State and a belief in the wide distribution of individual *private* property, then they are certainly what I am trying to defend.'

In many people's eyes the Tory Party had faltered in support of these values—'and why should anyone support a party that seems to have the courage of no convictions?' This article was obviously useful, but Margaret had to get her message across to more than the readers of one newspaper.

Her 'manifesto', directed at Conservative supporters and the public generally as well as at MPs, was issued in two parts on the week-end before balloting commenced. The first part, in a speech to her own association officers in Finchley on Friday, January 31, explained her reasons for standing and the values the Tory Party was in danger of forgetting; the second, in a letter to her constituency chairman released the following evening, set out how she believed the party could be led out of its difficulties. In view of the central importance of both documents, they are reprinted in full in Appendix C.

In her Friday speech she pointed out that since 1965 there had been four general elections and scores of new faces on the Tory benches, but since then there had been no fresh election for the leadership. The demand for an election now was 'all the more reasonable when you realise that the Leader of our party in Opposition personally appoints—without any procedure for election or confirmation by Conservative MPs—the whole of the Shadow Cabinet and those who control the party machine at Central Office. Many Members felt that they should be given a chance formally to express their views not simply about an individual as Leader, but about the whole nature and style of party leadership since 1965 and the general tenor of its policies.' It was for this reason that she had allowed her name to go forward.

Then, turning to the allegations of her opponents, she declared: 'You can forget all the nonsense about "defence of privilege"— I had precious little "privilege" in my early years—and the suggestion that all my supporters are reactionary Right-wingers. . . . . This is not a confrontation between "Left" and "Right". I am trying to represent the deep feelings of those many rank-and-file Tories in the country—and potential Conservative voters too— who feel let down by our party and find themselves unrepresented in a political vacuum.'

There was, she added, a widespread feeling that the party had not defended sufficiently strongly its traditional ideals of 'compassion and concern for the individual and his freedom; opposition to excessive State power; the right of the enterprising, the hard-working and the thrifty to succeed and to reap the rewards of success and pass some of them on to their children; encouragement of that infinite diversity of choice that is an essential of freedom; the defence of widely-distributed private property against the Socialist State; the right of a man to work without oppression by either employer or trade union boss'.

Her speech was reported well in the Press, as was her open letter the following day, in which she portrayed the different style of leadership she offered : 'People are daily becoming more aware of the need for leadership of the kind that only we can give. But it must be leadership that listens. Perhaps our greatest fault in Office was that we did not listen enough to what our supporters and sympathisers were saying. We allowed ourselves to become detached from the many who had given us their support and trust.'

She then went on to promise a broader consideration and representation of views within the party than had been permitted at the top in recent years : 'I believe our great need now is to *open out* the dialogue within our party, and to bring together a broader spread of talent from within our ranks. Let none feel excluded from this great dialogue by past differences or commitments. We cannot afford any section to feel estranged. Ours is a national party, and it must be an *open* party.'

Finally, she pinpointed the failure in political leadership by the 1970–74 Government : 'To listen and to lead—that is our role. True leadership offers inspiration and hope, but it also explains honestly the severe economic constraints under which we work. And this means that our future programme must be built on a bedrock of practicality. It is not enough to find the right economic formulae, the neatest administrative solutions. They will never work unless they are first made *acceptable* to the people.'

Even before this speech and letter were published, Shelton's canvass returns were highly encouraging. The latest tally before the week-end showed 120 votes for Margaret, 84 for Heath, and nine for Fraser. This meant that Heath had *already* lost the 42-vote lead he needed for an outright first ballot win. Neave duly reported this fact, but not the figures, to the political correspondents of the Sunday newspapers, though he cautiously admitted that Heath could still finish up ahead. Walker and Baker, however, were presenting a very different picture, claiming that the result on Tuesday would be a clear win for Heath.

From these two assessments much of the Press concluded that Heath was well ahead. Some Sunday papers also made much of Margaret's assertion, in a recorded television interview to be screened on the Monday, that she had no intention of appointing

Enoch Powell to her Front Bench team : 'I cannot forget that Mr. Powell deserted his own people who had supported him. I know just how those people felt when the person for whom they'd worked suddenly turns round and says, "I'm not going to fight for you any longer. Indeed, I'm going to advise people to vote for the person you've been fighting against".'

This struck Tory MPs as a statement of the obvious : Powell was no longer in the party, and was as likely to find himself on the Tory Front Bench as Jeremy Thorpe. However, her words came as a shock to those of the Press who still regarded her as a candidate of the far Right.

Meanwhile the papers had their feast of pictures. On Saturday Margaret allowed photographers into her kitchen as she got on with the week-end task of washing up, while the driver of the train from Doncaster to King's Cross was surprised when Heath appeared at his cab with photographers to shake his hand and thank him for a smooth run.

Thus by the time the strategy group met at Flood Street on Sunday, February 2, the lines of battle had been clearly drawn. Margaret had set out her position in two week-end statements. Heath was campaigning on the correctness of his past policies, and on his belief that his brand of Conservatism was more likely to retrieve electoral support than the policies of Margaret and her backers. In fact, though at the start of the campaign a substantial number of those publicly supporting her might have been labelled as Right-wing, this became far less true as the days went by. After I joined the campaign committee in the last week in January it was noticeable how at each meeting the active workers represented a broader and broader spread of opinion in the party.

The most puzzling aspect of the situation that Sunday was the obvious disparity in the canvass returns of the two sides. When Walker and Baker told the Press and backbenchers that Heath would win outright there may have been an element of calculation that MPs would rush to be on the winning side, but they were not lying. They had their canvass figures, and they genuinely believed them. Yet clearly one of the campaign groups must be working on faulty figures. It was therefore agreed at Flood Street that in the next two days the Thatcher campaign team would check back on as many of their promised supporters as possible, to ensure that Shelton's figures were accurate.

However, over that final week-end before the first ballot there were two developments which were judged to have strengthened Heath's cause. The first was a statement by Lord Home on BBC Radio that in his judgement Heath was the best person to lead the Conservative Party in the future. This, it was thought, might swing some votes in view of the high respect in which he was held on the Tory benches. The second was the sounding of constituency opinions by the officers of the National Union, through their area chairmen, which appeared to be coming down strongly in Heath's favour.

This was partly because Margaret's 'manifesto' statements had come too late to be absorbed by the majority of local association officers throughout the country; but ironically it also owed something to the fact that backbenchers had not reported to their local supporters the rotten state of the party at Westminster for fear of further damaging morale. Meanwhile, each backbencher was informed by his constituency chairman of the result of the soundings within his own association. In my constituency the verdict was 3–2 in Heath's favour, with support for Margaret apparently being stronger among branch officers than among those lower down.

The outcome of these soundings was formally reported to members of the 1922 Executive by Sir John Taylor, chairman of the National Union, on Monday, February 3. This was that 70 per cent of the constituency associations throughout Britain supported Heath. However, some four-fifths of these indicated that they would have preferred a wider choice of candidates. This pattern was conveyed by the 1922 Executive to any Tory MP who asked, some of whom then relayed it to the Press as evidence that the party in the country was solidly behind Heath. This was not necessarily true, of course, since the National Union's figures were perfectly compatible with a substantial minority of Margaret supporters in each constituency. However, it was certainly true that the majority of Tory workers away from the internal strife at Westminster were rallying loyally to the man they had followed to defeat only four months before—a not unworthy quality in the Tory Party.

It was at this point, as the Press reported Heath's position to be strengthening, that Neave decided something must be done to remind backbenchers at the last minute of the basic issues at stake. For a while we considered circulating photo-copies of the leading article in *The Times* on Saturday, which had concluded :

HOUSE OF COMMONS
LONDON SWIA OAA

ELECTION OF A LEADER OF THE CONSERVATIVE PARTY

The votes for each candidate in the Second Ballot
were as follows:

Geoffrey Howe *19*
John Peyton *11*
James Prior *19*
Margaret Thatcher *146*
William Whitelaw *79*

Scrutineers

The conditions of the procedure having been fulfilled
Margaret Thatcher is elected.

Chairman, 1922 Committee
11 February, 1975

The notice declaring Margaret Thatcher elected Leader of the Conservative
Party in Parliament, signed by Edward du Cann as presiding officer, other 1922
Committee officers, and the candidates' scrutineers. This was immediately
displayed in the Whips' Office.

Margaret Thatcher, Leader of the Conservative Party.

Mr. Heath has not freed himself from his mistakes and does not seem capable of doing so. However much one may appreciate his high standing in the world, and his honourable character and strength of purpose, Mr. Heath, whether elected or no, cannot offer a future to the Conservative Party so long as he is the prisoner of his past.

However, it was thought wiser instead to send letters to both *The Times* and the *Daily Telegraph* to appear the following morning before MPs cast their votes. So the letters were drafted, signed by Neave and Shelton, and sent off—a kind of final appeal to the voters by the Thatcher campaign committee. The two letters were worded differently, but both made the point that the party needed the inspiration of a new Leader to win back the ground it had lost. And both concluded that 'a majority of Conservative MPs know in their hearts that we cannot go on as we are.'

Late that night, on eve-of-poll, the Thatcher campaign committee met. As always the proceedings were good humoured, even jocular, but this time there was a nervous edge to the laughter. Shelton collected the final canvass reports; Neave said that after all the re-checking the vote was going to be close, and warned against any premature jubilation. Then the two campaign managers went to Neave's room to add up the canvass figures. Altogether 23 backbenchers had either not been contacted, would not say or were abstaining. Of the remainder 122 were for Margaret, 122 for Heath, and nine for Fraser. The two looked at each other in wonderment. This was better than they had dared to hope.

As the day of the first ballot dawned Margaret was up early to cook breakfast for Denis before he drove to his office in Swindon. At 8 am Shelton phoned to give her the previous night's canvass return. No one was going to secure an outright win, he said; it was going to be close, and with a bit of luck she might actually pull ahead. At 9 am Margaret drove to the Commons, where she faced another busy day on the Finance Bill. At noon, in Committee Room 14, the voting began, under the supervision of du Cann as 1922 chairman and members of his Executive. Margaret voted just before 1 pm before leaving for a working lunch on the Finance Bill provisions with some businessmen in the City.

Meanwhile, however, the Press had been inquiring from the

campaign managers about the closing state of play. Walker and
Baker were full of confidence; they had no doubt their man
would win outright. But when Neave was approached he seemed
surprisingly cautious. The result would be close—that was all he
would say. So the evening newspaper political correspondents
drew their own conclusions. 'Ted Forges Ahead', proclaimed the
headline in the London *Evening Standard*. For the Thatcher
camp this presentation could not have been better. For the small
number of backbenchers who were intending to abstain in the
hope of opening the field to other candidates in the second ballot
realised with a start that if Heath got his 42-vote lead their
purpose would be frustrated. Their only way of bringing the
reported Heath bandwagon to a halt was to vote for Margaret
in the first ballot—which was what they did. Thus the confident
claims of the Heath camp were counter-productive; Neave had
been politically far more astute.

When Margaret returned from her lunch she went straight to
her room, then on to Neave's office to await the news. The ballot
closed at 3.30, whereupon officers of the 1922 Executive began
counting the votes, scrutinised by Shelton representing Margaret
and by Kitson representing Heath. Kitson was confident of his
candidate's strength till the very end. Before the counting began
the two principal scrutineers made bets with one another; Kitson
bet £1 that Heath would get more than 130 votes, and Shelton
bet £1 that Margaret would get more than 110. By this time
about eighty Tory MPs were waiting in suspense in the corridor
outside. First sign of the way the voting had gone came when
the scrutineers emerged to rush the news to their candidates.
Shelton's face was expressionless, but Kitson's was ashen. Clearly
Heath had not done well. Then, after the MPs had trooped into
the Committee Room, du Cann announced the result :

Margaret Thatcher	130
Edward Heath	119
Hugh Fraser	16

Thus Margaret was ahead by 11 votes. The figures brought
first a gasp of astonishment, and then a cheer from backbenchers.
Outside the Press could scarcely believe it either. The situation
in the Tory Party had been transformed.

On the floor above Shelton gave the figures to Neave, who
went in to see Margaret alone.

'It's good news,' he said. 'You're ahead in the poll. There will be a second ballot, and you got 130 votes.'

Soon afterwards, to a mass of jostling photographers, television cameras and political correspondents in a hastily commandeered Committee Room, Margaret declared that 'the result is a very good basis on which to go forward. We believe that our vote will remain firm in the second ballot, and we hope to attract a few more. We go forward on the basis of quiet confidence.' Then, declining further interviews, she returned to her work on the Finance Bill Committee, breaking off later to attend a short celebration in Neave's Westminster flat.

The result could hardly have been worse for Heath. However you looked at the figures, more than half the Parliamentary Party had voted against him as Leader.

Looking back, one can easily see how his supporters had set about their task the wrong way. First, weeks before, they had shielded him from the strength of backbench dissatisfaction with the state of the party and with his own rigid policy position. Whether this was because they genuinely believed the dissatisfaction to be only skin deep, or because they refused to face its implications, none can tell. However, the very fact that there was such a gulf in understanding between Heath's immediate circle and the majority of backbenchers is itself a revealing comment on the state the party was in. Second, and arising from this, they had totally misjudged the mood of the party in the way they had run their campaign. On the policy level it smacked of complacency, and on the organisation level of condescension. The contrived flattery of lunch invitations probably offended as many as it impressed, and was lost on many of the 1974 intake.

Third, it was a major mistake to have as campaign managers those who were tied quite so personally to Heath. He did not have a reputation for ever advancing those who disagreed with him, and when canvassed for support by the Leader's Parliamentary Private Secretary there must have been many backbenchers who gave an ambiguous reply. After all, if Heath did win they did not want a black mark against their names for ever. In much the same way, over a lunch table, many naturally shrank from offending their hosts. And so it came about that the Heath team's canvass returns were so hopelessly optimistic. Heath would have done much better to appoint as his campaign manager one of those senior and well-liked backbenchers who still gave him their support.

Finally, even if his strength had been what their canvass figures suggested, it was a psychological blunder to claim, both before the previous week-end and on the day of the ballot itself, that Heath was home and dry, since this served only to drive a number of intending abstainers into the Thatcher camp.

Heath awaited the news in his Leader of the Opposition's room with his old friend Lord Aldington for company. As soon as Kitson gave him the figures he knew his leadership was over. 'So we got it all wrong,' was his reported comment. For twenty minutes he and Aldington talked the situation over. Then he announced his resignation, and asked Robert Carr to act as Opposition Leader until his successor was finally elected. Heath's ten years of leadership, which began with such promise and reached such a high peak of hope in 1970–71, were at an end.

CHAPTER FIFTEEN

The Backbench Revolution
February 11, 1975

Several in the Shadow Cabinet had already wondered whether they should throw their hats into the ring in the event of Ted Heath securing only a small lead over Margaret Thatcher. Now his sudden resignation had the effect of a starter's gun. Soon afterwards Party Chairman William Whitelaw announced his candidature, saying, 'I can only hope that I might be able to do something to unite our party.' It was not long before others joined in—Jim Prior, a very old friend of Heath's; Sir Geoffrey Howe, rather more detached but still a Heath supporter in the first ballot; and John Peyton, the sharply witty Shadow Leader of the House. Then came the news that ex-Ministers Maurice Macmillan and Julian Amery were thinking of joining in the race too. It looked like a long field, which would make it more difficult for any contestant to get the necessary 139 votes—50 per cent plus one—to secure victory this time round. If there was no conclusive result again, then the top three would have to go forward to a third ballot, to be decided by single transferable vote—in which case almost anything could happen.

On the evening of October 5 a still larger Thatcher campaign committee, now including some former Heath voters, met in the Commons basement. The mood was buoyant and elated. There was a cheer when Norman St. John-Stevas, Shadow Education Minister and a former Heath voter, joined the committee, and another for Keith Joseph. But a lot of work lay ahead, for a completely fresh canvass was necessary. Neave and Shelton had always known that some forty of those voting for Margaret in the first ballot did so only to keep the door open for someone else— generally Whitelaw—in the second. Heath's official campaigners were urging their followers to swing behind Whitelaw in order to block Margaret, yet it was among the remaining sixty or so former Heath votes that Margaret had to look to offset her losses

and then give her the further nine votes she needed to win. Some
Thatcher committee men arrived at the October 5 meeting
having already canvassed afresh a number of their colleagues.
Shelton called through the roll of Tory MPs and marked 160
straight away.

At this stage the tally was : Margaret, 99; Whitelaw, 41;
Peyton, 8; Howe, 7; Prior, 5. The following night, after
nominations had closed, and it was confirmed that neither
Macmillan nor Amery was standing, the figures were : Margaret,
106; Whitelaw, 46; Howe, 11; Peyton, 8; Prior, 6. Margaret
was indeed set up well. Her lead in the first ballot had given
her further credibility in the eyes of many, and she also gained
credit for having had the courage to risk all in the first ballot.
Many MPs were saying they wanted the leadership issue settled
without further ado. Margaret had the advantage, too, of having
already established the values in politics and the approach to
leadership which she represented. The others had to start from
scratch. Meanwhile, as they tried to cover the ground in seven
days that she had already covered in fourteen, she continued to
lead her team on the Finance Bill Committee, occasionally into
the early hours of the morning. And she still used Robin Cooke's
room to answer any questions from former Heath supporters
who wished to see her.

Margaret was now the front runner, and the others appeared
as challengers. Whitelaw was the strongest, and built a good deal
of his appeal upon his reputation as a conciliator. He believed
that party unity had been damaged as a result of MPs voting in
the first ballot contrary to the expressed wishes of constituency
workers, and that with his experience as Party Chairman he
could cement the two parts of the party together again. Further,
since he sat for a Cumberland seat, he had a popular appeal
and understanding of life further afield than the suburban
South-East.

However, Whitelaw had his difficulties. Though he needed to
pick up all the former Heath votes he could get, there were
evident dangers in being associated too closely with Heath's style
of leadership. So Whitelaw promised that under him 'no one
will be excluded because his or her ideas are different from my
own'. And, though some of Heath's closest circle were now backing him, their expressions of support did not carry great weight
since only a week or two before they had been busy trying to talk

down his leadership qualities. All in all, though he had considerable support in the leader columns of the Press, Whitelaw's task was a formidable one.

The only other candidate to cause the Thatcher campaign committee any anxiety was Howe. He had a small team around him composed largely of other lawyers, but unlike Whitelaw he had a reputation as a policy rethinker, which gave him some appeal among the younger and intellectually questioning MPs who had tended to line up behind Margaret. During this week Shelton had to warn the committee that, though Howe was not a serious challenger, any growth in his support was likely to be at the expense of Margaret, thereby denying her the necessary clear majority.

For a couple of days after the first ballot Margaret issued no further statements on her policy position. However, several of us were anxious that the myth that she was 'cool on Europe' was proving an impediment in attracting those who had voted for Heath largely on the grounds of his European commitment. So it was decided that on Friday, February 7, she would issue a statement clearing the matter up beyond all doubt. In this she said that Heath's outstanding achievement had been to lead Britain into the European Community. 'This torch must be picked up and carried by whoever is chosen by the party to succeed him. The commitment to European partnership is one which I fully share.'

The political week was due to end with the Young Conservatives' national conference in Eastbourne, at which both Margaret and Whitelaw had been invited to speak on the Saturday. There was some nervousness at Westminster over this. Parts of the YC movement had been strong supporters of Heath, and during the first ballot special YC T-shirts proclaiming 'Vote for the Grocer, not the Grocer's Daughter' (an allusion to the nickname given to Heath by the satirical journal *Private Eye*) had been sported by attractive young girls for the benefit of the Press. There were some fears, therefore, of hostile demonstrations at Eastbourne against the woman primarily responsible for displacing him. Some of Whitelaw's backers also feared the two candidates would be caught up in demonstration and counter-demonstration, and there was some talk of neither of them attending. However, both did—and the fears proved groundless. The very strong pro-Heath feeling had come very much from the Greater London YCs, who had some good campaigners as

leaders, but who were not typical of YCs throughout the country.
Whitelaw began with a question session on party organisation
which offered little scope for stirring statements, though his plea
to broaden the base of the party earned a warm response.

Margaret's task was to reply to the economic debate—an
opportunity of which she took full advantage. After reviewing
the speeches from the floor, she launched into a statement of
belief which had the delegates cheering almost every sentence :

'Our challenge is to create the kind of economic background
which enables private initiative and private enterprise to flourish
for the benefit of the consumer, employee, the pensioner and
society as a whole. But that is not everything. You can get your
economic policies right, yet still have the kind of society none of
us would wish. I believe we should judge people on merit, and
not on background. I believe the person who is prepared to work
hardest should get the greatest rewards and keep them after tax;
that we should back the workers and not the shirkers; that it is
not only permissible but praiseworthy to want to benefit your
own family by your own efforts. Liberty must never be confused
with licence, and you cannot have liberty without a just law
impartially administered. You would not have political liberty
for long if all power and property went to the State. Those who
prosper themselves have a duty and responsibility to care for
others. Individual responsibility does not stop at home, but
extends to the community of which we are all a part.'

This was Margaret speaking straight from the heart, developing in her own words the same theme of a free and responsible
society which Heath had expounded with such effect in Blackpool's Winter Gardens in October 1970, the theme which is the
very core of Conservatism. Her reward was a standing ovation
from the 1,300 delegates representing the youth wing of the Tory
Party. The message got across to a wider television audience too,
for this was Margaret's first big platform occasion since the start
of the leadership contest.

This triumph behind her, she strolled out into the sunshine
with Whitelaw to get some lunch. There was the now familiar
jostle of Press cameras as photographers clamoured for pictures
of them together. 'Closer together, please . . . closer.' 'Give her a
kiss,' said one Pressman jocularly—and Whitelaw, on the spur
of the moment, did. Pictures of the two embracing were in
virtually every Sunday newspaper, and provided Press and public
with some light relief. But the incident, though trivial, illustrated

well the changed temper of the leadership contest. The tension and at times personal animosity between rival supporters that had characterised the first ballot stage was gone; now it was a much more rational contest between colleagues who knew they could work together happily when it was over.

In the closing stages of the second-ballot campaign every candidate was stressing the need to recreate party unity, and indeed unity within the nation too. On Sunday Margaret had an article on the leader-page of the *Sunday Express*, which enabled her to give her view.

After the leadership contest, she wrote, 'there will be no difficulty about uniting the Tory Party. What unites a party in Opposition is the consciousness that it has a valid and appealing *message* for the British people. And this I am determined we shall have. The party will unite itself. What *I* want to do is to unite the country . . . This will not be done by vague appeals for "national unity". Still less can it be achieved by a mish-mash of compromises designed to try to please everybody. That would only get us deeper into trouble. The job of politicians is not to please everyone—which is impossible—but to do justice to everyone.'

That afternoon I gave the Press Association her final policy statement, projecting the unity theme to achieving a proper regional balance within the party :

'Real unity will not be secured simply by declaring that one will unify. Unity is achieved through *involvement* . . . We also secure unity by seeing that the different parts of Britain are represented in our team. It is true that as a party we have too narrow a South-East base. We must regain the ground we have lost in the industrial areas of the Midlands and North, in Scotland and Wales. This will be my priority if elected Leader.'

When Keith Joseph, Neave and Shelton conferred with Margaret at her home that evening they knew that her appeal had now been broadened to embrace many from all sections of the party who had not been with her at the start of the campaign. The further factor that was running in her favour was the general wish in the party to bring the contest to an early and conclusive end. In the first ballot a number of MPs had voted tactically to produce a second ballot. If anyone voted tactically this time it would be to avoid a third.

This factor was reinforced the following day, when the officers of the National Union reported to the 1922 Executive the result of the constituency soundings taken that week-end. The pattern was strongly in Margaret's favour, with a strong plea to produce a conclusive result as soon as possible.

This was in line with soundings in my own constituency association. At a meeting of my Executive Council on Friday night I had explained my support for Margaret, then taken a secret ballot on whom members would themselves vote for at the second stage. The result was 34 for Margaret and 17 for all other candidates.

Besides strengthening Margaret, the National Union's recommendation also weakened Whitelaw's position in a different way. For through the previous week he had been projected as the man to bring together the party in Parliament and in the country, following the damage inflicted by MPs spurning the first ballot advice from the constituencies. But now the constituencies' advice was to vote for Margaret, thereby turning the argument against him.

At 10 pm on Monday, February 10, the Thatcher campaign committee held what was to prove its last meeting. By then virtually all MPs had either declared their support or been canvassed, and as Shelton called through the roll the final gaps were filled. Neave took a quick look at the list, and again warned that a conclusive win was still not certain. A few defections could easily tip the scales to a third ballot. Then, after the rest of us had left, the final canvass count was made. It was: Margaret, 137; Whitelaw, 78; Howe, 19; Prior, 11; Peyton, 9. Another nine were 'doubtful-plus' (believed on balance to favour Margaret), and 13 doubtful or uncanvassed. Thus while her total was 137, all the other figures totalled 139. However, it was reasonable to suppose that enough of the doubtfuls would go her way to give her a narrow victory. At 11 pm the figures were given to Margaret.

As usual she left home early on Tuesday, February 11, to attend to her Finance Bill Committee business. By this time the sole question in the minds of Tory MPs was whether she would make it this time, or whether the party would be forced into the unsatisfactory procedure of a third ballot decided by single transferable votes. As before, the ballot opened in Committee Room 14 at midday, and closed at 3.30, whereupon a large crowd of Tory MPs waited outside for the result. Just before

4 o'clock the scrutineers emerged, their expressions inscrutable. But following them came the 1922 officers, one of whom gave me a sharp dig in the ribs. At that moment I knew Margaret was home and dry. After we had all entered the room du Cann announced the final figures :

Margaret Thatcher	146
William Whitelaw	79
Geoffrey Howe	19
James Prior	19
John Peyton	11

Margaret had gained her overall majority with seven votes to spare, and was 67 votes ahead of her nearest rival. In fact, her 146 total was exactly the sum of Shelton's 137 total from the canvass and the nine 'doubtful-plus'. His forecast figure for Whitelaw's vote was one out, and for Howe's exactly right. As backbenchers cheered the figures none could deny it was a convincing victory.

Again Margaret awaited the result in Neave's tiny office, with Joan Hall in support. But this time Neave broke the news to her more directly : 'It's all right—you're Leader of the Opposition !' For the next fifteen minutes her campaign supporters left her alone to prepare for the hectic hours that lay ahead. She rang Denis to tell him the great news, but he had already read it on the tapes. Then she began scribbling the simple message she was to read at the Press conference that had been arranged in the Grand Committee Room off Westminster Hall. She read it over to us, and it sounded just right. Some old friends looked in to offer congratulations, and a bottle of champagne was produced, though Margaret drank little herself.

Soon after, in the Grand Committee Room, she expressed her feelings : 'To me it is like a dream that the next name in the list after Harold Macmillan, Sir Alec Douglas-Home and Edward Heath is Margaret Thatcher. Each has brought his own style of leadership and stamp of greatness to his task, and I shall take on the work with humility and dedication.'

After thanking her helpers, she added : 'It is important to me that this prize has been won in *open electoral contest* with four other potential leaders. I know they will be disappointed, but I hope we shall soon be back working together as colleagues for

the things in which we all believe. There is much to do, and I
hope you will allow me time to do it thoughtfully and well.'

After this police and campaigners helped her through the
enthusiastic crowd outside the Commons to take her to television
interviews and another Press conference, this time before the
cameras, in Conservative Central Office, whose facilities were
now at her disposal as Leader of the Opposition. Immediately
after she attended her first official function by taking up one of
Heath's cancelled engagements at a supper meeting of the
Conservative Group for Europe in St. Stephen's Club, which
enabled her to underline again her commitment to the European
ideal. From there to a small celebration party in Shelton's flat
in Pimlico before returning to the Commons for dinner with
Humphrey Atkins, the Chief Whip. Finally, at the end of a
momentous day, she went again to the Finance Bill Committee
where she had spent so many late-night hours to take her leave.
As she did she was loudly applauded—by MPs on both sides.

So the Conservatives became the first party in Britain to
choose a woman as Leader and potential Prime Minister. For
that reason alone it was a historic decision. But, for the Conservative Party, something far more important had happened.
For the first time in its history, Tory backbenchers had carried
through a successful revolution of their own against the pressure
and advice of almost the entire party Establishment. It was
backbenchers, not the Leader or his Shadow Cabinet, who
forced a ballot, and it was a backbenchers' candidate who
emerged triumphant from it. When the election was announced
on January 23, and in the first ballot, Margaret had the support
of *only one* member of a Shadow Cabinet of twenty-three, she
was regarded with suspicion by most of those managing the party
machine at Central Office, and opposed by many in the National
Union. In short, she was an anti-Establishment candidate. Her
campaign manager was a backbencher, backbenchers of varying
shades of opinion made up her campaign committee, and it was
backbenchers who voted decisively for change.

It had never happened like this before in the party's history.
Under the old 'magic circle' system of consultations the party's
senior figures had the preponderant voice. When Eden followed
Churchill, it was a natural Establishment succession. When Eden
fell, it was the party's elder statesmen, Churchill and Lord
Salisbury, who advised the Queen to send for Macmillan. Again,
when Macmillan stood down the test of whether Lord Home

would succeed was whether he could form a Cabinet from the
existing Front Bench, and whether R. A. Butler would agree to
serve in it. This is not to say that these successors did not have
the support of backbenchers, they did; but it was at the *top* of
the party that the final decisions were made.

Even the formal ballotting process by which Heath was
elected in 1965 was not directly comparable with the very open
style of leadership election ten years later; rather, it marked the
transition to it. In 1965 the secret ballot was an innovation, but
the techniques of persuasion that preceeded it were very much
those of the old 'magic circle'·—discreet phone calls, and backbenchers following the leads given by an Establishment that was
divided on personal preferences rather than on any principles.
By contrast, those on both sides *in the first ballot* in 1975 felt
that vital party principles were at stake, and in both ballots
there was open campaigning with 'manifesto' statements and
candidates available to answer questions from the electors.

The result was that, after two sucessive election defeats, the
whole Conservative Party, outside the Commons as well as in,
was forced to ask itself and answer the vital questions of what
its real values and objectives were and how it could best secure
them. The therapeutic value of the exercise was proved after
her election by the surge of enthusiasm for Margaret's leadership
at every level of the party, and the receptions she received in
Scotland as much as in the South-East. It was as if something
pent up had suddenly been released.

Nine days after her election as Leader of the Opposition,
Margaret Thatcher was formally elected Leader of the Conservative Party to tumultuous applause from more than six
hundred MPs, peers and representatives of the National Union
at a meeting in the Europa Hotel. Lord Hailsham, who had
inspired her in politics when she was a student at Oxford,
proposed the motion, which was seconded by Whitelaw, now her
Deputy Leader on the Front Bench. In her speech, Margaret
said that 'somehow I feel there have been times when we have
lost our vision for the future, and we know that where there is
no vision the people will surely perish'. People throughout the
land were seeking two things above all—a forthright style of
leadership, and greater emphasis on principle. She would do her
best to provide both.

Lord Hailsham also read a telegram of warm congratulations
to the new Leader. 'It is an immense privilege to be elected to

this office and to be able to serve the party in it,' the message ran. 'Grave problems face us as a nation and as a party, which will not be overcome simply or easily, and which will need both skill and determination for their solution. Margaret Thatcher has both, and I sincerely wish her well.'

The message was from Ted Heath.

'What's Wrong With Politics?'

Margaret Thatcher's address to the Conservative Political Centre meeting on October 10, 1968, during the party conference at Blackpool, was the first comprehensive statement of her political philosophy to appear on paper. Though of course it was based upon her political experience up to that date, much of it is just as relevant today. Her paper is reprinted below, with only a few currently topical references deleted, by kind permission of the Conservative Political Centre.

Dissatisfaction with politics runs deep both here and abroad. People have come to doubt the future of the democratic system and its institutions. They distrust the politicians and have little faith in the future.

Why the present distrust?

Let us try to assess how and why we have reached this pass. What is the explanation? Broadly speaking I think we have not yet assimilated many of the changes that have come about in the past thirty to forty years.

First, I don't think we realise sufficiently how new our present democratic system is. We still have comparatively little experience of the effect of the universal franchise which didn't come until 1928. And the first election in this country which was fought on the principle of one person one vote was in 1950. So we are still in the early stages of dealing with the problems and opportunities presented by everyone having a vote.

Secondly, this and other factors have led to a different party political structure. There is now little room for independent members and the controversies which formerly took place outside the parties on a large number of measures now have to take place inside. There is, and has to be room for a variety of opinions on certain topics within the broad general principles on which each party is based.

Thirdly, from the party political structure has risen the detailed programme which is placed before the electorate. Return to power on such a programme has led to a new doctrine that the party in power has a mandate to carry out everything in its manifesto. I myself doubt whether the voters really are endorsing each and every particular when they return a government to power.

This modern practice of an election programme has, I believe, influenced the attitudes of some elections; all too often one is now asked 'what are you going to do for me?', implying that the programme is a series of promises in return for votes. All this has led to a curious relationship between elector and elected. If the elector suspects the politician of making promises simply to get his vote, he despises him, but if the promises are not forthcoming he may reject him. *I believe that parties and elections are about more than rival lists of miscellaneous promises—indeed, if they were not, democracy would scarcely be worth preserving.*

Fourthly, the extensive and all-pervading development of the welfare state is also comparatively new, not only here but in other countries as well. You will recollect that one of the four great freedoms in President Roosevelt's wartime declaration was 'freedom from want'. Since then in the Western world there has been a series of measures designed to give greater security. I think it would be true to say that there is no longer a struggle to achieve a basic security. Further, we have a complete new generation whose whole life has been lived against the background of the welfare state. These developments must have had a great effect on the outlook and approach of our people even if we cannot yet assess it properly.

Fifthly, one of the effects of the rapid spread of higher education has been to equip people to criticise and question almost everything. Some of them seem to have stopped there instead of going on to the next stage which is to arrive at new beliefs or to reaffirm old ones. You will perhaps remember seeing in the Press the report that the student leader Daniel Cohn-Bendit has been awarded a degree on the result of his past work. His examiners said that he had posed a series of most intelligent questions. Significant? I would have been happier had he also found a series of intelligent answers.

Sixthly, we have far more information about events than ever before and since the advent of television, news is presented much more vividly. It is much more difficult to ignore situations which you have seen on film with your own eyes than if you had merely read about them, perhaps skimming the page rather hurriedly. Television is not merely one extra means of communication, it is a medium which because of the way it presents things is radically influencing the judgements we have to make about events and about people, including politicians.

Seventhly, our innate international idealism has received many nasty shocks. Many of our people long to believe that if representatives of all nations get together dispassionately to discuss burning international problems, providence and goodwill will guide them to wise and just conclusions, and peace and international law and order will thereby be secured. But in practice a number of nations vote not according to right or wrong even when it is a clear case to us, but according to their national expediencies. And some of the speeches and propaganda to explain blatant actions would make the angels weep as well as the electorate.

All of these things are a partial explanation of the disillusion and disbelief we encounter today. The changes have been tremendous and I am not surprised that the whole system is under cross-examination. I welcome healthy scepticism and questioning. *It is our job continually to retest old assumptions and to seek new ideas. But we must not try to find one unalterable answer that will solve all our problems for none can exist. . . .*

In that spirit and against the background I have sketched, let us try to analyse what has gone wrong.

The great mistake—too much government

I believe that the great mistake of the last few years has been for the government to provide or to legislate for almost everything. Part of this policy has its roots in the plans for reconstruction in the postwar period when governments assumed all kinds of new obligations. The policies may have been warranted at the time but they have gone far further than was intended or is advisable. During our own early and middle period of government we were concerned to set the framework in which people could achieve their own standards for themselves, subject always to a basic standard. But it has often seemed to me that from the early 1960s the emphasis in politics shifted. At about that time 'growth' became the key political word. If resources grew by X per cent per annum this would provide the extra money needed for the government to make further provision. The doctrine found favour at the time and we had a bit of a contest between the parties about the highest possible growth rate. Four per cent or more? *But the result was that for the time being the emphasis in political debate ceased to be about people and became about economics.* Plans were made to achieve a 4 per cent growth rate. Then came the present government with a bigger plan and socialist ideas about its implementation, that is to say if people didn't conform to the plan, they had to be compelled to. Hence compulsion on Prices and Incomes policy and with it the totally unacceptable notion that the government shall have the power to fix which wages and salaries should increase.

We started off with a wish on the part of the people for more government intervention in certain spheres. This was met. But there came a time when the amount of intervention got so great that it could no longer be exercised in practice by government but only by more and more officials or bureaucrats. Now it is difficult if not impossible for people to get at the official making the decision and so paradoxically although the degree of inter-vention is greater, the government has become more and more *remote* from the people. The present result of the democratic process has therefore been an increasing authoritarianism. . . .

Recently more and more feature articles have been written and speeches made about involving people more closely with decisions of the government and enabling them to participate in some of those decisions.

But the way to get personal involvement and participation is not for people to take part in more and more governmental decisions but to make the government reduce the area of decision over which it presides and consequently leave the private citizen to 'participate', if that be the fashionable word, by making more of his own decisions. What we need now is a far greater degree of personal responsibility and decision, far more independence from the government, and a comparative reduction in the role of government.

These beliefs have important implications for policy.

Prices and incomes

First, Prices and Incomes policy. The most effective prices policy has not come by controlling prices by the government, through the Prices and Incomes Board, but through the Con-

servative way of seeing that competition flourishes. There have
been far more price cuts in the supermarkets than in the nationalised industries. This shows the difference between the
government doing the job itself and the government creating
the conditions under which prices will be kept down through
effective competition.

On the Incomes side, there seemed to be some confusion in the
minds of the electorate about where the parties stood. This was
not surprising in the early days because a number of speeches and
documents from both sides of the House showed a certain
similarity. For example, here are four separate quotations—two
from the Labour Government and two from our period of office.
They are almost indistinguishable.

1. 'Increases in the general level of wage rates must be related to
   increased productivity due to increased efficiency and effort.'
   (White Paper on Employment Policy, 1944)
2. 'It is essential therefore that there should be no further general
   increase in the level of personal incomes without at least a
   corresponding increase in the volume of production.' (Sir
   Stafford Cripps, 1948)
3. 'The Government's policy is to promote a faster rate of
   economic growth. . . . But the policy will be put in jeopardy if
   money incomes rise faster than the volume of national production.' (Para. 1 of Incomes Policy, *The Next Step*, Cmnd
   1626, February 1962)
4. '. . . the major objectives of national policy must be . . . to raise
   productivity and efficiency so that real national output can
   increase and so keep increases in wages, salaries and other
   forms of income in line with this increase.' (Schedule 2,
   Prices and Incomes Act, 1966)

All of these quotes express general economic propositions, but
the policies which flowed from those propositions were very
different. We rejected from the outset the use of compulsion.
This was absolutely right. The role of the government is not to
control each and every salary that is paid. It has no means of
measuring the correct amount. Moreover, having to secure the
state's approval before one increases the pay of an employee is
repugnant to most of us.

There is another aspect of the way in which Incomes policy is
now operated to which I must draw attention. We now put so

much emphasis on the control of incomes that we have too little regard for the essential role of government, which is the control of money supply and management of demand. Greater attention to this role and less to the outward detailed control would have achieved more for the economy. It would mean, of course, that the government had to exercise itself some of the disciplines on expenditure it is so anxious to impose on others. It would mean that expenditure in the vast public sector would not have to be greater than the amount which could be financed out of taxation plus genuine saving. For a number of years some expenditure has been financed by what amounts to printing the money. There is nothing *laissez-faire* or old-fashioned about the views I have expressed. It is a modern view of the role the government should play now, arising from the mistakes of the past, the results of which we are experiencing today.

Tax and the social services

The second policy implication concerns taxation and the social services. It is no accident that the Conservative Party has been one which has reduced the rates of taxation. The decisions have not been a haphazard set of expediences, or merely economic decisions to meet the needs of the moment. They have stemmed from the real belief that government intervention and control tends to reduce the role of the individual, his importance and the desirability that he should be primarily responsible for his own future. When it comes to the development of the social services, the policy must mean that people should be encouraged if necessary by taxation incentives to make increasing provision for themselves out of their own resources. The basic standards through the state would remain as a foundation for extra private provision. Such a policy would have the advantage that the government could concentrate on providing things which the citizen can't. Hospitals are one specific example. . . .

Independence from the state

To return to the personal theme, if we accept the need for increasing responsibility for self and family it means that we must stop approaching things in an atmosphere of restriction. There is nothing wrong in people wanting larger incomes. It would seem a worthy objective for men and women to wish to raise the standard of living for their families and to give them greater opportunities than they themselves had. I wish more people would do it. We should then have fewer saying 'the state must do it'. What is *wrong* is that people should want more without giving anything in return. The condition precedent to high wages and high salaries is hard work. This is a quite different and much more stimulating approach than one of keeping down incomes.

Doubtless there will be accusers that we are only interested in more money. This just is not so. Money is not an end in itself. It enables one to live the kind of life of one's own choosing. Some will prefer to put a large amount to raising material standards, others will pursue music, the arts, the cultures, others will use their money to help those here and overseas about whose needs they feel strongly, and do not let us underestimate the amount of hard earned cash that this nation gives voluntarily to worthy causes. The point is that even the Good Samaritan had to have the money to help, otherwise he too would have had to pass on the other side.

In choice of way of life J. S. Mill's views are as relevant as ever :

'The only freedom which deserves the name is that of pursuing our own good in our own way so long as we do not deprive others of theirs, or impede their efforts to obtain it. . . . Mankind are greater gainers by suffering each other to live as seems good to themselves than by compelling each to live as seems good to the rest.'

These policies have one further important implication. Together they succeed at the same time in giving people a measure of *independence from the state*—and who wants a people dependent on the state and turning to the state for their every need—also they succeed in drawing power away from governments and diffusing it more widely among people and non-governmented institutions.

The problem of size

The second mistake politics have made at present is in some ways related to the first one. We have become bewitched with the idea of size.

As a result people no longer feel important in the scheme of things. They have the impression that everything has become so big, so organised, so standardised and governmentalised that there is no room for the individual, his talents, his requirements or his wishes. He no longer counts.

It is not difficult to see how this feeling has come about. In industry the merits of size have been extolled for some years now and too little attention given to its demerits. Size brings great problems. One of the most important is the problem of making and communicating decisions. The task of decision tends to be concentrated at the top, and and fewer people get used to weighing up a problem, taking a decision, sticking to it and carrying the consequences. The buck is passed. But even *after* a decision has been made, there is the problem of communicating it to those who have to carry it out in such a way that it is understood, and they are made to feel a part of the team. In a large-scale organisation, whether government, local government or industry, failure to do this can lead to large-scale mistakes, large-scale confusion and large-scale resentment. These problems, can, and must be, overcome, but all too often they are not.

Government agencies and the public

The third mistake is that people feel they don't count when they try to get something done through government agencies.

Consider our relations with government departments. We start as a birth certificate; attract a maternity grant; give rise to a tax allowance and possibly a family allowance; receive a national health number when registered with a doctor; go to one or more schools where educational records are kept; apply for an educational grant; get a job; start paying national insurance and tax; take out a television and a driving licence; buy a house with a mortgage; pay rates; buy a few premium bonds; take out life assurance; purchase some shares; get married; start the whole thing over again; receive a pension and become a death certificate and death grant, and the subject of a file in the Estate Duty Office! Every one of these incidents will require a form or give rise to some office. *The amount of information collected in the various departments must be fabulous. Small wonder that life really does seem like 'one damned form after another'.*

A good deal of this form-filling will have to continue but I think it time to reassert a right to privacy. Ministers will have to look at this aspect in deciding how to administer their policies. There is a tendency on the part of some politicians to suggest that with the advent of computers all this information should be centralised and stored on magnetic tape. They argue that this would be time-saving and more efficient. Possibly it would; but other and more important things would be at stake. There would be produced for the first time a personal dossier about each person, on which everything would be recorded. In my view this would place far too much power in the hands of the state over the individual. In the USA there is a Congressional enquiry sitting on this very point because politicians there have recognised the far-reaching dangers of such a record.

Too much reliance on statistics, too little on judgement

Fourthly, I believe that there is too great a reliance on statistical forecasts; too little on judgement.

We all know the old one about lies, damned lies and statistics, and I do not wish to condemn statistics out of hand. Those who prepare them are well aware of their limitations. Those who use them are not so scrupulous.

Recently the economic forecasts have been far more optimistic than the events which happened. The balance of payments predictions have been wrong again and again. . . .

The truth is that statistical results do not displace the need for judgement, they increase it. The figures can be no better than the assumptions on which they are based and these could vary greatly. In addition, the unknown factor which, by its very nature is incapable of evaluation, may well be the determining one.

The party political system

Fifthly, we have not yet appreciated or used fully the virtues of our party political system. The essential characteristic of the British Constitutional system is not that there is an alternative personality but that there is an alternative policy and a whole alternative government ready to take office. As a result we have always had an Opposition to act as a focus of criticism against the government. We have therefore not suffered the fate of countries which have had a 'consensus' or central government, without an official opposition. This was one of the causes of trouble in Germany. Nor do we have the American system, which as far as Presidential campaigns go, appears to have become almost completely one of personalities.

There are dangers in consensus; it could be an attempt to satisfy people holding no particular views about anything. It seems more important to have a philosophy and policy which because they are good appeal to sufficient people to secure a majority.

A short time ago when speaking to a university audience and

stressing the theme of responsibility and independence a young undergraduate came to me and said 'I had no idea there was such a clear alternative'. He found the idea challenging and infinitely more effective than one in which everyone virtually expects their MP or the government to solve their problems. The Conservative creed has never offered a life of ease without effort. Democracy is not for such people. Self-government is for those men and women who have learned to govern themselves.

No great party can survive except on the basis of firm beliefs about what it wants to do. It is not enough to have reluctant support. We want people's enthusiasm as well.

'Education and Society'

On January 6, 1971, some seven months after becoming Education Secretary, Margaret Thatcher gave an address to the North of England Education Conference at Buxton, Derbyshire, on the theme 'Education and Society'. In this she stood back from immediate controversies, assessed the relevance of the Butler Education Act of 1944 to current society, and gave her view of the main forces shaping development within the education service. But in the course of this she also expounded a distinctively Conservative approach to education, and looked forward to defining more clearly the rights of parents in relation to their children's schooling. Beneath is a substantial section of her address.

We have lived this last quarter of a century with the Education Act of which Mr. Butler as he then was and his coadjutor Mr. Chuter-Ede, were the architects. And a very remarkable Act it was, remarkable for what it did not say as well as for what it did.

It has enabled the central Government and the local authorities and the Churches and the teachers to accomplish a very great deal—including many things which were not, and could not have been, in the minds of the legislators of 1944.

Like all great Acts it was the child of its time. The circumstances of 1944 required a settlement, a legal settlement in which all those with a stake in education, and in particular the local authorities and the voluntary bodies, could be allotted a place and given the appropriate rights and duties. The 1944 Act provided such a settlement and it worked.

It worked at its best where it was distributing broad powers and responsibilities. The broad structure still stands. But the fact that we have had nine Education Acts since 1944—or ten if you

include the Remuneration of Teachers Act of 1965—is a re-
minder not to try to do by legislation what is best left for other
techniques of government and administration.

The former [Labour] Government, by their promise of papers
white to green, gave the impression that this great structure had
outlived its usefulness and could no longer be adapted by periodic
amendment. A new, and they implied a greater, Act was needed,
a stronger structure better able to bear the loads that the following decades would put upon it. I do not share this view. It was
prompted, I believe, by a confusion between structure and
operation, between law and policy.

We would share their view if things we all want to do were
being frustrated by limitations contained in statute. It is true of
course that the Act does not give me the power to order education authorities to organise secondary education in any one
particular way to the exclusion of all others. But then I am not
asking for this power. It is true that the law does not permit me
to impose a central direction on the organisation of higher
education. But then I am not asking for this power either.

But while I believe that Lord Butler built better than he knew
there are some things that need amending. For one thing it would
be a boon to administrators central and local, if all the Education
Acts which now stand on the Statute Book could be consolidated.
For another, as happens with all Acts, some parts have proved
more difficult to administer while others have performed their
task and are no longer needed.

The clear-cut legal distinction between primary and secondary
schools embodied in the 1944 Act made sense in relation to a
much more uniform pattern of school organisation than we now
have or than we now want. A legislative device has been found
to accommodate middle schools, but the primary-secondary
dichotomy does not reflect the reality of the current situation.

Again the present legal distinction between secondary and
further education sometimes stands in the way of flexibility in
providing facilities for educating the sixteen to nineteens. In both
these respects some changes are desirable.

The provisions of the Act about development plans, development orders, and schemes of further education have served their
purpose. The concept of a fixed and detailed scheme or plan no
longer corresponds with the reality of an organically evolving
system of schools and colleges. These provisions could be
abandoned.

In other matters too it should be possible to adopt less rigid and less detailed formulations of the duties of local education authorities and school governing bodies—for example, in the sections of the Act dealing with special educational treatment, or with the sites and buildings of voluntary schools, or with special agreement schools.

I should like to do something to improve those parts of the Act that affect parents in the exercise of the choice of schools their child should attend. At present they are not very satisfactory. Sections which describe the rights of parents do not mean quite what they seem to the layman to mean; and if disputes arise they may have to be settled by recourse to a clumsy school attendance procedure and by correspondence with the Department entailing further delays while the full details are being investigated. We must try to make the arrangements for resolving questions about choice of school simpler and quicker.

These are examples of the sort of change that seems to me to be needed. I am not suggesting that I have cut and dried solutions to everything. But I hope that they will illustrate the general point that most of the changes I should like to see have the character of modifications or improvements, and that to enable us to advance as we would wish, major changes in the law are not necessary. The broad balance of powers and functions between central and local government, between local authorities and the voluntary bodies in the existing legislation seems to me to have stood the test of time pretty well.

There is one other general point. Section 7 of the 1944 Act which deals with the purposes of the statutory system of education has some challenging words in it. It says that 'it shall be the duty of the local education authority for every area, so far as their powers extend, to contribute towards the spiritual, moral, mental and physical development of the community'. That does not leave much that in theory is not the business of the educational system. These things are indeed the concern of the educationist. We consider that there is something lacking in an education service which merely provides instruction and ignores wider aspects of the development of the personality.

But the Act did say 'as far as their powers extend'. As used in this context the words have a legal application, but there is a wider sense in which we ought to recognise the limitations within which the schools must work.

It is very tempting, if one cares deeply about some problems in people's behaviour, as individuals or in society, to think that all would be well if only children were taught the right way to behave in this particular respect at school. And so representations are made that they should be taught to abstain from drugs, drink and smoking, to practise road safety, to exhibit racial tolerance and avoid throwing litter. These are actual examples, which have been put to me, but are by no means a complete list.

The motives of those who are urging this course are usually the highest. But I do ask them to remember that time in the schools is limited, and cannot be allocated to one purpose without reducing what is available for another; and this includes more traditional activities like teaching mathematics and history.

Young people are also subjected to powerful influences outside the schools, from home, from their contemporaries, from the mass media. The influence of the school is not likely to prevail unaided against these other forces unless it is reinforced by parents and the standards of adult society. It is unfair and unrealistic to expect teachers to shoulder these responsibilities alone.

Against this background let us consider what are the main forces that make for development within the education service.

I believe that ideas have always been, and still remain, as powerful an influence upon the development of our education system as the forms of its organisation and the availability of resources. Who produces these ideas and how are they propagated? Philosophers down the ages have been one source of ideas. More recently they have been joined by psychologists and sociologists. Teachers have both produced their own ideas and explored the possibilities of others.

This century has seen the massive expansion of what I might call corporate thinking about education. Parliaments, parties, associations, unions, committees, councils, ministries, experts have come forward with ideas of their own. Following the second world war we have seen the growth of organised research, to find out facts, to test existing ideas and to develop new ones.

But in the last decade or so I believe yet another, and in some ways more powerful agency has been at work. As our society has come to see the value and importance of education and come to demand more and yet more of it for its children and youth, so people have come to have ideas about the aims of education and about what they want to obtain from it.

I welcome this wealth of ideas, though it complicates the life of those who carry the responsibility for running and developing our national system of education.

Changes in ideas often involve changes in organisation.

There are basically two attitudes to organisation. One is to build up a structure which you believe is right—it might perhaps be called the architectural approach—and oblige people to work within it. The other is to go for a network of living institutions—call it the organic approach—where there is room for adaptation and experiment. I am myself convinced that the organic approach is better. It suits our way of life in this country. For the architectural approach you must be sure you have all the right answers, whereas good ideas can come from any part of the service at any time.

Children and students are not all the same, nor are their parents or their teachers. In my view the strongest and most generous education system is one whose organisation, whose institutions are as various and different from each other as the needs of people they serve and the people who serve in them. If schools are different from each other, it does not follow that the children in one kind are having a worse deal than the children in another.

From time to time there are pressures on the education service to embrace some one method of organisation whose advocates deem it to be so obviously right and just and so plainly of universal application that any conscientious Secretary of State must try to impose it and all conscientious local authorities and teachers must welcome its imposition. Fortunately the fashions in educational doctrines tend to wear themselves out long before they have done too much damage. One theoretical truth succeeds another. Meanwhile, in an illogical and untidy pattern, real schools, real colleges and real universities get on with the real work of education.

In the quarter of a century since we started to improve and expand the schools sector of the education service we have had many occasions to modify the law to match new ideas or to remove out-of-date inhibitions on experiment. But we have changed little of real substance.

We retain, as I believe we should, an independent sector alongside the vast public sector. Within the public sector a substantial stake is held by the Churches, and in between wholly public and wholly private there is the small but important direct grant system.

We retain in the State system, schools of a wide range of character. If those who enacted the 1944 Act had suffered from the delusion that secondary education could only be organised on the basis of different types of school to cater for different types of children the law would not have allowed for any development of non-selective schools—a fact which enthusiasts for non-selection should take to heart.

Platform in the Election for the Leadership

The reasons for Margaret Thatcher's candidature in the contest for the Conservative Party Leadership, and the 'manifesto' on which she was fighting, were set out in two separate statements. The first, explaining her reasons and giving her analysis of the situation then facing the Conservative Party, was contained in a speech to the officers of the Finchley and Friern Barnet Conservative Association on the evening of Friday, January 31, 1975, and read as follows:

Conservative supporters in my constituency have a right to know why I have allowed myself to be nominated as a candidate for the leadership of our party.

I hesitated for some time before agreeing to stand. It was obvious that I should be accused of disloyalty to Mr. Heath, of splitting the party and of unseemly personal ambition. Let me put the case to you as simply as possible.

In order to become a Conservative Member of Parliament, I like all my colleagues must be formally readopted as candidate before every election. My constituency Association can confirm or reject me as they please, even before the electorate is asked to vote on polling day.

Since 1965 there have been four General Elections. The Conservative membership of the House of Commons has changed substantially. Yet since 1965 there has been no election for the leadership of our party. There was, indeed, no provision for such an election.

It is therefore not surprising, particularly since our party has lost three out of the four elections since 1965, that there should have been a widespread demand for a procedure which would enable Mr. Heath to submit himself for re-election. The result might be that he was confirmed in the leadership—but at any rate his colleagues would have been given the chance to support an alternative candidate. Whatever the result, the party could then sink its differences and unite in support of its chosen leader.

This feeling among many of my colleagues appears all the more reasonable when you realise that the Leader of our party in Opposition personally appoints—without any procedure for election or confirmation by Conservative MPs—the whole of the Shadow Cabinet and those who control the party machine at Central Office. Many Members felt that they should be given a chance formally to express their views not simply about an individual as leader, but about the whole nature and style of party leadership since 1965 and the general tenor of its policies.

When Mr. Heath recognised the strength of this feeling, he very properly set in train the procedures for a leadership election. A number of my colleagues asked me to stand as a candidate and assured me of a considerable volume of support. I therefore allowed my name to go forward, since it seemed right that their views should be represented.

It is not a particularly easy time for me. Some people, in the Press and outside it, have not hesitated to impugn my motives, to attribute to me political views which I have never expressed and do not hold, and to suggest that the idea of a woman aspiring to lead a great party is absurd—a strangely old-fashioned view, I should have thought!

You can forget all the nonsense about 'defence of privilege'— I had precious little 'privilege' in my early years—and the suggestion that all my supporters are reactionary Right-wingers. It seems to me that those who propagate this idea do Mr. Heath a poor service by implying that his support lies only on the 'Left-wing' of our party!

This is not a confrontation between 'Left' and 'Right'. I am trying to represent the deep feelings of those many thousands of rank-and-file Tories in the country—and potential Conservative voters, too—who feel let down by our party and find themselves unrepresented in a political vacuum.

For past errors, in Government and Opposition, I accept my full share of collective responsibility. But I hope I have learned something from the failures and mistakes of the past and can help to plan constructively for the future.

In the desperate situation of Britain today, our party needs the support of all who value the traditional ideals of Toryism: compassion and concern for the individual and his freedom;

opposition to excessive State power; the right of the enterprising, the hard-working and the thrifty to succeed and to reap the rewards of success and pass some of them on to their children; encouragement of that infinite diversity of choice that is an essential of freedom; the defence of widely-distributed private property against the Socialist State; the right of a man to work without oppression by either employer or trade union boss.

There is a widespread feeling in the country that the Conservative party has not defended these ideals explicitly and toughly enough, so that Britain is set on a course towards inevtiable Socialist mediocrity.

That course must not only be halted, it must be reversed. The action by the Tory Party to carry out that reversal must begin now, while we are in opposition and have time to look at our policies afresh before the next election. That will be a priority task, whatever the outcome of the leadership ballot.

The second statement, indicating how she thought the party could be led out of its difficulties, took the form of a letter addressed to Councillor N. J. Sapsted, chairman of the Finchley and Friern Barnet Conservative Association, and released to the Press on the evening of Saturday, February 1, 1975. The text was as follows:

I have already explained why I have joined in the contest for the Leadership of the Conservative Party. I should now like to tell you, and through you our supporters, how I believe our Party must develop to win the next election and provide the leadership the nation needs.

We have just suffered the shock of two election defeats. Yet I am convinced the opportunity has never been greater for us to project our Conservative principles and beliefs to bring inspiration and hope to our people.

We start with many assets. We have a common purpose, as the Socialists self-evidently have not. We have an immense fund of talent in our ranks. And people are daily becoming more aware of the need for leadership of a kind that only we can give.

But it must be leadership that listens. Perhaps our greatest fault in office was that we did not listen enough to what our supporters and sympathisers were saying. We allowed ourselves to become detached from many who had given us their support and trust.

8—MT • •

How well I remember in the last election, when I put forward our policies to help more families own their own homes, people saying to me: 'If only you'd done this earlier, when you were in Government.'

If we had only listened more carefully to what our supporters and potential supporters were telling us we probably would have done. Then we might not have been in Opposition today.

But we do not inherit the future by dwelling on the past. I believe our great need now is to *open out* the dialogue within our Party, and to bring together a broader spread of talent from our ranks.

Let none feel excluded from this great dialogue by past differences or commitments. We cannot afford any section to feel estranged. Ours is a national Party, and it must be an *open* Party.

Let us also reach out to those whose hopes and ambitions are the same as ours yet who have grown apart from us, and listen to their real needs and wishes.

Listen to the younger generation. They don't want equality and regimentation, but opportunity to shape their world, while showing compassion to those in real need.

Listen to working families the length and breadth of Britain. They don't want growing State direction of their lives. They want more say over how the wealth they earn is used, more say over the quality of their children's schooling. More choice, not less.

Listen to men and women at work. They don't want to be propped up by subsidies, but to see their industries profitable, and Britain again the workshop of the world.

To listen and to lead—that is our role. True leadership offers inspiration and hope, but also explains honestly the severe economic constraints under which we work.

And this means that our future programme must be built on a bedrock of practicality. It is not enough to find the right economic formulae, the neatest administrative solutions. They will never work unless they are first made *acceptable* to the people.

Securing this acceptance, then mobilising our great skills and resources to get the job done—that is the challenge of national leadership today. With pride in our country, faith in our future, and courage now, that is the leadership we shall provide.

INDEX

Index